CAPE TOWN 2007

JOURNEYS – ENCOUNTERS
CLINICAL, COMMUNAL, CULTURAL

PROCEEDINGS OF THE
SEVENTEENTH INTERNATIONAL CONGRESS
FOR ANALYTICAL PSYCHOLOGY

D1798804

Cape Town 2007

Journeys – Encounters
Clinical, Communal, Cultural

Proceedings of the
Seventeenth International Congress
for Analytical Psychology

Edited by Pramila Bennett

DAIMON
VERLAG

The articles in this publication (CD included) were edited and compiled to
provide as true as possible a record of the Proceedings of the Seventeenth
IAAP International Congress held in Cape Town in August 2007.
The views expressed in them are those of the authors and are neither
endorsed nor necessarily held by the Editor or the Publishers;
they are meant to promote scholarship.

Cover design of African scene by Gary Stern

Contents

Tuesday, 14 August 2007

Wednesday, 15 August 2007

Thursday, 16 August 2007

Friday, 17 August 2007

Posters

Appendix

IAAP Executive Committee Officers

President: Christian Gaillard (SFPA)
President Elect: Hester Solomon (BAP)
Vice President: Astrid Berg (SAAJA)
Vice President: Joseph Cambray (NESJA)
Honorary Secretary: Tom Kelly (IRSJA)

IAAP Executive Committee Members

Ann Casement (AJA)
Danila Crespi (SVAJ)
Deborah Egger (AGAP)
Marianne Muller (SGAP)

Marjorie Nathanson (CGJISF)
Jörg Rasche (DGAP)
Pia Skogemann (DSAP)
Jan Wiener (SAP)

IAAP Secretary: Yvonne Trüeb
President's Secretary: Gloria Smith

IAAP Treasurer: Martin Amsler

Programme Committee

Joe Cambray, Chair
Astrid Berg (SAAJA)
Toshio Kawai (AJAJ)
Hester Solomon (BAP)
Gustav Bovensiepen (DGAP)
Denise Ramos (SBrPA)
Beverley Zabriskie (JPA)
Christian Gaillard (ex officio)
Patrizia Michan (IRSJA)
Marta Tibaldi (AIPA)
Joy Schaverien (SAP)
Tom Kelly (Honorary Secretary)

Local Organizing Committee

Rod Anderson
Paul Ashton
Astrid Berg, Chair
Sheila Cowburn
John Gosling
Tony Kelly
Peter Hodson
Elizabeth Martiny
Gary May
Gill Mudie
Ursula Ulmer

Congress Coordinators

Deborah McTeer
Jolandi Ackermann
Conference Management Centre
University of Cape Town Faculty of Health Science

Acknowledgements

The International Conference Volunteers is an international non-profit organization, specializing in the field of communication, in particular languages, and in Congress support. We are pleased that they agreed to participate in our Congress and provided translations of the plenary and some afternoon sessions.

Our thanks go the Art Exhibit Sub-Committee, Paul Ashton, Tony Kelly, Josie Grindrod and Kate Gottgens for the tremendous effort, enthusiasm and devotion with which they approached this project. It is unique that an IAAP Congress has dedicated space for the arts and we are particularly proud that it is all South African!

Preface

> 'People want somebody to listen to them. ...
> People are prejudiced against mental illness'.
> (Balint-Kurti 2008)

I have travelled and worked in several countries in Africa, both French- and English-speaking, for over thirty years but editing this book has occasioned my first visit to South Africa. It may be appropriate therefore to start by stating what I discovered through my attendance at the first Jungian Congress held in that country and my engagement with the papers given there. South Africa is 'not just another country', to borrow Richard Dowden's chapter title on the country in his book *Africa. Altered States, Ordinary Miracles.* It is the African country that most resembles Europe, and also I am told Northern California and I would even imagine Sydney, Australia. Visitors to Cape Town feel less of a culture shock in this handsome coastal city with its marvellous views, gardens, and wines than they would on arrival at almost any other part of Africa. My role as editor of the IAAP proceedings brought me to a new country which has strong links, culturally and historically, with my own – the island of Mauritius, which, like the Cape, was a link in the 19th Century British sea-route to the sub-continent.

Not all of us, of course, feel perfectly at ease in a society that is still emerging from years of apartheid. But this complex young democracy is incubating attitudes and practices about mental problems that could be seminal to all of Africa, and especially to the unstable and often impoverished nations to its north. Working on this publication gave me the opportunity to see how Analytical Psychology can be of help with the issues of mental health in Africa. It also helped me to arrive at a better understanding of the world in which I have been involved as managing editor of the *Journal of Analytical Psychology* over the past twelve years.

In a BBC *Focus on Africa* magazine article in their Jan-March 2008 issue, on pages 48ff, Daniel Balint-Kurti reports about mental health and religion in the Ivory Coast and other sub-Saharan countries, saying: '[the] mentally ill [are] considered at best as public nuisances and at worst as being possessed by evil spirits'. Post-traumatic stress for the victims of a war receives little attention, and in Rwanda, after the genocide of 1994, 'mental health is a national issue', but not much, if any, attention is accorded the problem. Cases of depression abound with the majority showing trauma: somatic symptoms of a mental illness.

Mamphela Ramphele admits that the profession of psychology remains an alien one for the majority of people in South Africa. At the same time, she opens the door to the psychological attitude with a depth and clarity that could not have emerged out of anywhere else. In her eloquent paper on social psychology in a nation in transition she makes a plea to professionals to examine their own roles as healers in the societies they hail from. Similarly, Suzanne Maiello's *Encounter with a Traditional Healer* gave her an opportunity to think about similarities and differences in the therapeutic approach to mental distress, as well as in the training of therapists/healers in the two cultures. Her sympathetic reaction to the *sangoma* Makaba underlined what Ramphele calls the complexities of our interconnected world, all of which are epitomized in South Africa's nascent democracy.

While this publication cannot convey the atmosphere and excitement about being in an African country, the papers here speak for themselves of the extensive research and enormous endeavour the presenters brought to their efforts to connect their work to this environment. The links start of course with Jung's 1925 psychologically informed journey to East Africa (he had travelled to North Africa in the 1920s) and his attempt 'to connect to the "primitive" within himself' and his emotionality. The continent was lit for him, as John Beebe points out, by the 'glare of unconscious complexes'.

Clearly, the usefulness of the profession of psychology in Africa, as I understand it, is too close to its beginnings for us to make a judgement. In Sierra Leone there is one mental health specialist in a country of five and a half million. Let's hope that our discussions in Cape Town did go some way to inspiring South Africans to build upon the psychological language they have already started to use to speak even more deeply of matters they still find too painful to confront (Ramphele).

I would like as a closing remark to once again quote John Beebe who spoke for many of us at the conference when he told us that he had undertaken this journey to South Africa in the expectation of 'getting closer here to his identity as a human being'.

Methodology / How this Publication and the CD are organized

The change that was introduced for the Barcelona Congress Proceedings of 2004 is followed: the plenaries are printed in the book while the attached CD contains all of the proceedings submitted, including photographs, drawings, illustrations, graphs and diagrams.

The printed contents are organized in chronological order as are the breakout sessions, Monday to Friday. The pre-Congress activities on Sunday 12 August 2007 appear at the end with the special presentations (posters). The plenaries were delivered in English except for two: one in German, the other in French. These versions are in the appendix in their original languages. This section also includes the full original programme together with an explanation of the Congress logo. There is an index in the publication as well as on the CD-rom.

While care has been taken to make the papers uniform in format and the references conform to a particular style, any departure is inadvertent. I apologize for any mistake that may have crept in, or indeed any omission.

Acknowledgements

I would like first of all to thank Joe Cambray, Chair of the Programme Committee, for his confidence in me to undertake this editing task, Bob Hinshaw for his generous support, Angela Connolly and members of the Publications Committee for their unfailing encouragement, and John Beebe for his incisive advice. Jan Wiener while endorsing this new role for me said that it was a daunting project and I did find it so! Lyn Cowan shared her methods of operation with me, and several friends helped with the technical intricacies and general computing work, among them to be singled out is Helen Evans of the Society of Analytical Psychology. I am especially grateful to Indrani Gardner and to Robert Imhoff of Daimon Verlag, both for their unwavering support. My husband, George Bennett, a broadcast journalist with several years of working in Africa, gave insightful help throughout the project, and encouraged me in this emotional return to work in an African context as I did before I joined the *Journal of Analytical Psychology*.

Pramila Bennett
London, January 2009

Monday, 13 August 2007

Opening of Congress

Astrid Berg
Vice-President
Chair of the Organizing Committee

Dear Colleagues,

It is with enormous pleasure that we welcome you to the XVIIth IAAP Congress in Cape Town. This is the first time that an IAAP Congress is held in the Southern Hemisphere. For all of our visitors this is also a journey home, to the continent where our species evolved and began the journey to populate the world. At this time humanity faces major challenges relating to the environment, global warming, and increasing polarization of religious and political groups. It therefore seems appropriate to contemplate the future from this vantage point.

The motto on our National Crest is in the ancient language of the Khoi San people and loosely translated calls on us to find strength in diversity.

We have 11 official languages and our National struggle to know and respect each other is a microcosm of the global challenge facing humanity. You will not regret having undertaken this journey: Our logo with the dancing shaman encountering the snake of renewal captures the essence of our endeavour.

The programme is representative of the richness and diversity of South Africa and the world, as so many of the proposals quite spontaneously reflected thinking which had to do with encounters on many levels – collectively, culturally, politically, interpersonally and intra-psychically. This is an opportunity to not only continue with our intellectual debates, but to also engage in a more concrete way with a country and its people that is unique.

We have chosen the Cape Town International Convention Centre to be our Congress venue. We are sure that you will agree that it provides the space, the light and the atmosphere which we are looking for in order to bring people together. All the activities will be there, and the hotels are within walking distance, as is the Waterfront, a most popular shopping and entertainment area for all Capetownians as well as tourists.

Present at the Congress will be Robin Troup, the local Tour Operator, who will be happy to assist you with planning your pre and post Congress safaris ahead of time, as well as arranging local day trips during the Congress. You will be able to go to Robben Island where Nelson Mandela was imprisoned, and visit various sites – museums and townships – which played significant roles in the political struggles of this country.

The social programme will enable you to participate in more informal meetings and will make possible spontaneous encounters. Please join us to make this a memorable happening.

Welcome Address

Hester Solomon
President-Elect

Dear Friends and Colleagues and Esteemed Guests,

It is both a pleasure and an honour to address these opening, welcoming remarks to the more than 500 participants for the 2007 17th IAAP Congress in Cape Town. The title of this Congress is very apt indeed: 'Journeys and Encounters'. Most of those assembled here today have travelled across one or two or even three continents to participate in this illustrious Congress. To those who have made a significant journey, I bid you a hearty welcome. Your efforts, I am sure, will be well rewarded by the content of this Congress and by the experiences you will have with your fellow Congress participants – journeys and encounters, indeed! To those many who are from South Africa, your wonderful country and your splendid welcome have been very moving for us, we who have travelled from afar, and I thank you on behalf of us all. I know that you have many other delights and excitements in store for us.

The IAAP has indeed gone global. Seated here together today are representatives from all the five continents. Implicit in this fact, as extraordinary as it is, is the reality that lies underneath, those elements that make us human: the excitement of coming here to Cape Town, natural apprehensions in face of the unknown, the joy of meeting colleagues and friends from diverse cultures and environments, and, finally, those journeys and encounters that we have embarked upon, individually and collectively to attend this Congress. We are immensely privileged to be here in South Africa, a country that has gone through its own remarkable journey since the first European settlers travelled here from afar and encountered members of varied local populations. And what an extraordinary overarching transition – from indigenous cultures, through the hard times of colonization, through the even harder times of apartheid, and then finally through democratization and the rigours of truth and reconciliation. The history of this country will no doubt cast its own light and shadows across some of the debates and discussions we will have at this Congress, be they clinical, communal, cultural or indeed organizational. This extraordinarily diverse land, with its wilderness and wildness, its first manifestations of human culture on rock faces, through to complex human invention and exchange, is itself embedded in the psyche and impacts upon us. By the end of this journey and these encounters we will all be touched by it, moved by it, and changed by it.

My time is brief here today, but I want to say a few words about some of the directions that the IAAP is set to be heading towards in the next period of time. An important reason for members of the IAAP to convene every three years, apart from the programme content of the Congress and its attendant encounters with colleagues from disparate parts of the world, is to reflect on and to do the business of our organizational governance. We are, after all, an international professional body, and we have a constitution with stated aims and ways of functioning. This is a moment for us all to reflect on how we have functioned in the recent and not so recent past and to consider together how we wish to proceed into the future, especially in the next three years. I cannot stress enough how important this opportunity is to hear from you about how you would wish the IAAP to develop into its future. We will have ample opportunities to do so informally as we meet throughout the coming days, and also, most importantly, at the Delegates' Meeting on Wednesday afternoon, when we do the official business of the IAAP.

I have been privileged to serve the IAAP now during a number of administrations. I wish to emphasize what an extraordinary job the Executive Committee, the Officers, and the numerous Sub-Committees and Working Parties do on behalf of and for the IAAP. This is sustained and dedicated work, done on a shoestring budget, thriftily and with enormous thought and careful, ongoing discussion. We seek to carry on the business of the IAAP in the most judicious way we can. This has been my impression since I first became a member of the Executive Committee to the present time. As we know, at both individual and collective levels, current functioning rests upon and is inherited from the past generation's functioning. I believe that we have inherited a generational hand over of remarkable quality. Of course, in such an increasingly complex and diverse organization, ranging globally over the five continents, our ways of functioning need to be adaptive to new circumstances and new times. I have learned much since my early years in the IAAP, and I have been thinking a lot about what I have learned. As we continue to respond and adapt to the growing complexity of the IAAP in the next three years, I think we will be addressing a number of important areas, many of which are already in the process of evolution. For example, traditionally the Officers have chaired the important Sub-Committees. I hope that it will be possible to delegate some of their responsibilities to other members of the Executive Committee. This is a process that has already begun and I hope that it will continue. Included in that broadening we will be extending the membership of the Sub-Committees beyond that of the Executive Committee by bringing on consultant IAAP members with particular expertise in relevant fields. I hope that this will lead to greater communication between the Executive and its President and the entire membership, so much more possible now with email and other types of telecommunications.

I would like the Executive Committee to cast a more conscious eye in its own governance and that of its member societies. A discussion has already begun here in Cape Town in the Council of Societies, the Executive Committee and among the Officers on this. We have also begun to engage in discussions regarding matters of training requirements and standards. We are the professional body that grants accreditation to practise as a Jungian analyst, but how do we define what it means to be a Jungian analyst, or what is a Jungian identity? How do we hold the tension in a creative and flexible way between the two perspectives of maintaining our constitutional commitment to high levels of training and ethics, while at the same time allowing room for flexibility, innovation and diversity as respected by our constitutional provisions as a federal organization?

These are some of the challenges that we can and must begin to address in this next administration. I have also been thinking about how we manage our finances at a time when the IAAP is growing in scope and organizational complexity. The Officers have overall responsibility to manage our finances, which they do with serious care, including a newly instituted yearly internal audit. Our finances are wonderfully overseen by our lawyer and treasurer, Mr. Martin Amsler, who will be joining us at the Delegates' Meeting on Wednesday. At the same time, I think that we would benefit greatly from having our own IAAP Finance Officer in charge of a Sub-Committee with further financial responsibilities, for example, for fundraising. This will help ensure that we can have confidence in our ability to honour our continued undertakings and commitments to support various IAAP-sponsored activities such as granting funds for IAAP research projects, conferences, publications, as well as to support our responsibilities to be responsive to calls for assistance where interest in the Jungian project cannot be met by local resources, such as the Developing Groups projects and the Router programme.

Finally, I wish to turn our attention to two extraordinary people without whom this Congress would not have been possible, Astrid Berg, Chair of the Congress Organizing Committee, and Joe Cambray, Chair of the Congress Programme Committee. They have also served during this past administration as the IAAP's two Vice-Presidents, with already a great deal of work and responsibility on their plates. They have put into the realization of this Congress their vision, striking dedication, and sheer hard work, along with the members of their respective Committees. What is remarkable is the quality of their partnership in doing so. I understand that they habitually exchange emails 15 to 20 times a day about Congress matters. The content, organization, and the very choreography of this Congress have depended on their remarkable, professional and friendly partnership – a true *coniunctio,* indeed.

And now it is my great pleasure to announce that it is time to say: Let the Congress begin!

Thank you.

Journeys – Encounters
Clinical, Communal, Cultural
Introductory Remarks

Joe Cambray
Vice-President
Chair of Programme Committee

To begin I would like to thank the Organizing Committee for their extraordinary work in arranging this congress, especially the chair of the Organizing Committee Astrid Berg. Hester Solomon has just given us a wonderful start with her cogent remarks. Several other key individuals who have been most helpful to me as chair of the Programme Committee are: Toni D'Anca who ably assisted me in coordinating the programme from start to finish, Pramila Bennett who I am delighted to announce will serve as the editor of the Proceedings of this Congress, and Don Williams the IAAP webmaster who has been essential in communicating the information about this Congress. Don has been with the technical staff here so that we will have audio/visual capture of the plenary sessions which will then be transferred to the IAAP website – we will make these available to our members in the autumn. Further, I would like to express my appreciation for to the audience for attending, many of you have travelled great distances at considerable expense and even some hardship, to be a part of this great endeavour of the IAAP and Analytical Psychology here in Africa; I also want to acknowledge those who are unable to make the Journey and be with us – from letters, emails and various other correspondences I know that many in the larger Jungian community are present in spirit.

Over the past three years it has been my good fortune and pleasure to chair the Programme Committee, a wonderful assembly of seasoned analysts, each with their own well-articulated views of our field. The group is culturally diverse, coming from 10 different countries representing all the official languages of the IAAP and several other important others (Portuguese and Japanese). Truly a working group, the committee demonstrated remarkable mutuality and respect for one another, and for the diversity found in our field. The committee consisted of the IAAP officers (Christian Gaillard-France, Hester Solomon-UK, Astrid Berg-SA, Tom Kelly-Canada, Beverley Zabriskie (past chair-US), Gustav Bovensiepen-Germany, Toshio Kawai-Japan, Patrizia Michan-Mexico, Denise Ramos-Brazil, Joy Schaverien-UK, and

Marta Tibaldi-Italy. It was an honour to lead this group and I learned much about our organizations worldwide in the process. Working together we evolved a creative, emergent, democratic process for the many dimensions of our task, starting with our theme, which arose directly out of the context of our experience of considering this Congress, in this location.

While analytically oriented presentations, clinical and theoretical, form the backbone of this Congress, a spirit of openness and desire for encounter brought this Programme Committee to broaden the conceptions of our call for participation. We thus invited the IAAP community, to consider actively engaging others working in kindred fields, hence the inclusion of scholars and practioners from various disciplines (e.g., paleoanthropology, psychoanalysis, psychology, sociology, the neurosciences, African healing systems and so forth – see the programme) to join us in presenting, and to interact with us. For the first time we also have poster sessions allowing more presenters, with works in progress, to be engaged.

In studying the 185 plus proposals submitted, pouring over them in detail to build this Congress, I realized what good fortune we had. The richness of the offerings required the Programme Committee to go through a selection process of protracted discussion and reflection to elaborate the form and content of the whole enterprise. Personally, I felt I had received an unexpected gift through this process and that the work the committee has done to craft the programme has become our opportunity to offer back to you a measure of what it received.

The uniqueness of this Congress, the first one in Africa, will start with the recognition of the importance of hearing African voices tell us of their experiences. All of the plenary sessions today will feature individuals who either live and work here now or have a deep history of connection with this place. African themes and concerns will also be found dotted throughout the congress; it is an essential part of the encounter already underway.

The themes of journey and encounter, however, are not only defined by our physical location, psychological and spiritual dimensions open us to a tremendous range of possibilities as you will see even in a quick perusal of the programme (see further). While you will each select your own unique journey through this congress, I would like to say a few words about a way of journeying. In Jungian fashion, I will draw upon a fairytale, one, which by the time it was first published in Venice in 1557 [called the *Peregrinaggio*], was itself already a traveller, having been translated from Persian into Italian. In English it has become known as 'The Three Princes of Serendip' where Serendip refers to the name of the island the princes were from, sometimes called Sarandib or Simhala-dvipa, more commonly known in the west as Ceylon, now Sri Lanka.

While there is no time to explicate the tale itself, it is the source of the term 'serendipity' coined in 1754 by a British man of letters, Horace Walpole. The definition offered by Walpole derives from the behaviour of the heroes of the tale, who as they travelled 'were always making discoveries, by accidents and through sagacity, of things which they were not in quest of'. It is the gift or capacity of the well-informed mind which is open to chance that can make or turn the curious or odd, often seemingly minor occurrence in an encounter into a meaningful, at time momentous, event. Therefore, in addition to your conscious plans, I wish you a serendipitous journey through the next five days and to start us off, I will turn the podium over to our Past President Professor Dr. Verena Kast who will introduce our morning's keynote speaker.

How Does One Speak of Social Psychology in a Nation in Transition?

Mamphela Ramphele
South Africa

Abstract

Although South Africa's transition into nationhood has been remarkable by all measures, persistent inequalities remain. These are directly traceable to the impact of the social engineering of apartheid which has left a legacy of poverty and a lack of education. In this talk, I focus on three key dilemmas for South Africans: identity as a nation of citizens with multiple identities, capacity for self-knowledge and self-acceptance and openness to new impulses. Acceptance of multiple identities is widespread but how deep is the acceptance of difference, especially when conflicts of opinion emerge? Finding a language of self-knowledge and acceptance requires a language that enables us to gain greater mastery of the complexities of living in a diverse society. How can psychology help with this task? In African cultures illness is described as a visitation from the ancestors: affected persons become wounded healers whose healing powers come from their acknowledged weakness. To what extent might you, as analytical psychologists, help find the ritual processes and language to be effective healers of your own nation?

Introduction

Practitioners of psychology might perhaps not be ready to hear that their profession remains an alien one for the majority of people in South African society. Psychological needs and issues related to mental health problems are not matters that are discussed in the public domain. They belong to the private domain. Even in that private domain psychological and mental health challenges are inaccessible to the individual involved and to those closely related. There is no universally accepted language to speak of problems of psychological and mental ill health. The worst insult you could level at anyone amongst those who have this sense of alienation from bio-medical psychology or neuroscience approaches to mental health is to suggest that there might be something wrong with their mental state.

What of the past and its language of psychological and mental ill health? Is there indigenous wisdom we might draw on to open up dialogue on mental health and psychological phenomena without causing offence? Most languages have evolved metaphors for speaking about matters that cause discomfort for individuals and communities. Such metaphors permit conversations that bring relief to those affected without such individuals feeling that their self-respect, human dignity and sense of belonging are under threat. Even during the Victorian era problems of members of the upper class affected by depression, anxieties or any mental or psychological disturbance, were described in the most delicate terms. 'They were off colour'. Some were said to be 'poorly'. Many euphemisms were employed to disguise any reference to matters psychological or mental.

In most African cultures mental illness is described in different ways as a visitation from ancestors of the affected person who are said to speak to one through ill health. The nature of ill health is often psychosomatic. Such ill health forces one to pay attention to the voices of ancestors through rituals that bring back harmony between the living and the dead. Discernment by traditional healers of the need for such rituals elevates the affected person's status into that of an interlocutor between present and past generations. Their status is transformed from being psychologically or mentally ill to being high priests for their families and the community. They become the centre of attention of not just living members of their families but also of those who have passed on. Their well-being improves and they find new meaning in their lives as useful members of their families and communities.

I would like you to come with me on a journey of exploration of my country's transition into nationhood and the dilemmas it faces in finding a language to speak to those challenges. Our transition has been remarkable by all measures. To move from being a society associated with some of the worst of human rights abuses against the majority population, to one lauded for one of the best human rights based national constitutions is a big leap forward. Nor should anyone underestimate the efforts that have moved us from a technically bankrupt economy to one that has seen uninterrupted growth for over ten years.

We are acutely aware of the persistent inequalities in our society even as we enjoy the benefits of a booming economy. Persistent inequalities of our society are directly traceable to the impact of the social engineering of apartheid. Not only was impoverishment of black people a planned state project, but also the under-investment in human and social capital in the majority population has left us with severe capacity problems at all levels of our society. The apartheid system understood that education is the one tried and tested way out of poverty, and they made sure that that route was blocked for the majority of the population. We are still struggling to deal with the burden of the legacy of divisions in our society and the designer poverty that has trapped the majority of citizens as we search for a definition of ourselves as citizens of a united nation.

We are only thirteen years into this journey. We are but a teenager in democracy terms. We like to think of ourselves as one of those '*Wunder kinder*' who are performing ahead of their peers on many fronts. The political will to get things right is in no doubt, but the capacity to do so is uneven. In those areas where we do well we excel, but where we have capacity constraints we tend to struggle to come to terms with our own failures and acknowledge them. Like many over-achieving teens, psychological and mental stress is a major risk as we wrestle with the challenges we face.

In this presentation I would like to focus on three key dilemmas we are wrestling with:

- Identity as a nation of citizens with multiple identities;
- Capacity for self-knowledge and self-acceptance;
- Openness to new impulses.

Identity as a Nation

We have tended to assume that our identity as a new nation would follow naturally from the political settlement agreements we reached and the rituals we enacted to signal our transition to democracy. We have under-estimated the challenges of migrating from our divided past towards a united nation.

None of the segments of our population that came together on this journey to South African nationhood have had any experience of citizenship in a democracy on our own home ground. In addition, all citizens come into this new democracy with deeply fragmented identities. Fragmentation exists and persists within both black and white communities as well as between them. Those fragments are not only defined by the predictable fault lines of categories defined by race, class, gender, sexual orientation, language and beliefs. Fragmentation also relates to political affiliation both within and between political parties.

The challenges of identity as a nation are not necessarily related to the multiplicity of fragments, but to the willingness to accept that multiplicity of identities can co-exist within a united nation. Multiplicity of identities is part of who we are and needs to be accepted and incorporated in our definition of ourselves. There are still too many instances where 'them' and 'us' are cast in immutable terms in our society. The experience of racial categorization has left many South Africans with a notion of 'different races' that defies any scientific evidence to the contrary. The idea of one single human race is hard to accept for many South Africans across the historical racial divide.

For example, there are still many white people who deeply believe that there are irreconcilable differences in essence between black and white people. Equally true is the persistence of belief amongst black people in essentialist differences between white and black people that are seen as unbridgeable.

The persistence of essentialist beliefs in unbridgeable differences between historical categories would not necessarily pose insurmountable difficulties in forging a united nation. What is critically important to test is acceptance of multiplicity of identities in people with whom we share citizenship of our nation. I can confidently say that acceptance of multiple identities is widespread in our nation. What I perceive to be a challenge is the depth of that acceptance when differences of opinion arise. How far and deep is the acceptance of difference as a positive attribute in a nation with such a diversity of experiences, cultures, physical attributes and opinions on a wide range of subjects?

There are challenges on all sides of the historical divides. Racist and sexist propaganda about inferiority and superiority has left deep imprints on our psyches as a people. Whilst black men react very strongly against any suggestion that they might be inadequate in the roles they have assumed, many of them do not bat an eyelid in expressing the most sexist views about women as leaders. For example, Fred Khumalo, one of the *Sunday Times* columnists, quotes a young man who was a student who said he would never work for a woman boss. When asked why he said: 'Women are too emotional and illogical. They do not have intellectual wherewithal to run organizations or companies. They can't make sound decisions unless there is a man they can use as a crutch[1].' Ouch! Imagine if a white person were to say the same thing about the inability of black people to manage and lead institutions by merely substituting 'black person' for 'woman' in the above quotation.

The same conceptual blindness applies to some white women who might be very sensitive about sexism and its impact on them as women, but find nothing wrong with their own deeply held racist views about both black men and women. *'You know what they are like!'* is a throw away line that is sometimes made in my presence with that look that says *'but you are not like them'.* The assumption is that I should understand what my fellow South Africans are saying to me about people who look like me and that I am *'good enough'* to be included in the *'in-group'.* The idea of freedom from discrimination as indivisible has yet to take root in our nascent democracy across the fault lines of our legacy.

Another manifestation of our continued wrestling with multiple identities as a nation is the tendency to silence others by labelling them as racist or agents of racists. For example, white people are

---

1 Fred Khumalo, *Sunday Times*, 12/8/07.

great South Africans for as long as they do not criticize black people in leadership positions, both in the private and public sector. In too many cases criticism of public officials immediately evokes negative reactions bordering on accusations of treason. How could such criticism be levelled at 'our people' given the successes we have under our belt? Even constructive criticism and fair comment on public issues are often dismissed as racist attacks.

There are also dangerous tendencies amongst public commentators who deny fellow black people the right to disagree or criticize public officials in both the private and public sectors. There is an unstated assumption that as a black person one should hold certain views that are aligned to the dominant political establishment. An example of debate on this tendency is captured in two recent articles: one by Christine Qunta in the *Star* newspaper (25/7/07) and the other by Sipho Seepe in *Business Day* (8/8/07).

Christine Qunta's point in her column in the *Star* was very clear that black people who criticize a black government are agents of destruction:

> Their willingness to be deployed to discredit African people is not only motivated by material gain or flattery. Like black policemen and askaris during apartheid, there seems to be a genuine belief deep within their consciousness of the omnipotence of white power and, conversely, the inherent powerlessness and inferiority of Africans.

There are interesting assumptions embedded in the above statement. First, the idea that black critics of the government are unable to act as independent people with views that happen to be different from her views and those of the government. This view of black people who are critical of some aspects of public policy reflects her own inability to imagine that some black people could have autonomous and diverse views on affairs of their nation without being 'deployed' by white people to express those views. This is a serious vote of no confidence in the intellectual independence of black people. Second, there is an assumption that those in government embody everything there is about 'African people'. What about those black people, African or not, who hold different views and express them in their membership of political parties that are in opposition to the dominant ruling party? Are they not 'African people' too? And what about white people who identify themselves as African, are they not allowed to be 'Africans' and yet hold different views from the dominant political party?

Third, there is also an implied understanding of critical comment as condemnation. There does not seem to be room in Qunta's view for citizens to agree with some aspects of public policy and its implementation whilst disagreeing with others. Hers seem to be an all or nothing law. It cannot be true that criticism of a majority black government is equivalent to rendering them powerless. Nor should we accept that criticism of a majority black government implies an affirmation of 'white omnipotence'. A majority black government like any other government in the world can and will make mistakes. It is the duty of citizens to engage in constructive criticism of their governments to ensure that we learn from mistakes and not be condemned to repeat them.

Finally, of greater concern to the values of our nascent democracy is Qunta's commentary that equates criticism with treason. The reference to 'askaris' is ominous. Askaris were former liberation movement operatives who were arrested, tortured and turned into agents of the dreaded intelligence services of the apartheid state who killed and maimed with abandon. It is very dangerous to use such language in our young democracy in which we should be encouraging not discouraging critical comment on affairs of state by all citizens. If critical comment becomes synonymous with treason then we are likely to weaken the democratic foundations of our society.

Sipho Seepe's critique of Qunta's approach to public discourse is not dissimilar to the points I make above, but eloquently emphasizes the dangers of her comments to our nascent democracy:

conflating a black government's interests with those of all black people,

the discrediting of black intellectual capacity to hold a diversity of views,

the lack of appreciation of the role of debate in a democratic society,

the intolerance of criticism that might incite violence,

and finally the too familiar notion that 'criticism of black government can only be motivated by racism'.

Amartya Sen characteristically makes incisive comments about the dangers of the tendency to impose a unique and singular identity on people in a complex world:

> The illusion of unique identity is much more divisive than the universe of plural and diverse classifications that characterizes the world in which we actually live. The descriptive weakness of choiceless singularity has the effect of momentously impoverishing the power and reach of our social and political reasoning. The illusion of destiny exacts a remarkably heavy price[1].

We will do well to resist the temptations of classifying people into irreconcilable categories in a country where diversity is our biggest strength. There are black and white people who support our majority

---

1 Sen, A., *Identity and Violence – The Illusion of Destiny*, New York: WW Norton, 2007, p. 17.

black government, but are critical of some aspects of its policies and/ or implementation approaches. They are as loyal as any other South African. There are black and white people who never criticize our majority black government but are betraying the very basic tenets of our national constitution by failing to perform their duties to provide public services to the poorest amongst us. Many of these under-performers are capturing the state for their own personal enrichment. Support for the government whether public or silent is not necessarily a measure of good citizenship. It is the discharging of our stewardship as citizens that should be a measure of our patriotism and loyalty to our democracy.

We are a nation that is still coming to terms with the cognitive dissonance that comes from moving from the 'known' – white male leadership – to the 'unknown' – non-racial and non-sexist leadership and social relationships. It is all the more important that there be open exploration of what it means to be citizens of this new democracy without excluding certain views simply because they raise uncomfortable issues. The identity of our nation by definition embraces multiple identities of the diversity of citizens making up our nation. Coming to terms with this diversity and embracing it as part of 'us' remains the biggest challenge of our evolution into a mature democracy.

Neville Alexander's book, *An Ordinary Country*, required reading for those interested in understanding the soft underbelly of our young democracy, cautions us against the simplistic notion of a 'rainbow nation' as a metaphor. Rainbows celebrate and showcase different colours as separate. He suggests that we rather embrace the Garieb, Nama word for Great river, to signal our unity and diversity as is the case of a great river that draws strength from its tributaries. We need to learn to celebrate cultural diversity and defend individual equality. The title of this book also serves to caution us against the temptation of believing the myth of ours is 'a miracle transition' that marks ours as a special country[1].

Self-knowledge and Acceptance

One of the markers of maturity is self-knowledge. Knowing one's strengths and weaknesses enables one to play to one's strengths and manage one's weaknesses. Self-knowledge comes from looking at oneself in the mirror and accepting what one sees as 'self'. Self-knowledge also comes from others holding the mirror to one. Therein lies the dilemma. If we are so sensitive to criticism, how are we to develop self-knowledge that includes positive and negative feedback? Smashing the mirror does not help us out of the dilemma of self-acceptance.

---

1 Alexander, N., *An Ordinary Country*. New York, Oxford: Berhahn Books, 2003, pp. 102-06.

Going back to the metaphor of our democracy being in its teens should help us to deal with the dilemmas of developing self-knowledge. As a privileged mother of two grown sons I have vivid memories of the challenge of giving positive and negative feedback to my teenage children. It did not matter how often I praised my sons when they did well, as the one criticism often drew the pained response, 'but you *always* criticize me'. Forgotten were all the praises of a few minutes before the critical comment. Much of this intolerance to criticism stems from insecurity that is part of the burden of youth. Even the brightest amongst young people are deeply insecure for very good reasons. The world they are entering is a complex, uncertain place.

South Africa is developing into a well performing young nation in an uncertain and complex world. Its insecurity is well founded. It is understandable that we sometimes seem to be having a bad case of teenage blues. When we do well we lap up the praise, but heaven help you if you catch us on a bad day and point to a weakness in our performance. We have difficulty in banking the often repeated and much deserved praises we get for the rainy day when we are fairly criticized for weaknesses we display in both public policy and implementation.

What do all these comments have to do with psychology you might well ask? I would like to take you back to my introductory remarks. We live in a society in which we are not comfortable with any reference to psychological or mental phenomena and the disciplines that deal with those matters. Yet from some of the comments I referred to about our insecurities and the challenges of self-knowledge we face indicate that we do need a language to speak of matters of positive and negative feedback. We need a better language framework to gain greater mastery over how to deal with the complexities of living in a diverse society without falling into the trap of 'choiceless singularity' that Amartya Sen warns us about.

For such a language of self-knowledge and acceptance to emerge we need ritual masters and mistresses. Is psychology up to the task of helping us find that language? What wisdom can it draw from to accompany us as a young democracy in search of self-knowledge and self-acceptance? How would such a language help us to dig deep into ourselves to name what we fear to acknowledge? How can you as analytical psychologists who deal with individuals make the journey with us as a nation in transition to enable us to find an appropriate medium to communicate our anxieties and triumphs?

The beauty of African traditional healing approaches to mental illness is the focus on embracing the affected person as s/he is. The demons that haunt the person are transformed into members of the family. The demons are transformed into ancestors who have come back to inhabit the body of the affected person. Interestingly, one never hears any ill spoken of such ancestors in this context. Their weaknesses are transcended and only their strengths are sought as pillars for the affected person to use to rise to the challenges s/he faces. The affected persons become inducted into the role of being wounded healers. By going through the woundedness of psychological anguish they develop the empathy for fellow sufferers. Their healing powers come from their acknowledged weaknesses.

It could be said that as a nation we have also gone through a ritual healing process in the Truth and Reconciliation Commission. We were blessed with one of the best ritual masters one could wish for, Desmond Mpilo Tutu. Tutu coaxed both survivors and perpetrators of human rights abuses into becoming wounded healers of their nation. By unburdening themselves, perpetrators allowed survivors to embrace them as part of the future we are all yearning for. We were enabled to embrace our demons represented by the ugly things we did to one another in defence of an indefensible system, as well as in fighting that system. We have all become infected by the violence of division and abuse of human rights over many decades. The TRC rituals helped to lay some of the demons in us to rest. But the job is far from done. One need only feel the seething tensions underneath the surface of our 'reconciled' society. Healing takes time and thirteen years is not long enough.

Is there openness to new impulses?

I would like to conclude with a plea to you as professionals to examine your own roles as healers in the societies you hail from. I particularly address myself to those of you who are South Africans living in a nation that is going through acute growing pains. To what extent can you be effective healers of your nation? How can you use your own woundedness as citizens to help our nation to acknowledge its own woundedness? How can you help us to generate a momentum for self-acceptance as a teenage nation that can both celebrate our successes and acknowledge and learn from our mistakes?

It is my hope that your deliberations at this conference will stimulate the kind of discussions that will inspire us to find the language to speak of matters we still find too painful to confront. I firmly believe that being able to speak of those deep matters that continue to cause us anguish will help us to transcend the divisions of our past and realize the vision spelt out in our constitution: to be a non-racial, non-sexist egalitarian democracy. But I also hope that your presence here in our nation will inspire you to rise even higher in your search for better ways of being healers in our increasingly complex and interconnected world.

Our nascent democracy embodies many of the complexities of our interconnected world – it is a microcosm of our world. May your presence in Cape Town become an important marker of growing openness to new impulses to help us and you to acknowledge and accept us as we are. I firmly believe that it is out of self-acceptance that we can find it within ourselves to transcend the legacy of our past that still holds us hostage in some aspects of our life as a nation. Out of that transcendence lies the possibility of a nationhood that is able to speak to its multiple identities with pride.

[This paper was first published in the April 2008 issue of the *Journal of Analytical Psychology*, Vol. 53, 2.]

Forgiveness After Mass Atrocities in Cultural Context: Making Public Spaces Intimate

Pumla Gobodo-Madikizela
South Africa

Abstract

In this paper[1] I explore the concept of forgiveness as a response to gross human rights violations. I present a conceptual examination of the effects of massive trauma in relation to what I refer to as the 'unfinished business' of trauma. Using a psychoanalytic framework, I consider the process of 'bearing witness' about trauma and examine how this process opens up the possibility of reciprocal expressions of empathy between victim and perpetrator. I then argue that, in this context of trauma testimony and witnessing, empathy is essential for the development of remorse on the part of perpetrators, and of forgiveness on the part of victims. Using a case study from South Africa's Truth and Reconciliation Commission (TRC) I clarify the relationship between empathy and forgiveness, and show how the restorative model of the TRC can open up an ethical space and create the possibility of transformation for victims, perpetrators and bystanders. In my conclusion I suggest that forgiveness in politics is the only action that holds promise for the repair of brokenness in post-conflict societies, particularly if, as in South Africa, victims have to live together with perpetrators and beneficiaries in the same country.

* * *

The title of this congress of the IAAP, 'Journeys' Encounters', is appropriate at this time when the escalation of violence and war, past and current as well as threats of wars to come, hover at the edges of our collective consciousness. We live in difficult and challenging times, times where political leaders do not value the very basis of the things that represent the core of what it is to be human. The work of healing, peace, and justice has never been more urgent.

At the same time, people involved in healing and peace building work perhaps have never experienced such challenges to the values that define their work, the value of care, justice and compassion. For so often, when we express moral indignation in protest against the injustices we see around us, we may find ourselves falling into the trap of speaking the language of hate. So, our journeys of healing and encounters with our enemies lead us back to ourselves. Yesterday's

---

I Title amended: in the Congress Programme it was 'Trauma, Forgiveness and the Witnessing Dance: Making Public Spaces Intimate'.

victims become tomorrow's perpetrators, and so the proverbial cycle goes. Our journey of healing in difficult times in our world is a daunting one. How do we transcend the cycles of hate and vengeance, while facing daily the forces that produce it?

My experience on South Africa's Truth and Reconciliation Commission, the TRC, has been the most profound moment in my life. The days, weeks, and months of journeying with victims and survivors' pain and trauma, and of encounters with perpetrators – their terror, depravity, and sometimes their brokenness because of the very horrendous crimes they committed – confronted us more closely with the complexity of the human condition. At the end of those many hours and days spent on the TRC, I came out with this one lesson, that there can be no adequate reparation for the horrors we have witnessed on the public stage of the TRC. It seems to me that forgiveness is a compelling and healthy response to the horrors committed in the name of totalitarian regimes. The subject of forgiveness continues to spark major disagreements, both among the public and within the scholarly community. Hannah Arendt, who, among her writings, is most famously known for her reflections on the trial of the Nazi concentration camp commander Adolf Eichmann in Jerusalem (Arendt 1965), refers to the atrocities committed under the Nazi regime as 'radical evil'. She writes that these acts transcend the realm of human affairs, and are therefore neither punishable nor forgivable (Arendt 1998). The radically evil are un-punishable because no amount of punishment can restore a sense of symmetry that would balance what they have done. They are unforgivable because no yard-stick exists by which we can measure what it means to forgive them, and there is no mental disposition we can adopt towards them that would correct the sense of injustice that their actions have injected into our world. Thus, for Arendt, there are certain acts which lie beyond the purview of forgiveness and for which contemplating forgiveness for them would be unethical.

In this paper my discussion will rest on two assumptions. Firstly, that forgiveness in and of itself is not necessarily an ethical issue, but derives its ethicalness from an ethical encounter between individuals.

Secondly, I will argue that understanding the *possibility* of forgiveness requires that we have a full grasp of the impact of trauma on both the external and the internal world of victims, an appreciation of the psychological reparation necessary in the working through of trauma at a deeply internal level, and the role of perpetrators' remorse in this process. I will argue that a psychoanalytic understanding of what is involved in the process of forgiveness can help us to appreciate the intersubjective dimension of the encounter between victim and perpetrator and its significance for the working through of the 'unfinished business' of trauma.

Distinguishing Between 'The Forgivable' and 'The Unforgivable'

Arendt (1998) argued that there are limits to what can be forgiven: some acts are so heinous as to render forgiveness for them morally inappropriate. I believe that Arendt's enduring insights on the subject of forgiveness cry out for re-examination. This is so particularly in light of the work of South Africa's Truth and Reconciliation Commission and other similar examples of attempts at national reconciliation and healing such as the *Gacaca*[1] process in post-genocide Rwanda. Applied even to the few examples of forgiveness after mass atrocities witnessed across the globe in recent years, the notion of 'the unforgivable' fails to illuminate the complex set of factors that may be at play when forgiveness is granted in the context of human rights abuses. In order to understand the dynamics that inspire the emergence of forgiveness we need a theoretical perspective that goes beyond notions of the ethical '*should*' or '*should not*' that set limits to what can be forgiven, to the psychological '*can*' or '*cannot*' which is determined by the nature of the encounter between the person/s asking for forgiveness and those granting or refusing to grant forgiveness. This approach to the analysis of the process of forgiveness will deepen our understanding of the relational dynamics that emerge in encounters that lead to forgiveness after mass atrocity.

Arendt's worldview was shaped and inspired by her observations and reactions to the events of World War II, particularly the Holocaust. Her thesis about the limits of forgiveness made sense at a time when the world was confronted with the unimaginable atrocity of the Holocaust, and when concepts of justice for dealing with crimes against humanity were based on the Nuremberg trials model. Thus, in the literature on forgiveness, the Holocaust became a type of yard-stick for the unforgivable – the Holocaust is unforgivable psychologically, ethically and politically.

The question one has to ask is whether it is conceivable to regard forgiveness as an impossibility with regard to the Holocaust but not inconceivable to regard forgiveness as a possibility with regard to present-day atrocities such as apartheid in South Africa and the genocide in Rwanda. We cannot compare the anguish caused by these horrific events on individuals, families and societies – pain is something that we should not rate or compare. The qualitative difference between present-day examples of mass traumas and the Holocaust may not be a useful measure for determining the possibility of forgiveness. Rather, a useful point of comparison may be that the post-World War II context did not necessitate forgiveness or

---

1 The *Gacaca* (pronounced 'gachacha') court is part of a system of community justice inspired by tradition and established in 2001 in Rwanda in the wake of the 1994 Rwandan genocide. It is believed it can provide justice for the victims and also aid reconciliation.

reconciliation (on a practical level because Germany no longer had a Jewish population), whereas in South Africa and Rwanda, where victims and perpetrators continue to live alongside each other, talking about forgiveness and reconciliation is imperative. In this sense then, the possibility of forgiveness would hinge on its necessity.

I find Cheney Ryan's (cited in Govier 2002) description of unforgivable acts as those which destroy hope, thus precluding positive possibilities, interesting. Govier explains:

> Ryan suggests that because infants and children represent hope, atrocities in which they are killed are especially likely to seem unforgivable. Such atrocities may seem so terrible as to eliminate the distinction between the acts committed and the agents who commit them.
>
> (Govier 2002, p. 102)

But now thinking about forgiveness becomes context-specific and dependent on the nature of transgressions. Here I am reminded of Elie Wiesel's words in Auschwitz in 1995 at the ceremony commemorating the camp's liberation: 'Although we know that God is merciful', Wiesel said, 'please God … do not forgive the murderers of Jewish children.… God, merciful God, do not have mercy on those who had no mercy on Jewish children' (cited in Roth 2006, p. 8).

It seems to me that a useful way of thinking about forgiveness in the general, that is, in the universal, is by adopting the language of Derrida (2002) and his notion of 'pure forgiveness' or Jankélévitch's (2005) 'unmotivated forgiving' – notions of forgiveness that transcend the deeds which make forgiveness necessary. When an act 'has neither mitigating circumstances, nor excuses of any sort', argues Jankélévitch, 'and when hope of regeneration has to be abandoned, then there is no longer anything else to do but to forgive' (2005, p. 106).

Correspondingly, Derrida (2002) contends that the essence of forgiveness is in forgiving the unforgivable: forgiveness acquires its true meaning only when it is called upon to forgive the unforgivable. He characterizes his understanding of forgiveness as 'the madness of the impossible'. Derrida considers circumstances where victims have been so dehumanized and abused that they lose the freedom, the power and the 'right to speak' the words 'I forgive'. In such cases, Derrida argues, the victim is a double victim because not only is the injury an irreparable violation, the victim is also stripped 'of the minimal, elementary *possibility* of *virtually* considering forgiving the unforgivable' (2002, p. 59). Derrida seems to be suggesting here that perpetrators who commit unspeakable atrocities dehumanize victims to the point where victims lose the very essence of their humanity, which is essential for making choices about the dilemma of whether to forgive or not to forgive. I have suggested that the emergence of forgiveness is deeply embedded in the capacity for empathy (Gobodo-Madikizela, 2002), so I want to elaborate briefly on this theme.

The validity of Derrida's (2002) argument above is borne out in the work of Fonagy and his colleagues on the effects of trauma on the development of the capacity to recognize the thoughts and feelings of another (Fonagy & Target 1996, 1997), a process which is the bedrock of the development of the capacity for empathy. The relationship between trauma and the capacity for empathy has been most impressively articulated by Laub & Auerhahn (1993), whose scholarship on Holocaust testimonies has been remarkable. Laub & Auerhahn's position is that extreme trauma leads to the dissolution of the empathic and attachment bonds within the human community.

To the extent that in our relationships with fellow human beings we seek to respect the dignity of others, our engagement with the community of human others is endowed with an ethical morality of care. Inherent in this *human* orientation is the assumption – particularly in societies that value communal existence – that one's livelihood is inextricably interwoven with that of others. When there has been a breakdown in this perception of the relational sphere, however – that is, when the human capacity to experience others and perceive them as real has been obliterated, when there's been a dearth of empathic capabilities (Laub & Auerhahn 1993; Laub & Lee 2003) – then extending care and empathy to others is severely diminished. There is, in a nutshell, little or no concern for the dignity of the other and no commitment to the expression of empathy for the other. My argument in this paper is that when the conditions for the emergence of forgiveness are created, they serve to re-animate the empathic sensibilities damaged by violence both between individuals and within communities. The process of restoring the human capacity for empathy and the intrinsic sense of human possibilities that are destroyed by violence requires a working through of trauma, which in essence is the reparation of the brokenness brought about by traumatic experience in the lives of victims.

The Need for Working Through Trauma

The story of forgiveness begins with the story of trauma. It is important to highlight what we all know, which is that the experience of trauma is one that remains 'unfinished' for many people who have been affected by trauma. Traumatic experience is referred to as an experience of loss: loss of control, language, power and self. It is a moment of rupture that produces what has been termed 'speechless terror' (van der Kolk 1996) and causes disruptions of personal identity. As Harjula and Heiskanen (2002) remind us, when people are traumatized, a 'silent language' begins to occupy the space between words, rupturing speech and changing its rhythm (p. 198). This 'silent language' in essence conveys the *'lived* memory' (Gobodo-Madikizela 2001, 2003) of trauma and the struggle with its disruptive impact. In the words of one scholar, Brison (2002), trauma is the 'unmaking' of the self – without language and without a feeling of a sense of control there is no self. The connections between the self and the rest of humanity are severed as victims are reduced to objects by their tormentors and their personhood treated as worthless. The process of working through the effects of trauma, Brison argues, involves an attempt to *remake* the self, the internal self as well as one's external world.

In her seminal work on the relationship between trauma and narrative, Caruth (1995, 1996) conceives of trauma as an 'unclaimed' experience, an event 'experienced too soon, too unexpectedly, to be fully known and … therefore not available to consciousness until it imposes itself again, repeatedly, in the nightmares and repetitive actions of the survivor' (1996, p. 4). The inassimilable nature of the traumatic experience results in the victim or survivor's re-enactment of the trauma. Re-enactment is a means of dealing with the unfinished business of trauma, aspects of an event that cannot be fully integrated into consciousness. For Caruth, the defining feature of trauma is therefore its 'belatedness', or the fact that the full meaning of the trauma can only be recovered subsequent to the event.

It has been suggested that the 'unclaimed experience' (Caruth 1996) of trauma leads to some kind of psychic rupture and a fragmentation of traumatic memories that remain unresolved, which dominate the mental life of many victims of trauma. There is sufficient evidence showing how these traumatic memories, and difficulties in their assimilation, often return as behavioural re-enactment, both at the interpersonal level as well as within societies (Bloom 1996; Herman 1992; Laub & Lee 2003; McFarlane & van der Kolk 2000). The phenomenon of re-enactment and its centrality in the lives of people who have been exposed to life-threatening experiences of trauma is well established in traumatic stress research (Beveridge 1998; van der Kolk 1989). The connections between traumatic experience and behavioural re-enactments are manifestations of the return of trauma as observed in therapy with individuals with a history of traumatic stress (Kernberg 2003; Laub & Lee 2003), as revictimization of self in battered women and sex workers (Herman 1999) and victimization directed at others in criminals who suffered physical or sexual abuse as children (Gilligan 1997).

These findings provide compelling evidence to influence significantly the way we think about the continuing effects of trauma and its impact in the lives of victims and survivors of mass violence. The language of violence is etched in the memory of many victims of violent conflict, and passed on to the next generation, and to the next, in the way that traumatic memory so often does, in ways subtle and not so subtle (Laub & Lee 2003).

Re-enactments can be seen as expressions of that which cannot be spoken – that which is as yet 'unclaimed'. This repetition of real events from the past is, perhaps, a cathartic way of putting into action the struggle to find language to express the frustrations, helplessness, disempowerment, and humiliation suffered by those who have faced extremely traumatic events in their lives, especially human-induced trauma such as mass political violence.

Re-enactments are triggered mainly at an unconscious level. In this sense then, re-enactment of trauma is both a manifestation of the presence of something that cannot be articulated and the expression of its *absence* – it is 'absent' because it is as yet unknown. Caruth (1995) carefully captures this idea of trauma as absence when she points out that trauma is a story of 'a wound that cries out' in an attempt to 'tell us of a reality or truth that is not otherwise available' (p. 4). The psychic imprints of trauma 'cry out' for articulation even if they are not fully grasped, or indeed known, by those who experience them. Caruth insists that trauma is identifiable only in the way in which 'its very unassimilated nature – the way it was precisely *not known* in the first instance – returns to haunt the survivor later on' (Caruth 1995, p. 4).

Caruth's (1995) analysis of trauma as 'a wound that cries out' is particularly helpful for understanding the notion of the 'unfinished business' of trauma which I have advanced in this article and elsewhere (Van der Merwe & Gobodo-Madikizela 2007). As Caruth points out, the traumatic wound is unspeakable and inarticulable until it 'imposes' itself through re-enactments. The insights that can be drawn from this understanding of the dynamics of trauma sketched out by Caruth are that the experience of trauma leads to deep psychological injury at an unconcscious level. Thus, re-enactment of trauma derives from unconscious processes. These re-enactments are symbolic of unacknowledged events finding voice in the present – a repetition of old scripts – what Volkan (2006) refers to as 'chosen traumas.' When these scripts are played out in the social domain, the consequences can be quite explosive. Re-enactment of trauma, scholars in the trauma field inform us, is a major cause of violence in society (Van der Kolk 1989).

At an individual level, victims who are vulnerable to repeating past traumas remain in a crisis precisely because of this 'unfinished business' of trauma, and they need help to regain control over their current lives. In the following section I want to draw from the theory advanced by Caruth (1995, 1996), Herman (1992), Felman (1991),

(Felman & Laub 1992) and others that trauma needs to be spoken in all its horror and violation to a listener or audience. These authors have suggested that the incidence of trauma overwhelms the affective region of the mind and renders cognitive processing of the event impossible, and as Caruth states, making it impossible for the event to be 'known'. The process of rendering the trauma knowable then requires speaking out about trauma and 'telling' it to someone who is a listener. Thus, testimonial narratives or 'witnessing' about trauma provide moments that illuminate the victim's traumatic experiences in a way that not only helps the victim to integrate the trauma into their lives, but, perhaps most importantly, invites others to bear witness to another's pain and suffering.

Trauma and the Witnessing Dance

The relationship between trauma and testimony has emerged as a major area of study in the scholarship on trauma, particularly trauma in the aftermath of gross human rights violations. The seminal work of literary scholars and psychoanalytic theorists Caruth (1995; 1996), LaCapra (1994), Felman & Laub (1992), has focused mainly on the testimonies of Holocaust survivors. This work explores the relationship between narrative and traumatic memory, particularly the potentially reparative elements of narrative testimony. The scholarship on testimony has profound implications for the way we think about how people tell and share stories about their traumatic experiences, and the role of narrative in dealing with traumatic pasts.

There are three levels of witnessing that I would like to address. Firstly, there is the witnessing through language – witnessing with words that try to capture what happened, the retelling of the story in the presence of an audience. The second level of witnessing is one that I think is much more important than the narrative rendering of the traumatic experience, and that is witnessing about trauma at an internal level. This level of witnessing is critical since the problem of trauma re-enactment occurs at a deeply unconscious level. The observation – of transgenerational transmission of trauma, e.g. Yehuda et al. (2000) – that the stories that victims and survivors carry internally as 'unfinished business' of trauma may be passed on to, and live on in the experiences of a second generation is not an exaggeration.

Thirdly, perpetrators, through their own presence and participation as listeners in public testimony such as those conducted by South Africa's Truth and Reconciliation Commission, insert yet another layer of witnessing. There is, also with perpetrators, an internal dynamic in their bearing witness. And here is what I mean by this: perpetrators, particularly those whose testimonial narratives carry an element of remorse bring a story of their own turmoil, a story of their destruction, not only in the world around them but also the self-destruction that comes with a life of violent aggression. When perpetrators feel a sense of remorse, they are likely to experience internal turmoil, shame and guilt for their actions. Thus, there is, potentially, a two-fold outcome in the process of witnessing about a violent and traumatic past. On the one hand, victims find their voice to speak the unspeakable and to confront the 'impossible history within them' (Caruth 1995, p. 4), and on the other hand, perpetrators are forced to confront the consequences of their actions in public, which may open up the possibility to 'bare their soul' and for expression of remorse. In this 'dance' of witnessing victims face the rupture within – the unfinished business of trauma – and perpetrators the internal stirrings of their depravity. At the same time, victims and perpetrators *speak* to each other and bear witness to the stories they bring from all levels of their experience of the past: the stories which find expression through words, and those which are inexpressible. In this sense then, the 'witnessing dance' on a public stage binds victims and perpetrators together in the act of bearing witness, through speech and through the very subtle elements of intersubjectivity in their encounter.

In bearing witness, confronting their depravity and coming face-to-face with the pain and suffering they have caused victims, perpetrators are re-humanizing not only the victims whose lives were shattered by their actions, but through their remorse they are also reclaiming their own sense of humanity, a humanity shattered by the atrocties they committed. The first step of dehumanization, of rendering the other invisible, is silencing the voice of conscience. The dehumanization of the self is the beginning steps of that slippery slope into a life of destruction against others who are considered to be enemies. When remorse is triggered in the moment of witnessing, however, the perpetrator recognizes the other as a fellow human being. At the same time, the victim, too, recognizes the face of the perpetrator not as that of a 'monster' who committed terrible deeds, but as the face with enough humanity to feel remorse. This does not deny the horrific deeds or set them aside as such; by showing remorse the perpetrator is showing his human side. This becomes an opportunity to integrate these human elements of someone who was perceived as other so that the perpetrator becomes less threatening, and more attuned with the victim's human identity.

The expression of remorse and the 'pain' (Duff 1986; Rollin 2006) associated with feelings of remorse carry a paradox that seems to present the perpetrator as the 'wounded other'. Woundedness – moral or psychological – is a sign of ethical responsibility towards the other. This responsibility towards the other invites victims and villains to share in the common idiom of humanity. It also provides an opportunity for reflection on the historical circumstances which dangle like the sword of Damocles, threatening to divide groups and individuals within the larger society in its efforts to heal after a violent and hateful past.

This woundedness, and the remorse that animates it, draws the perpetrator into a *relationship* with the victim. It is the recognition of the victim's pain that awakens remorse in the perpetrator, and it is remorse that lays the ground for the emergence of empathic sensibilities expressed on the part of the victim towards the perpetrator.

Empathy and Forgiveness

The essence of empathy is the capacity to feel *with* and to participate in shared reflective engagement with the other's inner life. Most scholars recognize some form of identification with the other at a deeper internal level as central to the capacity for empathy. Merleau-Ponty (1968), for example, defined empathy as 'the intertwining of our lives with those of others' (p. 49).

In psychology, and particularly within the psychoanalytic discipline, we recognize the critical role of secure attachment relationships in early childhood development, particularly the emergence of what Fonagy and Target (Fonagy & Target 1996, 1997; Target & Fonagy 1996) have termed the capacity for mentalization. Fonagy and Target have argued that the emergence of the capacity for mentalization, that is, the infant's awareness of her own feelings and thoughts and her ability to appreciate and distinguish the feelings and thoughts of others, is a process rooted primarily in the child's mirroring relationship with the caregiver. Mentalization, then, is the capacity to reflect on one's mental state and the mental state of others. The development of the capacity for empathy is deeply embedded in this early developmental process of mentalization. As pointed out in an earlier section of the paper, these authors have suggested that early trauma interferes with this developmental process. To reiterate, similar findings have been reported in studies of the effects of trauma in adulthood (Laub & Auerhahn 1993; Laub & Lee 2000).

The exercise of witnessing and bearing witness about trauma creates the possibility for the restoration of these empathic bonds with others, even those who are our former enemies. In my book *A Human Being Died That Night* I write thus about the quality of empathy:

> The power of human connectedness, of identification with the other as 'bone of my bone' through the sheer fact of his being human, draws us to 'rescue' others in pain, almost as if this were a learned response embedded deep in our genetic evolutionary past. We cannot help it. We are induced to empathy because there

is something in the other that is felt to be part of the self, and something in the self that is felt to belong to the other.

(Gobodo-Madikizela 2003)

I present this quote here in its entirety because I believe that contemplating the human capacity for empathy – the possibility of a moment when an empathic bond is established between victims and perpetrators and between any two parties who were previously adversaries – might help us to understand better what happens in encounters that lead to forgiveness. I believe that the psychoanalytic explanation of empathy opens up interesting possibilities for understanding the dynamics of forgiveness. One of the most useful aspects of psychoanalytic notions of the development of consciousness and of the self in relation to empathy is the focus on relationality and intersubjectivity.

What animates forgiveness lies in that intersubjective realm where we encounter the other's humanity in its 'purest sense'. I mean by this the interplay between the subjectivities that pertain to each 'side' of the forgiveness dyad and the emotional contexts within which these subjectivities are embedded. According to this perspective, there is a 'reciprocal mutual influence' between the subjectivities of two people engaged in an encounter and interacting in dialogue with one another (Stolorow & Lachmann 1987, p. 42). Insights from this perspective suggest that intersubjectivity recognizes that emotional responses and understanding that emerge from an encounter where one person asks for forgiveness and the other offers it, accrue from an interaction between two subjectivities – the forgiver's and that of the person who desires forgiveness. Therefore, the process of forgiveness is always specific to and 'co-created' within the particular dialogue encounter that produces forgiveness.

The *process* that entails granting forgiveness is more pertinent here than the 'act' of forgiveness as such. It seems to me that the term forgiveness, as an outcome of dialogue in the encounter between two people, may mean different things for different people. Genuine forgiveness, argues Horowitz (2005), 'involves significant intrapsychic work, conscious and unconscious working through of one's anger, and *putting the offence into the context of an integrated view of the whole person of the offender*' (p. 485, italics added). What Horowitz suggests here is that the underlying process that inspires forgiveness involves reflection and developing a sense of understanding of the other as well as gaining some degree of insight into what motivated the other to engage in the painful and cruel action.

I want to draw attention to Horowitz' notion of an intrapsychic dynamic at work in the process of forgiveness, and, in particular, to the pivotal turn to perspective taking and gaining an integrated view of the other – here is the essence of empathic movement towards the other, an experience of transcendence beyond oneself, but one which is inspired by both conscious and unconscious dynamics of the intersubjective engagement with the other.

The example I want to share is a story drawn from South Africa's Truth and Reconciliation Commission (TRC). It involves a group of seven mothers whose sons were killed by the apartheid government's police in an incident that came to be known as the Gugulethu Seven. Seven young men who were activists, and who, like many of us in our youth, were angry about apartheid and wanted to do something, were identified by black police collaborators who infiltrated Gugulethu Township near Cape Town. In the 1980s apartheid South Africa, police collaborators were known as *askaris*. When the group of *askaris* arrived in the township of Gugulethu they brought firearms and other kinds of combat paraphernalia and gave the young activists a crash course in the use of grenades, AK-47s, and other army equipment known at the time to be the signature of the ANC liberation army. The young activists believed that the *askaris* were comrades in the anti-apartheid struggle. After gaining the activists' trust, the *askaris* identified a false target which turned out to be a road block set up by an army of police to ambush the seven activists from Gugulethu. They were all brutally killed, shot in the head and suffered numerous other gunshot wounds. Evidence produced at the TRC hearing on the Gugulethu Seven shooting showed that some activists were shot from the back as they tried to flee and others from the front as they tried to surrender.

The narrative that emerged at the time in the media, however, suggested that the killing was a result of an anti-terrorist attack: government security forces had succeeded to prevent a bloody terrorist attack before it could happen! These kinds of murderous plots with the aid of police collaborators, and the media reports that accompanied them, were widespread during apartheid South Africa. It emerged during TRC public hearings that this kind of targeted killing of activists was used by security departments across the country to boost the image of the security police in the eyes of white voters and the Minister of Police. Reportedly, after these 'success' stories, the security budget was increased on the grounds that the police were doing their job well.

The policemen applying for TRC amnesty for their involvement in the Gugulethu Seven shooting were a white security police who was in charge of the murderous operation, and a black policeman who was one of the *askaris* who led the seven activists to their deaths. At the end of the public hearing the black policeman, Thapelo Mbelo, approached us as members of the TRC and asked if we could set up a meeting with the mothers of the seven victims. Mbelo wanted to apologize to them and to ask their forgiveness. After the mothers agreed to the meeting, and before setting up the meeting, I met with the mothers and other family members over a week, preparing them for their encounter with the man who had lured their sons into an ambush. I also met Mbelo for a few hours to prepare him for the meeting.

Encounter Between Victims and Perpetrators: Making Public Spaces Intimate

Public acknowledgement of responsibility for human rights crimes allows for the construction of narratives that are not simply individual and private matters, but are also expressions of collectively shared understandings of the past by those who contributed in whatever way to the perpetration of the crimes in question. 'Bearing witness' about a traumatic past, argue Feldman & Laub (1992), is a response to an ethical and moral imperative that compels the witness to confront a deeper level of truth by testifying in public. Feldman & Laub (1992) draw our attention to the fact that the most urgent claim of public testimony is to listen to it and to *hear* what is being communicated to us. The authors point out that the conjuring up of traumatic memory in the process of witnessing is done 'in order to address another … to impress upon a listener, to *appeal* to a community' (Feldman & Laub 1992, p. 204).

Confronting the past in this way demands a deeper affective connection to the witness on the part of listeners; it provides the possibility for the listening audience to deepen its own participation in the 'witnessing dance'. Perpetrators are invited to reflect on the suffering of victims and survivors and on the direct role they played. Bystanders, on their part, are forced to consider, if they may, the consequences of their *indirect* role which they played by turning the other way and doing nothing while enjoying the benefits associated with their position of privilege. Thus, public acknowledgment of atrocities and of the suffering and pain endured by victims is an important restorative step not only for individual victims and survivors, but also for the broader society. Encountering 'the other' through public testimony about the past, *hearing* the depth of the other person's story creates a space for the emergence of moments of transcendence. The encounter between Mbelo and the mothers of the seven young men was illustrative of these moments of transcendence. In the following section I focus only on critical moments in their encounter which led to the expression of forgiveness for Mbelo by some of the mothers of the seven young men.

It is important to note that in my sessions with the mothers in preparation for their meeting with Mbelo there was a sense of readiness expressed by some of the mothers of the murdered victims to forgive Mbelo; but they said they first wanted to see whether Mbelo meant his apology. When Mbelo was given a chance to speak, he expressed his apology, telling the mothers and family members of the victims that his apology was 'from the bottom of my heart'. As the mothers of the murdered activists looked on, one could sense the rising anger in their faces. One of them asked how Mbelo could betray his own blood and sell his brothers' lives to white men. Another accused him of being a wolf dressed in sheep's skin; and yet another broke down and cried in deep anguish and impotence for her helplessness and inability to provide financially for her grandchildren left in her care as a result of her son's killing. As this went on with most of the mothers confronting Mbelo with their pain, anger and impotent rage, Mbelo sat motionless, with only his face twitching anxiously. He cast a lonely figure and seemed uncertain whether the mothers would grant him the forgiveness he wanted.

There was a turning point after Mbelo begged the mothers for their forgiveness saying: 'I would like to ask you to forgive me, my parents … I ask your forgiveness my parents'. It might seem strange, perhaps presumptuous, that the man responsible for the killing of their sons should refer to the mothers as 'my parents'. In any other context, this would have been inappropriate. But there was something else at play which made it possible for Mbelo to refer to the mothers in this manner.

Mbelo's choice of language demonstrates the multidimensionality of social relationships within the African cultural context. This context derives its meaning from a particular sociocultural ethos that takes for granted an approach to dialogue which seeks to preserve an element of humanity in social discourse. This approach that encourages others to assert their humanity is inspired by the abiding humanity of *ubuntu*. So, when Mbelo begged the mothers to forgive him in their own language: '*Ndicela uxolo bazali bam*' ('I ask your forgiveness my parents'), he was making an appeal that went beyond the words themselves.

Bazali bam – my parents – presents Mbelo as a child who has gone astray and now begs his parents to be readmitted into the family circle of love and care. By addressing the mothers in this way Mbelo was using the instruments of humanity available in the culture to reclaim his own sense of humanity and of acceptability within the community. His act of betrayal excluded him and placed him in the realm of unredeemable 'other'. Drawing on the values of *ubuntu,* of shared common humanity, his words confronted the mothers with their own sense of responsibility as *parents*, as such, as representative of every 'child's' extended network of parents, which operates within the African ethic of care and human solidarity. The potency of Mbelo's words in the mothers' own Xhosa language, '*Ndicela uxolo bazali bam*', is stronger than the English translation.

The response of one of the mothers, Cynthia Ngewu, can be seen as a humanizing one. 'My son', she said, 'you are the same age as my son, Christopher. I want to tell you today, that I as Christopher's mother, I forgive you my son'.

Here too, the force of Cynthia Ngewu's words is better captured in the original language in which she spoke: '*Ndiya kuxolela mntanam*' ('I forgive you my son'). She repeated these words a few times as if to convey the unconditionality of her forgiveness, '*Ndiya kuxolela*' ('I forgive you'), '*Ewe, ndixolile*' ('Yes, I have forgiven' or 'Yes, I'm at peace'). Her final words to Mbelo, 'Go well my child', seemed to be an expression of a message both of hope and of obligation. They suggest an affirmation of the humanity that now binds Mbelo to her, and to some extent, the other mothers' own humanity.

It was interesting to observe that this spirit of forgiveness expressed by Cynthia Ngewu was extended to other mothers in the room as they witnessed Ngewu's communication to Mbelo in words and gestures. The intersubjective engagement between on the one hand Ngewu as 'representative' of the dead victims' mothers, and on the other hand Mbelo as the perpetrator, seemed to invite the perception of Mbelo in a new light. The reciprocal recognition of each other's pain between Ngewu and Mbelo, triggered, it would seem, by Mbelo's passionate remorseful plea for forgiveness, seemed to expand to the larger space in the room and to the rest of the mothers and other family members. There was a shift from the mothers' initial response to Mbelo and one witnessed nodding around the room and sounds of 'Mh' and 'yes' as Ngewu reached out with forgiveness to Mbelo, signalling agreement with Ngewu's stance towards Mbelo. It was clear that something about the dialogue between Ngewu and Mbelo had 'touched' the larger group; other mothers of the slain young activists were also communicating forgiveness to Mbelo. What insights might be drawn from this shift, this empathic movement towards 'the other'?

These moments of empathic engagement between victims and perpetrators are rare and unprecedented in the history of atrocities in the twentieth and twenty-first centuries. Often we, as listeners and witnesses, are drawn into these kinds of encounters with our own internal stories that we bring into these spaces of dialogue about the past. We are not simply present to provide the containment that is a necessary part of the listener role. In the process we are drawn into participating with our own stories in their different forms, including our own 'unfinished business' from the past. Whether they are stories of the pain of trauma, or stories of the pain of guilt – that is, whether we are victims, perpetrators or bystanders – we become co-participants in the process of witnessing and we are moved to participate at a deeply personal level. I have referred to this tendency for an audience to be drawn to the stories of those bearing witness about the past through identification as a process of 'making public spaces intimate' (Gobodo-Madikizela, *in press*).

What the mothers seemed to be communicating in their collective response of forgiveness transcends the words of forgiveness themselves. As Mbelo prepared to leave, each of the mothers embraced him ('you are now one of us', they seemed to be saying). Their gesture of forgiveness expressed in an embrace could be seen as a sign pointing Mbelo towards his own sense of obligation, drawing him into a vision of shared humanity ahead, a vision he espoused through the promise inherent in his words of apology – 'from the bottom of my heart'. A door had been opened for Mbelo to go on and pursue the quest to re-claim his humanity. The embrace also seemed to gesture Mbelo and the mothers collectively to a position of mutual obligation towards building a more humane society.

Conclusion

This dialogue and encounter between family members of victims and a perpetrator conveys the power of words, emotions and gestures as *cultural language*. The nuances and intricacies of the 'cultural dance' of the communication between Mbelo and the mothers is illustrative of dialogue that is primarily concerned about giving a human face to a man who is begging, not for the slate to be wiped clean, but for a chance to take the first steps towards rehabilitation and to live among fellow human beings. The concept of *ubuntu* is probably the best ethical framework that sums up the response that unfolded in this encounter. Inspired by the concept of *ubuntu*, Steve Biko famously called for an approach which embodies hope to restore humanity in South African society at a time when the ravages of violent conflict were threatening to destroy that very essence of hope: 'the quest for true humanity,' Biko said, '[is] the greatest gift possible' (Biko 2002).

Although the concept of *ubuntu* is universally considered to be an African concept, I consider *ubuntu* to be a human concept. The notion of *ubuntu* invites us all as fellow human beings to truly listen to one another in our social and political engagement, so that during moments of witness about our past and our different roles in it we can *hear* and connect with one another at critical points when our humanness shines through. This, I think, is the essence of a justice based on the quest for human dignity and the restoration of a moral order in societies previously characterized by violence and hatred between groups and individuals. The ideas of social reconciliation and forgiveness that have emerged across the globe in recent years are not necessarily new, nor created by the Truth and Reconciliation

Commission. These ideas are drawn from the universal values of care, compassion and empathy, values that are central in our perceptions of moral humanity. Ordinary people under certain circumstances are capable of far greater evil than we could have imagined. But so are we capable of far greater virtue than we might have thought.

In our quest to restore the human spirit and to create opportunities that will open the door to the possibilities of transformation in societies struggling with traumatic pasts we must find ways of making the values of empathy and compassion, even for our former enemies, accessible in the aftermath of mass trauma. Societal groups *can* transcend cycles of violence and forgive, if not necessarily fully reconcile with, other groups. But that uncertain process is made more likely, and less tentative, when it is supported by an ethos of acknowledgment and accommodation and underpinned by the nationally constructed language, cues, and symbols of collective reconciliation. The result may not be reconciliation in its full sense but, through the vicarious experience of stories of forgiveness, a society can begin to heal itself, and a more authentic and settled sense of self-esteem and of collective worth can come to permeate public discourse about the past.

[This paper was first published in the April 2008 issue of the *Journal of Analytical Psychology*, Vol. 53, 2.]

References

Arendt, H. (1965). *Eichmann in Jerusalem: A Report on the Banality of Evil*. New York: Viking Press.

Arendt, H. (1998). *The Human Condition*. Chicago & London: The University of Chicago Press.

Beveridge, A., 1998. 'On the origins of post-traumatic stress disorder'. In *Psychological Trauma: A Developmental Approach*, eds. D. Black et al, 3-9.

Biko, S. (2002). *I Write What I Like: Selected Writings*. Chicago: University of Chicago Press.

Bloom, S. L. (1996). 'Every time history repeats itself, the price goes up: the social re-enactment of trauma'. *Sexual Addiction & Compulsivity*, 3, 161-94.

Brison, S. (2002). *Aftermath: Violence and the Remaking of the Self*. Princeton: Princeton University Press.

Caruth, C. (1995). *Trauma: Explorations in Memory*. Baltimore: The John Hopkins University Press.

– (1996). *Unclaimed Experience: Trauma, Narrative, and History*. Baltimore: Johns Hopkins University Press.

Derrida, J. (2002). *On Cosmopolitanism and Forgiveness*, translated by Mark Dooley & Michael Hughes. New York: Routledge.

Duff, R. A. (1986). *Trials and Punishments*. Cambridge: Cambridge University Press.

Felman, S. (1991). 'Introduction to Claude Lanzmann's speech, The obscenity of understanding: an evening with Claude Lanzmann'. *American Imago,* 48, 474-78.

Felman, S. & Laub, D. (1992). *Testimony: Crises of Witnessing in Literature, Psychoanalysis, and History.* New York: Routledge.

Fonagy, P., & Target, M. (1996). 'Playing with reality: I. Theory of mind and the normal development of psychic reality'. *International Journal of Psycho-Analysis,* 77, 217-33.

– (1997). 'Attachment and reflective function: Their role in self-organization'. *Development and Psychopathology,* 9, 679-700.

Gilligan, J. 1997. *Violence: Reflections on a National Epidemic.* New York: Vintage.

Gobodo-Madikizela, P. (2001). 'Traumatic memory'. In *Truth and Lies: Stories from the Truth and Reconciliation Commission in South Africa,* ed. J. Edelstein. New York: New Press.

– (2002). 'Remorse, forgiveness, and rehumanization: stories from South Africa'. *Journal of Humanistic Psychology,* 42, 7-32.

– (2003). *A Human Being Died That Night: A South African Story of Forgiveness.* Boston: Houghton Mifflin.

– (in press). 'Transforming trauma in the aftermath of gross human rights abuses: making public spaces intimate'. In *Intergroup Reconciliation,* eds. Arie Nadler, Jeffrey Fisher & Thomas Malloy. Oxford: Oxford University Press.

Govier, T. (1999). 'Forgiveness and the unforgivable.' *American Psychological Quarterly,* 36,1, 59-75.

– (2002). *Forgiveness and Revenge.* London & New York: Routledge.

Harjula, E., & Heiskanen, T. (2002). 'Trauma lives in speech: the rhythm of speech breaks, words disappear, a hole is torn in speech'. *International Forum of Psychoanalysis,* 11, 198-201.

Horowitz, L. (2005). 'The capacity to forgive: intrapsychic and developmental perspectives'. *Journal of the American Psychoanalytic Association,* 485-511.

Herman, J. (1992). *Trauma and Recovery: The Aftermath of Violence – From Domestic Abuse to Political Terror.* New York: Basic Books.

– (1999). 'Complex PTSD: a syndrome in survivors of prolonged and repeated trauma'. In *Essential Papers on Post-Traumatic Stress Disorder,* ed. M. J. Horowitz, 82-93. New York: New York University Press.

Jankélévitch, V. (2005). *Forgiveness,* trans. by Andrew Kelley. Chicago & London: University of Chicago Press.

Kernberg, O. F. (2003). 'The management of affect storms in psychoanalytic psychotherapy of borderline patients'. *Journal of the American Psychoanalytic Association,* 51, 517-45.

LaCapra, D. (1994). *Representing the Holocaust: History, Theory, Trauma,* Ithaca: Cornell University Press.

Laub, D. & Auerhahn, N. (1993). 'Knowing and not knowing. Massive psychic trauma: forms of traumatic memory'. *International Journal of Psycho-Analysis,* 74, 261-76.

Laub, D., & Lee, S. (2003). 'Thanatos and massive psychic trauma'. *Journal of the American Psychoanalytic Association,* 51, 433-63.

McFarlane, A. C., & Van der Kolk, B. A. (2000). 'Trauma and its challenge to society'. In *Traumatic Stress: The Effects of Overwhelming Experience on*

Mind, Body and Society, eds. McFarlane & Van der Kolk, 25-45. New York: Guilford Press.

Merleau-Ponty, M. (1968). *The Visible and the Invisible.* Translated by A. Lingis. Evanston, IL: Northwestern University Press.

Rollin, H. (2006). 'Remorse in melancholia'. *British Journal of Psychiatry*, 189, 471-72.

Roth, J. K. (2006). 'Forgiveness? Reflections on Ethics after the Holocaust'. The Ernest and Renee Samson 7th Anniversary Lecture, Cape Town Holocaust Centre. Unpublished.

Stolorow, R. & Lachmann, F. (1987). 'Transference – the organization of experience'. In *Psychoanalytic Treatment: An Intersubjective Approach*, eds. R. Stolorow, B. Brandchaft & G. Atwood, 28-46. Hillsdale, NJ: The Analytic Press.

Target, M., & Fonagy, P. (1996). 'Playing with reality II: the development of psychic reality from a theoretical perspective'. *International Journal of Psycho-Analysis*, 77, 3, 459-79.

Terr, L. (1990). *Too Scared to Cry.* New York: Harper & Row.

Van der Kolk, B. (1989). 'The compulsion to repeat the trauma: re-enactment, revictimization, and masochism'. *Psychiatric Clinics of North America*, 12, 389-411.

Van der Merwe, C. & Gobodo-Madikizela, P. (2007). *Narrating Our Healing: Perspectives on Working through Trauma.* Cambridge, UK: Cambridge Scholars Press.

Volkan, V. (2006). *Killing in the Name of Identity.* Charlottesville, VA: Pitchstone Publishing.

Yehuda, R., Bierer, L. M., Schmeidler, J., Aferiat, D. H., Breslau, I. & Dolan, S. (2000). 'Low cortisol and risk for PTSD in adult offsprings of Holocaust survivors'. *American Journal of Psychiatry*, 157, 1252-59.

Shifting Shadows:
Shaping Dynamics in the Cultural Unconscious

Catherine Kaplinsky
UK (SAP)

Abstract

Jung has suggested that wars, social upheavals and religions are 'but the superficial symptoms of a secret psychic attitude unknown even to the individual himself, and transmitted by no historian ...' (Jung 1964, para. 315). With a focus on South Africa and some dream material, I explore this idea with particular emphasis on the cultural unconscious and the emerging theory of cultural complexes. Different cultures demand the repression of different aspects of the self and have different ways of actualizing a moral code. These repressions are part of what make up a dynamic and shifting cultural complex which inevitably plays a part in historical change. In turn, historical change plays its part in shifting these dynamics.

In the analytic setting via the transference and countertransference, we are familiar with what is being repressed in relation to shadow dynamics, complexes and obsolete defences. Such dynamics relate to themes of boundary, identity and otherness which, in turn, reach back to early infantile strivings as well as forward in the service of unfolding. Central to this dynamic is the absorption of cultural attitudes – including that which must be repressed, allowed in or defended against. Major political shifts – historical change – inevitably affect cultural dynamics, 'secret psychic attitude(s)' and shifting shadows.

Shifting Shadows: Shaping Dynamics in the Cultural Unconscious

When we look at human history, we see only what happens on the surface, and even this is distorted in the faded mirror of tradition. But what has really been happening eludes the enquiring eye of the historian, for the true historical event lies deeply buried, experienced by all and observed by none. It is the most private and most subjective of psychic experiences. Wars, dynasties, social upheavals, conquests, and religions are but the superficial symptoms of a secret psychic attitude unknown even to the individual himself, and transmitted by no historian.

(Jung 1964, para. 315)

The Dream

I begin with a dream which was sent to me around the time of South Africa's democratic transition in 1994. The dreamer, now deceased, was an exiled White South African, a professor in a European University and a close friend. The dream – and the dreamer's exploration of it – addresses a particular 'secret psychic attitude' which will resonate with a particular population at a particular moment in time.

'From the ages of 35 to 40 or so I had a recurrent dream. The experience was always pleasant. It was very simple.

A small black boy, whom I somehow knew to be Xhosa[1], sat on a beach. The beach was very long and very beautiful, with heavy surf. If you looked at the surf from the beach it seemed high, with big waves banked up on one another. Above the surf, the air was filled with a light haze. The boy was about four years old. He played with a whole lot of cowrie shells which were 'cattle'. He was putting these cattle into a kraal [African enclosure] made of sand. He was happy. I was not present in the dream. I could not talk to him, only observe him.

I only understood the dream after a long internal voyage. The location – rather idealized – was the first thing I recognized. It was obviously Hamburg, South Africa, at the Keiskamma mouth, where I spent holidays between the age of 3 to 7 years and where I lived for about 9 months during those years. The sensation of waves banking up was exactly how I saw the sea from the beach. I checked this carefully a few days ago when I visited Hamburg after some 45 years and there was the haze too. You very often get it on still days when the surf is big. The cowries were clearly part of a childhood reality. I often played the cattle game mainly when alone.

The little boy was a puzzle, and I took a long time to home in on him. Then at one point I had a strong set of feelings about my identity which was somehow mixed up with being Xhosa. At that period I realized that the little boy was – in a curiously inadmissible way – myself. This I think was why I was not present in the dream except as an observer, unable to talk to the little boy.

Why was I the little boy? That took a while to answer. What I found was the following: In early childhood I was with my mother and little sister in the Ciskei where my cousins and uncles were farmers. My father was 'up north' in the army. During that time my 'relationship' with my mother was terrible. You can say that she was jealous of my childhood because she wanted to be looked after herself and resented having to be a responsible parent. She was,

---

1 The Xhosa are the second largest ethnic group in South Africa, predominantly settled in the Eastern Province. Nelson Mandela is a Xhosa.

to all intents and purposes, a competitive child ... only a grown up one, with great power over me. I have no recollection of meaningful love from her.

On the other hand I was loved and properly mothered by Rosie Ngwekazi who was a servant-cum-nursemaid in my aunt's house. As I came to realize bit by bit, Rosie had been my mother in every sense of the word. I depended on her far more than most White South African children might depend on their Black nursemaids because of my mother's opting out of her role – and because my mother actually hurt and humiliated me. Rosie on the other hand loved me and was my only source of unconditional loving.

The little boy was myself as Rosie's son which is what I dearly wished to be. When I discovered this some years ago, I experienced a sort of unbounded joy and freedom. The discovery that I had been loved like that was also my first adult recognition that, like everyone else, I was 'lovable' and that it was also OK to love myself.

I came to understand that I had been denied this recognition for so many years (recall only came to me at about 40) because after my father's return, we went to Cape Town and I was subject at home and at school to extremely strong racist conditioning. I simply could not own a Xhosa woman as my mother. It would have been unthinkable in the world in which I grew up. All the Black part of me which had come into being in the Ciskei became inadmissible. I could not allow myself to own the experience with Rosie. And although by the age of 25-30, I had disentangled a large amount of the racist shit that was pushed into me in the post-Ciskei years, this critical bit remained. After all, it raised very fundamental questions. At the same time, since Rosie's love was so central to my emotional survival, I held on to it in a subconscious way in the dream-sequence.

I saw Rosie at the Feni location when I visited the Ciskei region two weeks ago. It was a wonderful meeting. I was able to thank her for the love she gave me then. She knew perfectly well how important it had been and, very discreetly, made it clear that she knew a great deal about my mother's inabilities. She said that it was important that I had come back because I was Xhosa and because my 'navel is buried' in the Ciskei. I know what she means.

So there's your dream. Make whatever use you can of it. I share all the usual reasons for hating apartheid, but I have my own additional one ... it prevented me from owning the most important experience of childhood by making it inadmissible. I could not own the central Black part of myself. I don't have the dream any more. It must be because I can own the reality.

The unconscious has no sense of time'.

This dream was a gift – to the dreamer, to me and to us and we will all have been affected by it in different ways. Like all dreams, it expresses a secret psychic attitude which is both personal and collective. It also addresses a historical moment in time which relates to a particular culture. It speaks to the damaging and ruthless effects of a pernicious political system and how the dreamer's personal complexes were intricately tied up with this system. It reaches out to two segments of the dreamer's culture – the acceptable and the unacceptable. And it speaks to what is acceptable and unacceptable in his internal world, to his private unfolding and the integration of shadow. He 'does not have the dream any more', he says.

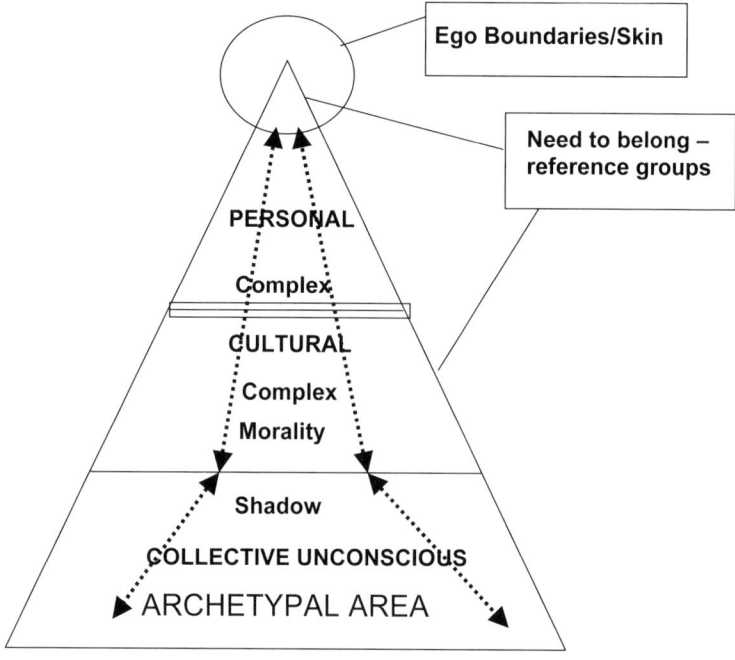

Theoretical Journey

First, it is important to recognize that this is not a dream about a patient – so this will not be a typically clinical paper, but one which I hope will further our thinking in relation to the effect of culture and history on the psyche. But before looking further into the dream, I would like to tease out some elements of Jungian theory which might assist in interpretation. In turn, of course, the dream informs theory.

My aim, more precisely, is to attempt to home in on some of the myriad of transitional areas which have the capacity for dialectical, transformative process – as well as the capacity for containment and for defence. These are the areas where boundaries evolve and shift and where shadows simultaneously follow and these are the areas which impact on psychic attitude.

The theories which I have found relevant are complex. In summary, the paper proceeds as follows: It begins by focusing on the relationship between the personal, the cultural and collective archetypal areas of the unconscious. This is followed by a discussion of the developing theory of cultural complexes. These are inevitably intertwined with personal complexes, the need to belong and specific reference groups. Since belonging implies denial of what does not fit, the paper then proceeds to explore the way in which Jung's concept of the shadow shifts with changing boundaries and relates to an archetypal morality. Morality is expressed differently in different cultures giving rise to varied and different cultural complexes. Finally, before returning to the dream, the paper focuses briefly on how infant research has expanded our understanding of early ego boundaries and of the importance of skin. All these themes are inevitably interconnected.

Personal Cultural Collective

To begin with what is distinctly Jungian, we are familiar with the dialogue between the personal and the collective unconscious or archetypal area. Significantly, Jung did not propose a particular intermediate realm between the personal and the collective – though he was clearly fascinated by the influence of culture and history on the individual psyche. As we know, he brought many insights to this realm. However he often seemed to lose sight of the fact that his own attitudes and theories were, themselves, a product of his particular time and place. This has been well documented, particularly by Farhad Dalal (1988). For instance, while we are aware that Jung was profoundly moved by his experience in Africa, he was in fact threatened by it. These anxieties further extended to America – about which he wrote in *Civilization in Transition*:

> Racial infection is a most serious mental and moral problem where the primitive outnumbers the white man. America has this problem only in a relative degree, because the whites far outnumber the coloured. Apparently he can assimilate the primitive influence with little risk to himself. What would happen if there were a considerable increase in the population is another matter.
>
> (Jung 1964, para. 966)

Also well documented, by Maidenbaum (1991 & 2002), Samuels (1992), Kirsch (1991 & 2001), and Singer (2004) amongst others, was Jung's interest in national character, through which he became entangled with accusations of anti-Semitism. As a result of this, analytical psychology's relationship to culture has, for many years, been an ambivalent one. It is taking time to sift through the difficulties.

H.E. Baynes first postulated a 'cultural psyche' in *Mythology of the Soul* (1939/1971). Subsequently, Joseph Henderson expanded our understanding of the cultural unconscious. He defined it as

> an area of historical memory that lies between the collective unconscious and the manifest pattern of the culture … it has a kind of identity arising from the archetypes of the collective unconscious, which assists in the formation of myth and ritual and also promotes the process of development in individuals.
>
> (Henderson 1990, p. 104)

As he pointed out, 'Much of what Jung called "personal" was actually culturally conditioned' (ibid.). And again later, Vannoy Adams (1996, p. 40) says 'much of what Jung called "collective" was actually "cultural".

Essentially, the cultural unconscious is a dynamic field, a living history, connecting simultaneously to both the collective and the personal. Culture influences the way individuation processes are lived out. In turn, individuation processes influence the culture. It follows that identity and culture are entangled. To quote from Orlando Figes,

> Identity … is not meaningful unless one can show how it manifests itself in social interaction and behaviour. A culture is made up not simply of works of art, or literary discourses, but of unwritten codes, signs and symbols, rituals and gestures, and common attitudes that fix the public meaning of these works and organize the inner life of a society.
>
> (Figes 2002, p. xxxii / iii)

Cultural Complexes

Of late, interest in cultural themes has been mushrooming as global communication continues to precipitate unforeseen clashes emphasizing problems of conflicting values and inequality and threatening the survival of life as we know it. This brings me to the idea of the cultural complex, recently developed by Singer and Kimbles (2004a; 2004b) in America which elaborates this energetic field. This concept facilitates the exploration of both the cultural unconscious with its impact on groups and institutions on the one hand and individual psychology on the other. I think it provides part of a theoretical framework for understanding the above dream. It also enables us to think about different cultures in a fresh way.

The idea of the cultural complex is clearly derived from a coupling of Jung's theory of 'complexes' with Henderson's theory of cultural unconscious. But I hope to extend this developing theoretical concept by attempting to home in on some of the intangible transitional areas where boundaries evolve and shift. As we know these areas are found in the relational spaces in time and space – which reach back to collective areas and archetypal potentials, as well as out into a cultural matrix. It is the energies and feelings which are 'trapped' in these spaces, in the ego-self axis, which we, as analysts, try to reach and join.

Recapping briefly on the theory of the personal complex, as we know, it was Jung's work on the Word Association Test that led to his theory of complexes. He also called these 'splinter psyches' (Jung 1960, para. 203) and then again, the 'architect of dreams' (ibid., para. 210). For Freud, Jung's work using the galvanometer became empirical proof of the unconscious. So the complex is a collection of images and ideas clustered round a core of one or more archetypes and crucially is characterized by a particular feeling tone. Complexes are rooted in the body and when activated, affect our behaviour. They are natural phenomena, essential to psychic life and can develop along positive or negative lines. They can therefore involve a certain turning back in on oneself, a recoiling – or an excited reaching out.

A cultural complex then is also an elemental aspect of any culture. To quote Singer and Kimbles,

> Cultural complexes can be thought of as arising out of the cultural unconscious as it interacts with both the archetypal and personal realms of the psyche [as well as] the broader outer world arena of schools, communities, media, and all the other forms of cultural and group life. As such, cultural complexes can be thought of as forming the essential components of an inner sociology.
>
> (Singer & Kimbles 2004a, p. 4)

This inner sociology, they go on to say, 'is a description of groups and classes of people as filtered through the psyches of generations of ancestors [and] has all sorts of information and misinformation about the structures of societies' (ibid., p. 5). This 'inner sociology' therefore is an essential aspect of the 'cultural complex'.

So, 'on an individual level, cultural complexes are expressions of a need to belong and have a valued identity within the context of a *specific reference group*'. However, the criteria required to belong might lead to splitting, rigidities and a whole range of phenomena that we recognize as psychological disturbance.

At the level of [the] group, cultural complexes seem to offer cohesion which provides a sense of kinship and group spirit. [But], at the pathological extreme, this kinship is expressed in archetypal defences of the group spirit.

(Singer & Kimbles 2004b, p. 201)

It is this 'need to belong' and the 'need for a valued identity within the context of a specific reference group' which I would like to focus on further. To belong to a reference group implies a particular 'fit', a similarity of identity, and clearly harks back to early attachment dynamics. Aspects of oneself that do not 'fit' must therefore be relegated, split off, repressed. Splinter psyches or complexes, as well as sub-personalities, which Redfearn (1985 & 1994) writes about, result from this.

Shifting Shadows, Changing Boundaries, Morality

This naturally brings us to Jung's concept of the shadow. The simple definition is 'that which a person does not wish to be'. This links to 'what is allowed' and 'what is not allowed' and the Freudian super-ego. The personal shadow, as we know, is more easily accessible and relates to the repressed and disowned part of the individual. It is *acquired* as an adaptation by the ego to outside demands. So, 'that which a person does not wish to be' is moulded by what mother and intimate others wish him or her to be, as well as by the ideology of the various groups which make up the interactive field of the culture in which they are contained.

With the concept of the cultural unconscious, also comes the cultural shadow. Anthony Stevens (1982) expanded on this idea in his book *Archetype*. Like the personal shadow, the cultural shadow arises out of the archetypal area – the area of non-ego. From this emerges ego development, me/not-me dynamics and good and bad values which extend out into the world. All cultures advocate good values and shun bad ones. This lends support to the idea of a kind of programming with a phylogenetic basis, or an archetypal basis, for morality which I will now focus on briefly.

The moral complex or Freud's super-ego 'is the psychic organ that makes society possible'. It monitors our behaviour so that cultural values are ensured. Non-conformity to the moral code brings threat of abandonment, ostracism or other forms of punishment. But there is a price and paradox to morality since, to quote Stevens, 'the very milieu that makes actualization of the Self possible also demands that aspects of the Self remain unactualized in the unconscious or be actively repressed there' (Stevens 1982, p. 211). There lies the cultural shadow.

With different cultures having different ways of actualizing the moral code, they demand the repression of different aspects of the self. From anthropology we know that what is defined as 'good' and 'bad' is culturally highly variable – thus now making the idea of universal values (common values amongst all cultures), also highly debatable. For instance, different cultures demand that such behaviours as adultery, homosexuality, incest, overt expression of aggression are suppressed to a greater or lesser degree. Therefore that which is required to be repressed varies from person to person and culture to culture. What does seem universal though are these particular nodal points around which all cultures develop moral codes – such as those above mentioned – incest, adultery etc.

There are some overlapping themes between Stevens's work on cultural shadow and Singer and Kimbles' cultural complex. Both address an archetypal form or pattern which is inherited in the form of an archetypal morality – of good and bad values. These are then fleshed out in moral codes which vary subject to environmental and historical changes. It follows that cultural complexes are particular expressions of an archetypal morality. Inevitably too, individuation processes are shaped to some extent by such cultural complexes.

It is clear that within this complicated dynamic web, born of archetypal longings to attach, to belong and be validated, are the manifold transitional spaces in which integration takes place – or in which splits and rigidities occur. These are the spaces where boundaries evolve and interact and in which personal and cultural complexes evolve. This is the stuff of our work within the analytic *vas* where these themes are played out via transference and countertransference and regressive states. The search for meaning is partly around a longing for a state of 'in-ness' and belonging which, in turn, involves a sense of agency and of being an effective part of life's drama and process.

Before returning to the dream, I would like now to focus more on this theme of 'belonging' since 'to belong' implies a boundary and while a boundary provides a sense of containment, it can also be an area of intercourse, or a point to be broken through – or out of – in order to 'become' and individuate. Boundaries also defend and give rise to shadow projections while keeping out that which is undesirable. And they are, of course, a source of conflict and war. Essentially, they are the transitional areas where choices are made and they are an intricate aspect of our analytic work.

I am reminded of a Bedouin saying quoted by Bruce Chatwin in *Songlines* (1988, p. 224). It reads:

> I against my brother
> I and my brother against our cousin
> I, my brother and our cousin against the neighbours
> All of us against the foreigner.

This saying has much relevance for this paper.

To quote from Kimbles, 'Intergroup conflicts, expressed through us/them dynamics, projections and righteousness, are the expression of normal group processes' (2000, p. 168). Essentially, on an individual level, processes of rejection and projection and boundary making are expressions of an archetypal push to separate out and individuate. With growth and development, various boundaries, containers and senses of belonging expand, spiral-like, out into the world. Rosemary Gordon (2005) explores this theme in her paper 'Do be my enemy for friendship's sake', a line from one of Blake's poems. She explores how our aggressive energy needs acceptable expression and how we need a place in which to put it.

There are inevitably pathological extremes which occur when these dynamics become rigidly defensive. The us/them dynamics of the apartheid ideology was such an example. The word 'apartheid' itself means separateness. The particular boundaries set up by this ideology, and the methods used to keep it in place, became some of the most rigid and notorious in history. As we know the colour of the skin indicated the positioning of in-ness or out-ness in society. As such it played into South Africa's cultural complex in which all manner of projections were aimed at those with non-white skin by the ruling white population. Skin colour therefore could trigger emotional reaction and was key to the cultural complex.

Infant Research, Ego Boundary, Skin

Infant research has expanded our understanding of the early drama involved in boundary formation. As we know, ego boundary and a sense of otherness have their roots in infancy. The ego evolves within the transitional boundary areas, where unconscious choices are continually being made. These are choices about what must be taken in and accepted and what rejected or projected. Such processes are involved too in the immune system. Here mechanisms within an organism protect against infection by identifying and killing pathogens. Such processes can become complicated: the immune system can become disordered and links have been found between emotional states and some immune deficiency disorders.

Fordham (1985) expanded our understanding of the early dynamics involved in separating out and the development of an ego boundary. Crucial to the process is the archetypal energy involved in the curious, exploratory reaching out of deintegration, followed by the re-integration of these experiences. The rhythm of deintegration and re-integration can be understood as a primary expression of the individuation principle.

The experience of skin is particularly important in relation to early ego boundary. Freud was the first to write about this. He wrote in a footnote that 'the ego is ultimately derived from bodily sensations, chiefly from those springing from the surface of the body. The ego is thus a mental projection of the surface of the body' (Freud 1927).

Esther Bick (1968), a Kleinian analyst, was the first to conduct an in-depth study of the psychological function of the skin, postulating that the skin is experienced as a sheath that holds together the psyche and soma. Through the experience of adequate holding and shared satisfaction, the infant is able to tolerate periods of separateness which then create spaces in which develop the imaginal and the capacity to symbolize.

Since Bick's research, much work has been conducted illuminating the relational significance of the skin to ego boundary. Anzieu (1990) speaks of the skin envelope, Feldman (2004, p. 289) of the psychic skin. Essentially, the 'skin … provides the point of contact with the external world … [and] acts as a delineator of boundaries between what is experienced to be outside and what is experienced to be inside the self'. The colour of the skin is of course irrelevant to the infant – other than signifying familiarity.

Dream Exploration

So now, following on from this section on early ego boundary formation, we can return to the dream.

For our dreamer, his mother was 'terrible' and 'she had great power over him'. Leaving himself open to her would have been damaging for him. As a result, he would have had to set up defensive structures, or a 'second skin' function, to protect his undeveloped, vulnerable self from impinging experiences. But meanwhile, he also sought appropriate responses elsewhere and, as we know, found them in Rosie. Rosie became the good object who stood in for mother. He said she 'loved and properly mothered' him and was his 'only source of unconditional loving'. We are aware that within these dynamics are the seeds for idealizing and denigrating. The dreamer was somewhere aware of this too when he alluded to his idealized memory of the beach in the Ciskei.

In the world of myth we know about the opposite poles of the archetypal mother. For an infant, the mother is not an individual in her own right, but the 'living embodiment of the Great Mother archetype' (Stevens 1982, p. 95). She can be both creative and loving on the one hand, and on the other, destructive and hateful – the Good Great Mother or the Terrible Mother.

We can see how the dreamer had been placed in a double-bind. He needed both to 'own' his experiences with Rosie in order to be 'true' to himself *and* he needed to 'disown' them in order to be 'true' to his white racist culture. Inevitably too, the 'disowning' involved a betrayal which resulted in guilt. So splinter psyches or complexes developed out of the intricate network of affect, absorbed via mother, Rosie and intimate others who, in turn reached out to and imbibed from this culture.

Thus there was a kind of layering of splits and shadow formation. Firstly, his 'terrible' mother required that he set up a defensive structure, a second skin function. Healing then occurred when he 'found' more appropriate responses from Rosie. Then, later again, in order to keep his identity within the family and to 'belong' to his particular white culture, he was required to deny his experiences with Rosie and split off from them. It is here that the personal complexes can be seen to be intricately linked to the cultural complex.

The positive outcome of the dreamer's 'required' denial of Rosie was his sense of acceptance by mother and intimate others as well as a sense of belonging and group spirit in the various white South African reference groups in which he was involved. This sense of belonging and 'in-ness' is necessary for healthy development. The negative outcome was that this aspect of denial became absorbed in the dreamer as an aspect of his shadow. There, it created a particular kind of rigidity which, in turn, linked to the rigidity of the cultural complex. Only after much personal work could this rigidity be loosened.

We cannot know what sort of transference experiences helped the dreamer with the healing process – though he did have some therapy. It is clear that he had a kind of bodily knowledge of his experience with Rosie and that he became conscious of this only after his 'long internal voyage'. The example certainly illustrates something of the way in which archetypal needs are sought out, and can be found, in another. Indeed, this archetypal need is the very foundation of our work as analysts in the transference and countertransference dynamic.

An important part of the dreamer's personal work involved understanding his dream, the game he played and the symbols therein. As we know, in analytical psychology, 'a symbol expresses a psychological function, which Jung later referred to as the transcendent function. This function mediates between opposites and effects transitions between, and transformations of psychic states' (Bovensiepen 2002). The transcendent function, Jung wrote, 'is a natural process, a manifestation of the energy that springs from the tension of opposites and consists in a series of fantasy-occurrences which appear spontaneously in dreams and visions' (Jung 1953/1966, para. 121).

The cattle game in the dream was crucial to the dreamer's personal work as well as an illustration of the work of the transcendent function. In this game, which he often played as a child, he used cowrie shells as pretend cows. The transition from cowrie to cows is particularly interesting and inventive – though he calls them 'cattle'.

The cowrie/cows were in a kraal container and were being moved about – in and out. So within this 'cattle game' there is a lot of valuable playing, experimenting, change and exchange, shifting.

As we know, the dreamer had lived with a traumatic conflict and had been split off from what might be seen as his 'true self' in Winnicott's terms (Winnicott 1971). Part of what was happening in this game was an attempt to 'disentangle' himself from what he called the 'racist shit that was pushed into [him] in the post-Ciskei years'. It is this 'racist shit' which makes up part of the cultural complex in which he lived and which affected his personal complex. One has a glimpse of his anger too, when he talks of this 'racist shit' – an anger he was unable to express while in a state of dependence and helplessness but which would probably be necessary for his healing. Through this game, he counters the helplessness while being omnipotently in charge of his cowrie/cows.

Cowrie shells are a particularly fascinating symbol. The shells exist on the sea shore, the transitional area, where the ocean and the land meet. This is where the dreamer also remembers the haze – the misty moist area above the turmoil of the surging waves – in-between the ocean and the sky. 'You very often get it on still days, when the surf is big', he wrote. This 'stillness' and the 'big surf' is an interesting set of opposites and I have a sense that they also represent the 'stillness' required by the dreamer to make meaning and to integrate the surging emotions so evident as he wrote. And, of course, shells, most obviously, have a hard, rigid defensive surface. This surface shields and contains the vulnerable, hidden, living inside. The underside of the shells has a feminine vulva-like opening. The dreamer was finding his way to reach into his hidden, vulnerable underside.

The shells were pretend cows in the dream. Cows are a feminine symbol with a softer, loose skin. They are generally calm and can be looked after, fed and protected. They relate to each other and they relate to him, they provide milk and nourishment and they shit easily – evacuating their waste. The dreamer could have a responsive interaction with them, a dialectical interplay. It was as if he was playing with the idea of softening up his defences as he shifted his cowrie-cattle-complexes about in the 'secure' kraal-container. Part of his 'working through' would necessarily be about his rage and wish omnipotently to control his cow mother as well as his cow Rosie – but also he was finding his way to acknowledge and accept his internalized Rosie – the love he had had for her and the love she had apparently had for him.

This theme of dominance, power and dependency can easily be linked to the cultural level. The Whites in the apartheid era dominated and controlled the Blacks who depended on them economically. But here there is an interesting twist because of the dependence the

Whites had on Blacks – not only for their labour but very often for their emotional care – and in the dreamer's case, he said he depended on Rosie 'for emotional survival'.

Power and control are linked to cowrie shells in yet another way. Historically, the cowrie shell was the most popular currency in parts of Africa. Only in the sixteenth century did their value diminish. During the slave trade, cowries were among the items Europeans exchanged with coastal West African groups for slaves. Also in West Africa they were sometimes used for counting since it was considered taboo to count animals or people. And they were used in many other ways. They could be used for decision-making – thrown like dice for a yes/no answer; they were used in bride-wealth, divination, funerals, initiation rites and for all manner of decoration. And in other parts of the world too, including China and Arabia, they were also used as money – units of exchange and value. Archaeologists have excavated millions of them in the tombs of the Pharaohs. So the cowrie is a rich symbol, a valuable unit of exchange, reaching back to ancient cultures.

The dreamer would have been aware of the high value both of cowrie shells as well as cattle in African cultures. Particularly for the Xhosa tribe, cattle are highly valued. They are a symbol of wealth as they ensure nourishment – milk and meat. In addition, in many African tribes, certainly with the Xhosa tribe, cattle are given as dowries, offerings, at marriages. They too are therefore units of exchange. Importantly, it is widely believed that the ancestors are all around, making themselves and their wishes known through creatures and happenings. Often it is through animals, such as cattle, that they speak – particularly in dreams. So, not only can cattle link the families of newly weds, but they can also link back to the ancestors.

The colouring of the cowrie is of particular importance. Colours vary, but in South Africa they are generally a mixture of white with blotchy brown, black or caramel markings on them. The dreamer's sister confirmed that that was how she remembered them in the Ciskei. The link to cows is again evident – both have similar colouring – though for cows, the markings are generally more defined.

The patterns and colouring of the cowrie/cows are clearly significant in relation to the dreamer's personal complexes as well as the cultural complex. And the generally more defined markings of the cattle may well link to a firming up of his colour consciousness and all that it meant. So, as the dreamer watches the game from a removed position, in the knowledge of his 'white' background, he knows he 'simply could not own a Xhosa woman as [his] mother'. He writes, 'All the black part of me which had come into being in the Ciskei became inadmissible'. It seems here that the infant dreamer assumed he was black and Xhosa – one and the same as the woman with whom he experienced 'in-ness' and 'belonging' and attachment – part of her and part of her culture.

As we know, aspects of the later conditioning experienced by the dreamer, involved the colour of the skin. His early self knew of the skin in terms of responsiveness to touch, warmth, smell. With his mother this had presumably been inadequate. But with Rosie, the experience was 'good' and containing and he associated dark skin colour with these positive sensations. His personal complexes then, embodied both a 'terrible mother' – as well as the 'good mother' which he found in Rosie and which 'countered' some of the inadequate experiences with his mother.

Later when the dreamer 'belonged' to other reference groups, he became aware that the colour of the skin marked out acceptable and unacceptable groupings. It was this which made up part of the cultural complex which further affected his internal world. To belong to these reference groups meant he 'should not know' about his relationship with Rosie; he should repress the warmth, gratitude and longing he felt for her. Those with dark coloured skin, like Rosie, received any manner of negative projections which then colonized the cultural shadow. Additionally and inevitably, with the emotional abandonment of Rosie, came guilt and this guilt also lodged firmly and unconsciously both in the cultural shadow as well as in the personal shadow of the dreamer. As such, the dynamic interaction of these shadow contents, made up important aspects of the cultural complex.

In the dreamer's white culture, it was the colour of the skin which signified acceptance or non-acceptance – in or out, good or bad. But in the dream, the colours, black, brown and white all made up one skin – whether it was the rigid hard protective cowrie shell or the softer skin of the cows. The observing dreamer – the third position – was witnessing the cattle game in which the opposing colours made up one skin.

There is a sense of awe at the healing process at work – not only in the dreamer's split internal world, where the experience with Rosie resided as unacceptable – but also a healing process which reached back through cultural conditioning, back to the ancestors of the dreamer's culture and beyond.

Vera Bührmann (1986), the first Jungian analyst in South Africa, explores the role of ancestors and traditional healers for the Xhosa, making fascinating links to depth psychology. Her research interestingly was in 'the Keiskammahoek area of the Ciskei' (p. 23), the exact area where the dreamer had his experiences with Rosie. For the Xhosa, the ancestors are omniscient and omnipresent and Bührmann describes the belief that the ancestors have favourite places for 'lingering'. One is the 'entla' – opposite the entrance door – and the other is in the cattle kraal. These are also areas where traditional healers

sometimes perform their healing rituals – and calling up the ancestors is necessary for healing (p. 28). So the 'kraal' is also literally a
significant containing space in which healing processes can take place.

From our point of view, we see the cattle game was a means of
loosening both the personal complexes of the dreamer and of freeing
himself from the cultural complex in which he had been caught up.
Thus the symbols are a means of enlivening the past in the present.
Through them, it is possible to see the complexes unfold and the
transcendent function at work.

Later, the dreamer's account of his meeting with Rosie as a grown
man seemed to indicate that she too was aware of how important her
relationship had been for him. This is a most moving moment of his
account. She told him then that his 'navel was buried in the Ciskei'.
He said, 'I know what she means', but I am not sure whether he did
really know of the myth and tradition to which this statement refers.
It is worth describing.

Traditionally for the Xhosa, the 'dropping' of the umbilical cord has
particular significance. Until this happens the infant is not regarded
as a separate being. At the birth of the first child, the mother and
baby are ensconced in a room in the maternal home for a period of
time. (This can vary, but is essentially around the time it takes for the
umbilical cord to 'drop' and for the couple to heal). No one except
particular female elders can contact the nursing couple. These elders
cook, wash and care for them. They take their role very seriously and
have much influence on the unfolding life of the child.

The actual 'dropping' of the umbilical cord is an important moment
and, when it happens, the paternal grandmother is called for. She takes
it to the paternal home where it is ceremonially buried. This place of
burial is also where the ancestors are buried and where the baby too,
in time, will be buried. The ceremony marks the identity of the baby,
linking it to its ancestors as well as to the concept of 'ubuntu' which
is understood as an important aspect of its identity. This concept of
'ubuntu' is found in many African cultures and is defined as 'a spirit of
fellowship, humanity and compassion' (Berg 2004, p. 244). Thus the
burial of the umbilical cord has the literal function of 'grounding' the
identity of the baby, of linking it to the ancestors and joining it in the
fellowship of 'ubuntu' – in the spirit of humanity and compassion.

So, it seems, Rosie had taken her role of 'elder' very seriously –
both nursing the dreamer and probably trying to guide his mother. The
dreamer wrote, 'She very discreetly made it clear she knew a great
deal about my mother's inabilities'. Rosie had re-membered and given
him a sense of his 'in-ness' and belonging with her and her culture by
saying that he was Xhosa. It was this that left him with the experience
'of unbounded joy and freedom'.

Of course, Rosie's 'secret psychic attitude' would be another story and another paper. What we do know is that her history of exploitation had cultural ripples which finally led to the demise of apartheid. One might also ask though to what extent the groundedness of her culture in the spirit of 'ubuntu' helped prevent the predicted bloodbath and encourage forgiveness. Also one might ask whether the dreamer's 'unbounded joy and freedom' had something to do with a sense of forgiveness he received from Rosie.

It is significant that Jung too had an experience of something similar to the dreamer's. In *Memories, Dreams and Reflections* he wrote almost erotically about his 'maid'. 'I still remember her picking me up and laying my head against her shoulder', he wrote.

> She had black hair and an olive complexion and was quite different from my mother. I can see even now, her hairline, her throat, with its darkly pigmented skin, and her ear. It was as though she belonged not to my family but only to me, as though she were connected in some way with other mysterious things I could not understand. This type of girl later became the component of my anima. The feeling of strangeness which she conveyed, and yet of having known her always, was a characteristic of that figure which later came to symbolize for me the whole essence of womanhood.
> (Jung 1963)

What has happened in both situations is that at a crucial time in the early development of these two men, each experienced unconditional love, each felt possessed by and had the sense of possessing and belonging to another in a way which had suffused their sense of being. Jung has worked on this aspect of himself, has based his theory of the anima around it. It is possible also that his interest in other cultures was influenced by this experience. He has, after all, been called the father of transcultural psychology, an equalizer and unifier. But the conditioning in the culture in which he grew up and the cultural complex in which he was contained still left him wary and un-attuned to people with darker skins and which later led him to say many surprisingly ethnocentric things.

So it is hoped, from these examples, that the entanglement of the personal complex and cultural complex is evident. Each speaks to an unfolding identity and a dialectical interplay which involves networks of groups and institutions. As such the ego ideal is entangled with cultural ideals and is propelled by archetypal needs to belong, feel contained and to individuate.

What the dreamer has helped us to focus on is 'the secret psychic attitude' which Jung wrote about in the quote at the beginning of the paper. This attitude 'belonged' to a particular population at a particular moment in time. Exploring the dream helped us to focus on the transitional areas in which these attitudes mutate and where the transcendent function is at work expressing itself through symbols.

Cowrie shells and cattle as units of exchange were compelling symbols. Most significantly, the multi-colouring in a single 'skin' of both the shells and the cows speaks to the Rainbow Nation which Desmond Tutu famously referred to at the moment of democratic transition in South Africa. It was also the moment when formal permission was given for the loosening and shifting of shadows.

Acknowledgements

My particular thanks to Tom Singer for his valued help and comments on this paper. Thanks also to Warren Colman, Coline Covington, George Craig, Raphie Kaplinsky, Melissa Leach, Mpine Makoe, Nokuzola Mndende, Jef Pieres, Joy Schaverien, Kate Springford, Marcus West.

[This paper was first published in the April 2008 issue of the *Journal of Analytical Psychology*, Vol. 53, 2.]

References

Adams, M.V. (1996). *The Multicultural Imagination*. London & New York: Routledge.
Anzieu, D. (1990). *Psychic Envelopes*. London: Karnac Books.
Baynes, H.E. (1940). *Mythology of the Soul*. London. Bailliere, Tindal & Cox.
Berg, A. (2004). 'Ubuntu – a contribution to the 'civilization of the universal'. In *The Cultural Complex. Contemporary Jungian Perspectives on Psyche and Society*, eds. T. Singer & S. Kimbles. London: Brunner-Routledge.
Bick, E. (1968). 'The experience of the skin in early object relations'. *International Journal of Psycho-Analysis*, 49, 4, 484-86.
Bovensiepen, G. (2002). 'Symbolic attitude and reverie'. *Journal of Analytical Psychology*, 47, 2, 241-56.
Bührmann, M.V. (1986). *Living in Two Worlds*. New York: Chiron Publications.
Chatwin, B. (1988). *Songlines*. London: Picador.
Dalal, F. (1988). 'Jung, a racist'. *British Journal of Psychotherapy*, 4, 3.
Feldman, B. (2004). 'A skin for the imaginal'. *Journal of Analytical Psychology*. 49, 3.
Figes, O. (2002). *Natasha's Dance*. London: Penguin.
Fordham, M. (1985). *Explorations into the Self*. The Library of Analytical Psychology, Vol. 7. London: Academic Press.
Freud, S. (1923/1927). *The Ego and the Id. SE* XIX.
Henderson, J. (1990). *Shadow and Self*. New York: Chrion Publications.
– (1984). *Cultural attitudes in Psychological Perspective*. Toronto: Inner City Books.
Jung, C.G. (1912). *Symbols of Transformation*. CW 5.
– (1953/66). *Two Essays on Analytical Psychology*. CW 7.

– (1960). *The Structure and Dynamics of the Psyche. CW* 8.

– (1964). *Civilization in Transition. CW* 10.

– (1963). Aniela Jaffé: *Memories, Dreams, Reflections by C.G. Jung*. London: Routledge & Kegan Paul.

Kimbles, S. (2000). 'The cultural complex and the myth of invisibility'. In *The Vision Thing: Myth, Politics and Psyche in the World*, ed. T. Singer. London: Routledge.

Kirsch, T. (1991). 'Carl Gustav Jung and the Jews: the real story'. In *Lingering Shadows*, eds. A. Maidenbaum & S.A. Martin. Boston & London: Shambhala.

– (2001). Reports on the VIIIth international Meeting of the International Association for the History of Psychoanalysis (IAAHP). *Journal of Analytical Psychology*, 46, 3.

Maidenbaum, A. (ed.) (2002). *Jung and the Shadow of Anti-Semitism*. Berwick, ME: Nicholas-Hays.

Maidenbaum, A & S. A. Martin (eds.) (1991). *Lingering Shadows*, Boston & London: Shambhala.

Redfearn, J. (1985). *My Self, My Many Selves*. London: Orlando.

– (1994). 'Movements of the I in relation to the body image'. *Journal of Analytical Psychology*, 39, 3.

Samuels, A. (1992). 'National psychology, national socialism and analytical psychology: reflections on Jung and anti-Semitism. *Journal of Analytical Psychology*, 37, 1.

Singer, T. (2004). 'Archetypal defences of the group spirit. In *The Cultural Complex. Contemporary Jungian Perspectives in Jungian Analysis*, eds. T. Singer & S. Kimbles. Brunner-Routledge.

Singer, T. & Kimbles, S.L. (2004). *The Cultural Complex. Contemporary Jungian Perspectives on the Psyche and Society*. London & New York: Brunner-Routledge.

– (2004). 'The emerging theory of cultural complexes'. In *Analytical Psychology Contemporary Perspectives in Jungian Analysis*, eds. J. Cambray & L. Carter. London, New York: Brunner-Routledge.

Stevens, A. (1982). *Archetype: A Natural History of the Self.* London: Routledge & Kegan Paul.

Winnicott, D. (1971). *Playing and Reality*. London: Tavistock Publications.

Jung and Otherings in South Africa

Renos K. Papadopoulos
UK (IGAP)

Abstract

This paper is an attempt to examine the various intersecting para-
meters related to the early stages of the Jungian movement in South
Africa. It is not a history of the movement but an endeavour to identify
some key themes that characterize that development. The process of
othering emerged as an overarching leitmotif of the various dimensions
of that historical moment. These include theoretical and clinical dimensions, the wider socio-political and historical context as well as my own
personal circumstances. Within the climate of the overall polarization
imposed by the apartheid policies of the racist government, inevitably,
other events and activities were affected by this othering. Archetypal
othering is not always destructive. It can be an indispensable part of an
individuation process because it confronts an individual with polarized
forms of an archetype that may then lead to more moderate ways of
connecting with it. This process allows one to humanize an archetype, i.e.,
to relate to it in ways that are not overwhelming so that they obliterate
one's individuality, but rather enriching for the individual. It will be argued
that the early Jungian movement in Cape Town was also affected by a
process of archetypal othering before it found its own settled and mature
state. Examples are offered of the ways this othering permeated the early
period of the formation of a professional Jungian group in South Africa.

Background

In 1980 my PhD thesis at the University of Cape Town (UCT), '*The
Dialectic of the Other in the Psychology of C.G. Jung: a Metatheoretical
Investigation*', was the first PhD in Africa that dealt directly with
analytical psychology. From 1971 to 1981 I lectured in the Department
of Psychology at UCT teaching clinical psychology subjects and from
the beginning I began introducing Jungian ideas into these courses.

The dominant orientation of the Department, during that period,
was behaviouristic with an emphasis on positivistic research. The
Department had an experimental bias investigating different aspects
of learning theory using animals, mainly, rats. In opposition, a 'counter-
culture' movement of humanistic psychology (HP) developed that
challenged the dominant paradigm and teaching curricula and involved
students in extra-curricula activities such as weekend marathon
'Encounter', 'Sensitivity' and 'Training' groups which soon expanded

to include non-University persons and encouraged multicultural contact. This movement was one of the many actions that emerged in the South African society, spontaneously or by design, as a response to the dehumanizing effects of the apartheid policies. HP with its emphasis on the personal experience and responsibility, the authenticity of being, the I-thou encounter, the development of personality (including its transpersonal dimensions), and its holistic epistemology was extremely close to Jungian ideas. However, at the time, basking in its iconoclastic 'anti-establishment' euphoria, HP was not in a position to trace its theoretical ancestry; yet in South Africa (particularly in Cape Town), that movement created a fertile ground in which Jungian psychology was to flourish and some key persons of the current South African Association of Jungian Analysts (SAAJA) were centrally involved in HP.

The phenomenon of HP can be appreciated as part of the wider cultural response to the prevailing materialism of the post World War II years when people needed to reconstruct their cities and lives by privileging the external world and avoiding facing the incomprehensible horrors of the war. HP echoed the wider societal movements (in music, art, and life-styles), the students' revolt against impersonal curricula and bureaucratic authorities and added its voice to the cry for a more humane society with more individual and collective responsibility and compassion. Understandably, in South Africa, this movement had the additional anti-apartheid dimension. At UCT, the HP movement organized various events that promoted not only the human potential but also inter-racial contact. HP was characterized as the 'Third Force' in psychology (psychoanalysis and behaviourism being the first two) and was critical of the psychiatric establishment considering it responsible for distorting the human condition by medicalizing suffering. Therefore, it is not surprising that Jung, both a psychoanalyst (insofar as the unconscious was central to his theories) and a psychiatrist, was a *persona non grata* in the early HP and no wonder that in South Africa, at the time, he was neglected. However, the central message of HP (that human beings have an inherent potential for psychological and spiritual growth and development) was very close to the idea of Jungian individuation.

Arriving from Europe to South Africa, my academic psychology education was in positivistic and experimental psychology whereas clinically I had been introduced to psychoanalysis (Freudian) in a substantial way (my psychotherapy and psychopathology professor, Dr. med. V. Matic, had close links with the early Freudian circle in Vienna). However, I also had a strong (but undeveloped) affinity for Jung as I had attended many extra-curriculum lectures on his psychology and had read many of his writings.

Inevitably, my previous understanding of Jung needed to be recast to fit into the changed contexts that surrounded me in the socio-political realities of South Africa as well as the upheavals in the psychological paradigms; the reality of the racist government policies that othered all 'non-whites' was overwhelming and created an imposing theme with far reaching effects on most facets of life. It was in the context of this re-formulation that I began developing my ideas about the Other in Jungian psychology. Central to this was the appreciation of the Other not only as an intrapsychic condition of the dissociated psyche but also as an external and real Other that is in constant relational interaction with the subject. My PhD research proposed a reading of Jung according to which his theories could be understood as successive reformulations of his 'problematic of the Other', i.e., his life-long quest to comprehend the nature / functions of and interactions with the Other. I discerned various formulations of the Other within Jung's opus (e.g., the 'Other-as-complex', the 'Other-as-Self' etc.) and argued that 'dialectic' was the key process that characterized his way of relating to these Others.

Other and Othering

The Oxford English Dictionary defines the other as 'The perception of an entity as distinct in relation to other entities; the perception or representation of a person or group of people as fundamentally alien from another, frequently more powerful, group'. Thus, the other does not need to possess any specific qualities of 'otherness' as it is defined relationally. An entity becomes other the moment somebody perceives it as such; it is not that it intrinsically has any otherness in itself. Moreover, in interpersonal and social contexts, the perception of a person or a group as being other (to 'me' or 'us') often has power consequences such as exclusion or marginalization; examples are the divisions between factions in colonial and post-colonial contexts, segregations according to race, and disempowerment based on gender or ethnic differences.

With the emphasis on the differences between the first (the defining) entity and the second (the othered) entity, what is often forgotten is that the two entities share a lot of sameness and are different only in relation to some characteristics. Therefore, there can be four different combinations of connections between the first entity and the other, depending (a) on the focus (on similarities or differences) and (b) whether the relationship is appreciated as complementary or oppositional. Conflict tends to arise when the focus is on differences and the relationship is oppositional, whereas if the relationship is complementary, diversity could be celebrated as enriching.

Othering is the process by which the first entity constructs the second entity as other and Weiss emphasized that 'There is no knowledge unless there are at least two items interrelated. Because the items, to be two, must be other than one another, the relation which connects them is a form of othering' (1958, p. 93). Thus, othering is a universal cognitive process (conscious or unconscious). In the cases where the first entity is not a person, the othering is constructed by a third entity that could be a person, a group of people, an ideology or a theoretical position that observe the first two entities. In all cases, what is of paramount importance is to have an awareness, as complete as possible, (a) of the fact that the very actual perception or representation of an other is not a given but, in effect, a product of an othering process which had been performed by a certain body of knowledge (individual or collective, conscious or unconscious, intentionally or unintentionally), and (b) of the implications of this othering process. Without this vigilant awareness, the othering happens imperceptibly and, very likely, it will have detrimental implications. Always, it is imperative that we endeavour to explore the wider relevant contexts within which the othering has taken place. Often, these contexts extend to surprisingly wider socio-political positions where issues of power and privilege are endemic (cf. Rabinow 1984).

One of the difficulties in considering the process and value of otherings is that whereas in logic otherings are inevitable and potentially constructive, in interpersonal and social contexts they tend to have destructive effects. In the latter, a key consideration is the degree of permanence and reality that is attributed to the otherness: according to an *analogue* understanding of otherness, the other has gradations, shades, degrees and nuances of otherness, whereas according to a *digital* understanding of otherness, the otherness is taken to be complete and definitive. Racial otherings tend to be of a *digital* kind, assumed (by the othering group) to be *ontological* rather than a product of a *constructivist* operation; these types of otherings follow, erroneously, an *essentialist* epistemology.

It could be argued that the confusion among the various types of otherings (analogue or digital, essentialist or constructivist, etc) is responsible for the varieties of human tragedies in interpersonal and social situations. For example, the apartheid laws in South Africa were based on an *essentialist* approach (although, of course, they were a product of ideological *constructions* mixed with erroneous socio-economic considerations) and brought incalculable suffering to generations of groups of people that the white regime decided to other.

The Archetype of the Other

The tendency to perceive similarities and differences is a basic function of the cognitive processes of the human brain, regardless of culture, time, geographical location and circumstances; circumstantial factors affect substantially the way these similarities and differences are perceived. However, the function of perceiving them is universal and, therefore, it would be appropriate to appreciate the other-ing process essentially as an archetypal process. Once accepted in its archetypal context, then we are enabled to understand that its bipolarity (like with all archetypal phenomena) is an inherent quality of its nature; consequently, this should help explain the numinous effects of the resulting polarization involved in othering. The numinosity of polarization can be dangerous, leading to the entrenchment of the extreme positions people assume as a result of archetypal otherings.

In the context of personal psychology, the archetype of the other helps us appreciate its importance in the individuation process. More specifically, it can enrich our understanding of an individual's individu-ation process by introducing the significance (a) of dealing with the various others, not only internal but also external ones, and (b) of considering the centrality of the othering process and its implications.

Jung clearly indicated the importance of external and social dimen-sions in the individuation process (e.g., Jung 1916). The relationship between internal and external others is a very delicate one. Insofar as an external other (a person or a group) may stir up and grip an individual, it would be appropriate to consider that it also performs some internal (psychological) function for that person. It is well known that various internal others are projected onto external ones (e.g., shadow or anima images), but the opposite may also occur when external others may activate internal others, e.g., when the attractive or repulsive energy of an external other may trigger off the examina-tion of a corresponding internal process.

For a person to individuate a certain archetype, it would be impor-tant first to experience it in its polar extremities, connect with its full scope/range and then gradually integrate it by relating to it in its various shades and nuances (and not in its pure polarities); archetypal othering (both internally and externally) plays an indispensable role in this process. Polarization is essential in the individuation process and it could be argued that it is the othering that provides the mechanism by which polarization is activated.

Needless to say, difficulties occur when the othering process is not completed and resolved, when individuals or groups get stuck on one point along the entire continuum of the process thus remaining fossilized in various forms of otherings. Such unresolved otherings lock persons and groups in oppositional and conflictual positions.

Establishing Analytical Psychology in South Africa

It is important to emphasize that this brief paper is not intended to provide the history of Jungian psychology in Southern Africa but only to make use of certain historical reflections in order to address some relevant othering themes.

Dr Vera M Bührmann (1910–1998), the only Jungian analyst in Africa at the time, was neither a psychologist nor involved in HP. On the contrary, she was very much part of the 'establishment', being both a psychiatrist and an Afrikaner. She had trained as a Jungian analyst (with the Society of Analytical Psychology) during her specialization years in the UK (in Public Health in the 1950s). In effect, she was a 'crypto-Jungian' as she was extremely shy of her Jungian identity and was doing her utmost not to attract attention to it. She was an eminent psychiatrist, known for her passionate involvement with the plight of autistic children. As a loyal psychiatrist employed in the local hospital and university, Vera did not have a private practice, so she did not work as an analyst. Instead, she used her analytical knowledge in her psychotherapy work with children within a hospital context and also offered psychotherapy supervision to some young registrars in psychiatry.

The HP Movement in the Psychology Department was losing its momentum when Dr Graham Saayman (also an Afrikaner) was appointed Senior Lecturer (in 1974). Graham was an ethologist with impeccable credentials in scientific research in animal behaviour (mainly with dolphins and baboons) and he was also interested in Jung. However, his perspective on Jung was different from Vera's and mine as he connected the instinctual patterns he was observing in animals with the Jungian archetypes and also related to Jung through his personal Yogic experiences. In the Department, he initiated a series of scientific investigations to explore various Jungian themes, such as androgyny, dreams in groups, states of consciousness during transcendental meditation (Saayman *in this volume*); we even attempted to develop a scale to measure archetypality (Faber, Saayman & Papadopoulos 1983).

In 1974 I started coordinating the 'Jung Study Group' that was led by Vera and included professionals (academics and clinicians) who used to meet regularly to study Jung's writings and explore the application of Jungian ideas in theory and psychotherapeutic contexts. It started modestly, but soon became ambitious and in 1976 I organized a 'Jung Week' to mark the centenary of Jung's birth. For an entire week, on the UCT campus there were various events (lectures, seminars, film shows, book exhibitions) as well as the official Pro Helvetia mobile exhibition depicting Jung's life and work. That event put Jung and the 'Jung Study Group' firmly on the map and many interested individuals approached us requesting personal analysis or specialist training in Jungian psychotherapy. Increasingly, it was becoming evident that without Jungian analysts to offer analysis and supervision, there would be no further development to the Jungian movement.

In the mid/late 1970s South Africa was boycotted by most international academic and professional bodies due to its racist policies. Hoping against hope, we were expecting that some solution would appear to resolve our predicament and it was then that Sir Laurens van der Post connected with us. Sir Laurens (also an Afrikaner) then living in the UK always kept close contact with South Africa and Vera knew of him from her youth. From the outset, she was cautious of the image he cultivated of himself, as the grand old man of Africa, but Vera, a pragmatist, was keen to explore ways that Sir Laurens could help the Jungian movement in South Africa. Every time he came to the Cape, Sir Laurens used to invite Vera and me (occasionally also Graham) to have tea with him in the grand lounge of the colonial Mount Nelson Hotel. Sir Laurens would monopolize the conversation with endless ideas and dreams, often unrelated to the realities we were facing.

In the meanwhile, Robert Schweitzer, a bright psychology student, asked me for assistance with his research interest in the methods of indigenous African healers. He had met with a Xhosa healer (Mr Tiso) and had collected plenty of material that he wanted to analyse. I suggested that he should contact Vera and that marked the beginning of Vera's second professional life. She met with Mr Tiso and immediately developed a deep respect and affinity for his work. With the authority of a psychiatrist and an Afrikaner, Vera would give presentations in psychiatry departments all over the country about the striking similarities between Jungian analysis and the healing ceremonies of African healers. That was revolutionary. Vera was instrumental in generating a serious interest in professional circles about the wisdom of African practices much more effectively than any subversive, anti-establishment movement.

At the time, in parallel to my lecturing in the Department of Psychology, I was busy working on my PhD thesis attempting to articulate the psychology of the other. In addition, I was (a) coordinating the 'Jung Study Group' endeavouring to find ways forward, (b) running a small psychotherapeutic practice with a Jungian orientation, supervised by Vera, (c) involved in community projects in the 'coloured' suburbs ('townships') of Cape Town, e.g., training non-professionals in counselling skills to help their own community in various contexts (also, I had close connections with the local Indian community, studying Hindu scriptures), and (d) I began receiving training in systemic family therapy, inspired by the epistemological implications of its theory and the scope of its practice. In effect, whilst investigating the other, I was deeply involved, in close contact, with various others feeling the need to break the mould of polarized otherings that were activated within the overall climate of the racist othering of apartheid policies.

What we wanted from Sir Laurens was to assist the 'Jung Study Group' with bringing over Jungian analysts to offer analysis and supervision. However, soon we realized that he had his own vision of how a Jungian movement could be established in South Africa. By that time I had moved to London and I continued meeting with him on a regular basis in order to find ways to assist the Jungian group in the Cape.

Connecting Jung with Africa

The ways that members of the 'Jung Study Group' were connecting Jung to the African reality were through (a) the painful predicament of the marginalized urban Africans (and other 'non-whites') living in the segregated townships (and, consequently, related to the anti-apartheid struggle), and (b) the African traditional healing practices (Vera Bührmann). However, Sir Laurens had other ideas. He had close personal links with Zulu royalty and was strongly against the ANC movement, dismissing Nelson Mandela as a 'communist'. Characteristically, he said that 'The world has created a dangerous myth out of Mandela. They have made him into a God, much as they made Hitler and Stalin into Gods ... he is intellectually not very bright' (Jones 2001, p. 412). Sir Laurens was friends with Ian Player the owner of the 'Wilderness School', an exclusive business that catered for wealthy western executives organizing specialist safari tours so that they would experience the 'healing power' of the African wilderness. As Sir Laurens was providing the finance for the development of a Jung centre in South Africa, his wishes prevailed and instead of the Jungian training including a direct experience either of an urban African situation or of traditional healing, trainees were expected to undertake a 'wilderness' trip where they would get in direct contact with African nature and wild animals. Moreover, Sir Laurens prevented a plan I had developed, i.e., to establish simultaneously at the outset three Jungian centres in Africa: in addition to the Cape Town one, one in Accra (Ghana) and another in Nairobi (Kenya). Such a plan would have rooted Jung very firmly in the African context and the white Cape Town centre would have had two sister centres in Africa to grow up together as a family. Instead, the Cape Town centre was set up on its own and, in effect, as a centre for whites only; it still remains so. Finally, Sir Laurens, with his close connections to the Jung Institute in Zurich, imported an exclusively Zurich Jungian approach to the South African centre, thus ignoring Vera's (London-oriented) developmental approach and the existing sensitivity for HP and community psychology.

Therefore, at the point of its official formation as an actual institution, the Cape Town Jung centre had to abandon its roots and accept the inevitable compromise of altering its approach and orientation to suit the wishes of its donor, Sir Laurens. The existing sensibilities were othered and new priorities needed to be followed. The HP activities, the involvement with community projects, the connection with indigenous healers had to be set aside to make place for an archetypal approach to African wilderness. The positive consequences of this othering were that Jungian training was enabled and eventually SAAJA (which is now thriving) was established; on the negative side, analytical psychology lost a unique opportunity to fruitfully inter-pollinate with the genuine African realities (as well as get directly involved in the plight of brutalized people) and produce potentially enriching innovations to theory and practice. Instead, a Zurich transplant to the Cape produced only slight variations of its European prototypes.

Othering Jung in Africa

One way of understanding what happened with the Jungian movement in South Africa at that time is in terms of it being sucked into the whirlpool of archetypal otherings. Within the context of the sharp polarizations that were talking place in the wider contexts (socio-political, theoretical, clinical, etc) the Jungian initiative in Cape Town was inevitably influenced by them. Whereas the initial local movement (the early 'Jung Study Group') followed a direction that reflected an acute awareness of the various otherings and attempted to position itself in an appropriate way, that balance was lost when external assistance was offered. Sir Laurens was not a neutral person; he had a very long personal (and ambivalent) connection with Africa with a very strong set of firm positions (likes and dislikes). Consequently, the Jung centre had to locate itself within sharply polarized positions, mirroring the wider societal divisions and otherings. It is important to note that in time those othered positions changed and that now SAAJA embraces many trends the initial members of the early Jungian movement pursued, e.g., a sensitivity for community psychology and for the plight of the disadvantaged.

The option to connect Jung to the African wilderness (at the expense of other viable connections) reminds us of a form of othering that Jung himself had followed. As argued elsewhere, Jung tended to venerate the distant and Exotic Other, the 'primitive', whilst ignoring more familiar forms of others that are uncomfortably closer to us. This tendency 'at best, … [was, in effect] an attempt to critique the limitations of European rationalism' whereas 'at worst, [could be understood] as a subtle form of patronizing the 'primitive', idealizing the native, adoring the 'noble savage' and a form of post-colonialist othering; 'by idealizing the 'primitive', regardless of the genuine good intentions behind it, Jung ignored the socio-political and economic plight of the disadvantaged and created a romantic tendency for a return to the lost paradise of simplicity and pure and uncontaminated wisdom' (Papadopoulos 2002, p. 174).

Archetypes are not abstract and romantic ideas, but can be images that activate brutal realities, causing real suffering. People can be pulled into polarized positions with numinous powers, believing in the purity of their actions whilst, unknowingly, they are sucked into whirlpools of archetypal otherings. Ultimately, such extreme positions are not always destructive as long as they are part of an overall developmental process that enables people to relate to the archetype of the other (and the real other) in ways that eventually lead to less polarized connections. Archetypal othering is an inevitable moment in a process of individuation as long as it facilitates the humanizing of the archetype and enables real connection with it in appropriate and less polarized forms.

This is one way to understand the otherings of the Jungian movement in Cape Town.

References

Faber, P.A., Saayman, G.S. & Papadopoulos, R.K. (1983). 'Induced waking fantasy: Its effects upon the archetypal content of nocturnal dreams'. *Journal of Analytical Psychology*, 28, 141-64.

Jones, J.D.F (2001). *Storyteller: The Many lives of Laurens van der Post*. London: John Murray.

Jung, C.G. (1916). 'Adaptation, Individuation, Collectivity'. *CW* 18.

Papadopoulos, R.K. (2002). 'The other other: when the exotic other subjugates the familiar other'. *Journal of Analytical Psychology*, 47, 2, 163-88.

Rabinow, P. (Ed.) (1984). *A Foucault Reader*. New York: Pantheon.

Weiss, P. (1958). *Modes of Being*. Carbondale, IL: Southern Illinois University Press.

Journey to the Centre:
Images of Wilderness and the Origins of the Southern African Association of Jungian Analysts

Graham S. Saayman
South Africa (SAAJA)

Abstract

This review is derived from a programme of Jungian theory, research and applied clinical practice developed at the University of Cape Town between 1974 and 1989. Analytical psychology helped develop approaches to psychotherapy relevant to the South African context and appropriate to a world beset by much doubt, alienation, conflict, anxiety and trauma. A major objective of this research-practitioner model was to equip students with general principles and basic skills in cost-effective, preventive approaches. The central theme was the adaptive functions of the human family system. Jung was one of the first major western theorists to make evolution relevant to psychology and his theory includes the expansion of consciousness and the meaningful, purposeful, intentional nature of the psyche. Saayman argues that experiential spiritual disciplines such as yoga and aboriginal vision quest have Darwinian 'survival value'. He understands the therianthropes, particularly the antelope-headed human forms, in the Khoisan rock art galleries as depicting the tantric practice of 'thinking with the heart' during shamanic vision quests. These paintings capture the essence of spiritual generosity as practised by the Khoisan hunter-gatherer ancestors of modern people. In this world view, the ethic of generosity, making choices based upon positive, harmonious, empathic, compassionate, interpersonal feeling-toned values, is a core social ethic with survival value. Thus, the extermination of the great herds of animals and the genocide of aboriginal peoples during the colonial era accelerated the environmental impacts that presently threaten global ecology. Experts on combating climate change say the first step is to change the primary core value of technological culture, namely: economic growth is essential. Indeed aboriginal origin stories suggest a similar remedy, a return to the core values that were there in the beginning: respect the nature of reality, re-realize the survival value of generosity of spirit and honour all living forms.

* * *

Welcome to Cape Town, especially those of you who have travelled long distances. This is a heart-warming moment for those of us who made the leap of faith and began the journey here so many years ago.

This review is derived from a programme of Jungian theory, research and applied clinical practice developed at the University of Cape Town between 1974 and 1989 by Renos Papadopoulos and myself. This programme formed one of the pillars of The Cape of Good Hope Centre for Jungian Studies, founded in 1987 as the precursor of the Southern African Association of Jungian Analysts (SAAJA).

This presentation compares material from a variety of subjects, sometimes with different levels of explanation. The paper develops lateral connections between different disciplines and makes implicit connections between the following explicit steps:

- Clinical applications of psychobiological studies: stress reduction, dream groups, kinship, androgyny and family therapy.
- Wilderness and the Wounded Healer Paradigm.
- The Collective Unconscious and African Origins of the Human Species.
- Khoisan rock paintings of antelope-headed human figures as Archetypal signifiers of the evolution of the family system.
- Vision Quest and the Survival Value of Dreams – the major theme of this paper.
- Generosity, Eros and Selection of Adaptive Core Values.

The Human Family

The central theme of the University programme was the origins of the human family system. Analytical psychology helped us develop approaches to psychotherapy relevant to the South African context and appropriate to a world beset by much doubt, alienation, conflict, anxiety and trauma.

A major objective of this research-practitioner model was to equip students with general principles and basic skills in cost-effective, preventive approaches, including family therapy and group therapy based on dream appreciation, integrated within a Jungian psychotherapeutic model.

Western materialistic philosophy posits a *'Big Bang'*, a *'Struggle for the Survival of the Fittest'*, some *'Random Mutations'* and the arrival of humans at the apex of a 'Great Chain of Being' or *Scala Naturae*. This is a narrowly reductive, causal and ultimately depreciative and erroneous understanding of the process of human evolution. This view all too often justifies a power-based, winner-takes-all philosophy favouring ethnocentric socio-political and economic policies.

Jung was one of the first major western theorists to make evolution relevant to psychology but his theory includes the expansion of consciousness and the meaningful, purposeful, intentional nature of the psyche.

A course on psychobiology, with the 'Collective Unconscious' as the primary theoretical construct, laid the theoretical foundation for the Undergraduate programme. A major focus was on typically human 'patterns of behaviour', understood as a biopsychosocial developmental process: from infancy, through adolescence, young adulthood, middle age, and preparation for death. Another central focal point was the role of subjective inner processes in providing direction and meaning at the onset of specific phases of this maturational process.

Jung initially called these inner factors primordial images: 'the instinct's perception of itself, the self portrait of the instinct'. He later formulated a clear definition of the archetypal dream, those bizarre, colourful, emotionally-toned dreams with mythological motifs that help to illuminate the onset of critical transitions in the life of the dreamer.

Basic concepts from the classical ethology of Konrad Lorenz and Nico Tinbergen interface nicely with this formulation: in animals with relatively simple nervous systems, inherent proto-images or 'sign stimuli' evolve in synchrony to release pre-programmed sequences of instinctual behaviour as a key opens a lock. A well-known example of an expressive movement acting as a social releaser is snarling in the domestic dog: ears laid back, wrinkled face, fangs bared simultaneously communicates alternating intentions to flee or to attack. It is the ritualized threat posture: an inherent signal that adaptively resolves conflict without actual fighting and injury.

In humans, newborn infants gaze significantly longer at a stylized picture of a human face than at control material, suggesting an inherent attraction to the parental image, which is critically important for initiating the bonding and developmental process.

The central theoretical thrust of the undergraduate course, often overlooked by reductive approaches to human behaviour based on animal models, was that inner processes – dreaming, imagining, meditating – also have Darwinian 'survival value'. A primary function of archetypal dreams is to maintain systemic balance between the human community and nature.

The Determinants of Family Systems

During the 1960s ethologists began to study a wide variety of long-lived, large-brained mammals to develop models of the evolution of human social systems. In most of the primates and some other complex, long-lived social mammals with large brains, long lives and slowly developing offspring – dolphins for example – adult males and adult females live together with their young throughout the year as opposed to joining only during a limited breeding season. Here the central question is: what factors bind these groups together?

Figure 1. What Factors Structure the Family System?

Early primatologists believed that the dominance hierarchy of adult males was the ultimate authority in the primate social order. When women observers entered the field, the scientific community gradually recognized that it was the females – the mothers – who bind the social system together as the transmitters of kinship and relatedness.

Sexual Attractiveness and Receptivity

Figure 2. Menstrual vs. Oestrous Cycle Sexual Attractiveness and Receptivity

Sexuality in the Old World primates cycles continuously with the menstrual cycle as opposed to a circumscribed oestrous period during a limited mating season. Biologists initially identified sexual hormones and the pair bond as a primary cohesive force in the social life of primates.

Socio-ecological studies of large-brained, long-lived mammals – comparing primates and social carnivores such as the dolphin – provided models of the family system during hunter-gatherer times.

Figure 3. Social Carnivores as Models of Human Hunter-Gatherer Bands

Our studies of the Indian Ocean humpback and bottlenose dolphin schools on the south-east coast of South Africa revealed that their social system is flexibly organized. Subgroups separate and recombine as do bands of forest-dwelling chimpanzees and nomadic groups of human hunter-gatherer societies. The social systems are adapted for the efficient and sustainable exploitation of environmental resources – a critically important socio-ecological factor.

Figure 4. Care of the Young and Kinship in Large-Brained, Long-Lived Mammals

Clinical Applications of Psychobiological Adaptations

A black-coated pink-faced infant is a prime example of a primordial image in primates; a threatened infant releases a protective parental response of the entire troop. Field studies identified the survival value of attachment – the fulfilment of the nurturant and instrumental roles of mothers and fathers – as central to the adaptive functioning of family groups:

- the combined energies of the adults of both sexes are required to feed, protect, nurture, educate and socialize slowly developing young;

- our later research showed a similar pattern in humans – revealing Psychological Androgyny as a significant determinant of the psychological adjustment of children in intact and divorced families;

- when both husbands and wives have integrated their contrasexual aspects (anima and animus in fathers and mothers respectively) and both parents flexibly perform instrumental and affective roles, child adjustment benefits;

- this work identified the roles dimension of family functioning in a Jungian-oriented approach to systems therapy of the family – particularly the provision of nurturance and support – as a particularly important aspect of the family's ability to rear well-adjusted children.

The Stress Response

An aged and toothless male calls for assistance when attacked by a physically more powerful male. He mimics the highly-pitched scream of the fearful mother, gums bared whilst pointing the tail up straight. Mothers in this mode are usually immune from attack.

This alarm reaction, adaptive in hunter-gatherer times, has a parallel response in modern people, mediated by the neuro-endocrine system:

Figure 5 Fright Flight Freeze

adrenaline rush, increased red blood cell and sugar production, racing heart, rapid and shallow breath, sweating, trembling, cold hands and feet, pupils dilate, inhibition of digestion, mind goes blank, panic and terror. However, in modern times this inbuilt reaction manifests as chronic stress and pathological extremes of generalized anxiety, panic attacks and depression.

Meditational Approaches to Stress Reduction

Figure 6 The Kundalini Chakra System Image by Lee McIntyre

At postgraduate level, our honours, masters and doctoral students investigated the use of breathing techniques, relaxation, meditation and dream appreciation in a group setting, as adaptive, alternative interventions for anxiety reduction and stress management. At the same time, laboratory-based research explored the relationship between meditation, the sleep cycle, and the frequency and intensity of archetypal dreams. This was the era of the classical studies by

Wallace and Benson on transcendental meditation and the relaxation response.

Wallace and Benson demonstrated that decreases in heart rate, respiration, blood pressure, muscle tension, metabolic rate and analytic thinking are associated with increases in alpha wave activity of the brain. Nowadays many mental health professionals use biofeedback, breathing, relaxation, meditation and other visualization techniques as standard treatments procedures for youth and adults in psychiatric hospitals.

Wilderness Therapy

Figure 7. Imfolozi Rhino Trails

The theme of wilderness guided the developmental history of the Jungian centre as well as the university programme. The wilderness leadership school, supported by Laurens van der Post, pioneered a Jungian approach to the role of wilderness as a uniquely African training experience for Jungian analysts. We collaborated on participant-observer studies on the role of wilderness in healing alienation and imbalance in the modern psyche.

The African Origins of Homo sapiens

Let us shift now to links between evolution, dreams, meditation and vision quest. During the 1980s, the years of establishing the Jungian centre, geneticists were assembling an historic record of human evolution by analysing DNA sequences in samples of blood taken from thousands of men living in isolated communities throughout the world. The genetic data show that the human family, *Homo sapiens*, originated in Africa. Modern humans carry the genetic markers of a single ancestral stock.

Small bands of hunter gatherers made an epic journey out of Africa about sixty thousand years ago. Waves of migration went around the world.

The evidence suggests that the small number of Khoisan still surviving in the Kalahari today have the oldest genetic markers of all people living in the world.

Jung was among the first to clearly articulate how the evolutionary blueprint of ancestral structures, genetically programmed into the human nervous system, is fundamental to the dynamics of the modern human psyche. It is remarkable that Laurens van der Post, in a definitive paper entitled 'Race prejudice as self rejection', published as early as 1957, summarized how Jungian thought would anticipate the modern genetic findings.

Van der Post, entranced by the creation myths of the Khoisan, the first people of Africa, explained how nocturnal dreams, the dreams Jung called archetypal or big dreams, can put people in touch with the inner voice of ancestral wisdom. He deeply regretted that this voice has been rejected by the world.

Recalling how the first people of Africa would say, 'there is a dream dreaming us. It is a good dream', van der Post wrote, 'the only trouble is that we live it badly'.

Antelope-Headed Human Forms in Khoisan Rock Art

These antelope-headed human forms in Khoisan rock paintings are called therianthropes; they are partly animal, partly human. I talk about them with due humility, because they have sacred significance. Moreover, their interpretation is the subject of an expert debate and I hope to learn more about them later on in the conference.

My own understanding of their significance in the context of altered states of consciousness research owes much to Richard Atleo and a social scientist also named Umeek, hereditary chief of the *Nuu-Chah-Nulth* people on the west coast of Vancouver Island, British Columbia.

Figure 8. Thinking Through the Heart: The Feeling-Toned Function of Relatedness (Image: Rock Art Research Institute, Wits University. Photographer: Neil Lee)

Highly knowledgeable about aboriginal origin stories, Umeek is actively involved in developing a truth and reconciliation process on behalf of the aboriginal people and the government of Canada. When I showed him these images of the therianthropes, he immediately related them to mythological bear-, wolf- and raven-headed figures from aboriginal vision quest practices. In Umeek's view, origin stories – how the North American trickster figure son of raven, or mantis in the Southern African version, stole the light of consciousness and gave it to the people – map out a metatheoretical rationale for the practice of vision quest, an aboriginal experiential method of acquiring knowledge from the metaphysical realms.

Figure 9. Native American Origin Stories: Bear-Wolf- and Raven-Headed Figures

The practice of vision quest requires a systematic, step by step consciousness-altering discipline including fasting, ritual cleansing, trials of hardship and endurance, prayer, drumming, dancing and religious ceremonies.

From the perspective of states of consciousness research, meditating on the essence of the antelope recalls the Eastern tantric practice of 'heart-breathing', or thinking through the 'heart-brain' of the fourth chakrum. Focusing on the heart-brain bypasses the ego at the level of the cerebral cortex. As depth psychologists know full well, the greatest threat to safe, effective spiritual practice is inflation – a pathological syndrome Jung described as the mana personality. Supreme egotism predicts the primal fall from heaven. The antidote is humility.

The antelope-headed human figures reveal the wise prescription that you are safest in the realms of spirit when the most beloved animal leads and safeguards your consciousness.

When I first saw these images they reminded me of Chiron the centaur with the head and torso of a man joined at the solar plexus with the body and hindquarters of a horse. Chiron captures the essence of a therapeutic paradigm with nature at its core and connects the health of earth's ecosystems to the art and science of healing.

In contrast to the antelope-headed Khoisan images, Chiron has a human head. From the perspective of heroic

Figure 10. *Hamlet's Dilemma: Physical or Metaphysical Reality? Image by Kevin Atkinson*

Greek mythology, *the thinking function* is highly valued in Western technological culture – analytical logical objective, rational impersonal decision-making.

These reflections reminded me that in Jung's typology, in addition to the impersonal, logical thinking function, humans also make choices based on the *feeling function* – positive, harmonious, empathic, compassionate, interpersonal feeling-toned values – known to aboriginal people as 'thinking with the heart'. The African word *ubuntu* has a similar meaning.

The intent of a specific vision quest may be to make rain, heal the sick or negotiate the success of a hunt by requesting the spirit of the respected quarry to cooperate with the hunters. When the animal, be it antelope, bison or whale, keeps the agreement and offers itself to the hunters, all of the body parts are used, meat, gristle, bone and hide. Nothing is left to waste.

However, the major purpose of the vision quest process is to enable the community to access metaphysical guidance for the development of protocols or covenants in order to make positive, ethical choices based upon the feeling-toned values of human relatedness, to cater for their daily sustenance and to maintain a sustainable and harmonious existence between the social order and pristine nature.

In this world view, the ethic of generosity, part of the original design of creation, caring for the total web of life is as much a natural law as any known physical law. Generosity is a core social value with *survival value*, as pivotal as anatomical and behavioural adaptations such as hands, claws or teeth which have been selected by the process of evolution.

The principle of generosity of spirit embodies the essence of an ecological balance with nature; lived experience, based on community wide experiences of vision quest over millennia, demonstrated positive outcomes in the physical realm.

Khoisan Creation Stories and the Myth of Oedipus

The rock art galleries depict the entry of technological culture and the diametrically opposite decision-making process: the superior thinking function, with feeling as the shadow.

Figure 11. 'You must have forgotten the teachings of your Ancestors.'
E. Richard Atleo (Umeek)

Thousands of years after the epic exodus of the first people from Africa, the descendants of the Khoisan arrive from Europe. When they saw the original form of their ancestors, did they sense they were looking at the roots of their own beginnings?

Contemplating these records of colonial conquest the myth of Oedipus occurred to me: Sophocles, in the Greek tragedy *Oedipus Rex*, tells how Oedipus was cast out as an infant by his family for fear that he would fulfil an oracle and slay his own father. And indeed when Oedipus – attempting to escape the oracle – came upon his unknown father at a crossroads he killed him in an impulsive argument over the right of way.

Developments initiated during the colonial era have accelerated environmental impacts that have ultimately devastated global ecology.

Metaphorically, the descendants of the first family have slain their father, raped the forests, pillaged the great waters and contaminated the air above mother earth. From this perspective Oedipus is not a fantasy, or myth, but a fact of history.

The San were astounded when the newcomers began a slaughter en masse of their precious herds of antelope. They retaliated with tiny arrows anointed with a toxin that provoked a death as horrible as rabies. This sealed their fate. Their descendants declared them beyond the law and they were driven out of Eden.

In a parallel process in North America the plains buffalo became extinct east of the Mississippi by 1833.

The last commando rode against the vanishing bushmen in 1836.

The last pictures of the San were painted in about 1870.

This attitude to nature pictures a poor prognosis for the human race.

Modern civilization, obsessed by the conquest of nature, has arrived at terracide as a likely outcome of tinkering with technology. Distinguished earth scientists predicted long ago that manmade climate change, a side effect of science and industrial pollution, would produce effects as devastating as full-scale nuclear war. The countdown to catastrophe is under way.

Conclusions

The experts on combating climate change say the first step is to change the primary core value of technological culture, namely: economic growth is essential.

Indeed aboriginal origin stories suggest a similar remedy, a return to the core values that were there in the beginning: respect the nature of reality, re-realize the survival value of generosity of spirit and honour all living forms.

Clearly, changing this core value will not be easy. So what then can psychology offer the world at this time of accelerating crisis? Crisis intervention theory tells us that crises offer opportunities to make positive change but the threshold to irreversible climate change creeps up insidiously.

Is our species worried enough to shift from the pleasure principle to the reality principle? What hope is there to change a globally entrenched core value?

South Africa offers an example of a significant change in core values.

Modern South Africa is immensely important as a signifier. Once considered the archetypal shadow of the world, over 13 years ago the people dropped the politics of confrontation and armed strife and chose another core value: positive human relationships, acceptance of personal responsibility, reconciliation and peaceful transformation.

Can the human family benefit from this example, accept that positive change is possible, and begin to restore and heal the earth in the closing window of opportunity that remains?

References

Atleo, E.R. (2004). *Tsawalk: A Nuu-chah-nulth Worldview*. Vancouver: University of British Columbia Press.

Faber, P.A. & Saayman, G.S. (1991). 'On the relation of the doctrines of yoga to Jung's psychology'. In *Jung in Modern Perspective: The Master and his Legacy*, eds. R.K. Papadopoulos & G.S. Saayman. Bridgeport: Prism Press, 165-81.

Faber, P.A., Saayman, G.S. & Touyz, S.W. (1978). 'Meditation and the archetypal content of nocturnal dreams'. *Journal of Analytical Psychology*, 23, 1-22.

Jung, C.G. (1948). 'On the nature of dreams'. *In The Structure and Dynamics of the Psyche*, CW 8, paras. 281 – 97.

Jung, C.G. 1975. 'Psychological commentary on Kundalini Yoga'. *Lectures One and Two*. Spring, 1-32.

Saayman, G.S. (2007). *Hunting with the Heart: A Vision Quest to Spiritual Emergence*. Cape Town: Kima Global Press.

Acknowledgements

Figures 6, 8 and 10 are reproduced here with the kind permission from the photographers and copyright holders.

Tuesday, 14 August 2007

Race, Racism and Inter-Racialism in Brazil: Clinical and Cultural Perspectives

Walter Boechat & Paula Pantoja Boechat
Brazil (AJB)

Abstract

This paper approaches the complex problem of inter-racialism in Brazil from the psychological point of view. This country, with is multi-coloured society, has puzzled anthropologists and sociologists about the problem of differences, races living together. Brazilian society has reached a racial democracy? An historical background of crossbreeding since the colonization period is considered by the authors as of relevance. Also the permanence of stereotypical images of the slavery period in the cultural unconscious of Brazil is taken into consideration. The race prejudice is approached as being closely connected to a prevalent *social class prejudice*. Even the tonality of the skin colour is perceived as darker or lighter, according to the social class in Brazil's highly stratified social system. The authors provide some examples in history and actual society in Brazil comparing these anthropological findings to a clinical case. The authors present this clinical case to emphasize the importance of working out with the concepts of the cultural unconscious (Henderson) and stereotypes and stereotypical images (Vannoy Adams) to fully understand the individuation process in a multi-cultural society like Brazil. They also suggest the importance of the racial traits for the social affirmation of the individual, a feature they call *the racial persona*. The so-called *cordial racism*, typical of Brazilian culture, an expression recently employed by the daily paper *Folha de S. Paulo* in Brazil is considered highly meaningful and is interpreted in terms of the cultural shadow of Brazil.

* * *

No people that go through this [the slavery period] as its daily routine through the centuries would get out of it without being imprinted indelibly. All of us, Brazilians, we are the same flesh of those tortured blacks and Indians. All of us Brazilians are, in an equal way, the possessed hand that tortured them.

(Darci Ribeiro 1995, p. 120)

Introduction

We would like to thank Joe Cambray and the organization of this International Congress of IAAP for the opportunity to speak in this plenary session. As Brazilians and Latin Americans we feel this is a great responsibility but also a fantastic opportunity to speak on such an important and delicate theme as racism from a psychological point of view within a Jungian International Congress in a country such as South Africa, which has undergone so many developments in this field.

We would also like to thank specially Andrew Samuels for his creative mind and insistence, three years ago in Brazil, that we should present this paper here at the Congress.

When the Brazilian Jungian group was starting to form its first society in 1978 we received the visit of Adolf Guggenbühl-Craig. Although almost thirty years have passed, we can remember well the days he spent with us in Rio de Janeiro. Once driving close to the beach, he told us: 'The well known *racial democracy* in Brazil is widely commented on. The crowded beaches where everybody can go, no private places where people have to pay to go as we have in some public spaces in Zurich ... You can see, as we see now, white, Moreno and blacks all together on Brazilian beaches. But if you go to good restaurants, you can watch a *whitening* of the atmosphere, as long as you go to more expensive places. If you go to less expensive ones, small bars at the corner of the streets, it is the other way around: there is a *darkening* of the place, you see more black people'.

It is true that Rio de Janeiro is a city with a large Black population. However, coloured students are a minority at the university where we run a post-graduate (*lato-sensu*) course in Jungian Psychology. Also this is true for clients in our private clinic. Nevertheless, studying the social clinic for people of low income the Jungian Association of Brazil (AJB) holds in Rio de Janeiro we can observe a higher proportion of patients of dark colour. All these only confirm a verity largely demonstrated by statistics[1]: racial prejudice in Brazil is, in fact, a social class prejudice. We shall discuss this fact in its historical, sociological, archetypal implications and also through a clinical example.

Clinical Case

Some time ago Paula received a patient whose problems and concerns were deeply connected to the racial prejudice prevailing in Brazil. The patient, a female – we shall name her Maria – was 26 years old at the time. Maria was dark skinned, but not really black. In Brazil she would be called a *dark mulatto* (in South Africa the term I believe is

---

1 See the long and careful research done by the daily paper *Folha de S. Paulo*, *Racismo Cordial* [*Cordial Racism*], 1988.

coloured). She was a beautiful woman, although a little overweight. She was a virgin at the time, not ever having had a boyfriend. She came for analysis because, in her own words, 'she felt she was living in a parallel world', not in this real world.

This is her life story: Maria was an adopted child. Her parents travelled to south Brazil to adopt her because there one can find many emigrant-descendants from Italy and Germany and the population is mainly white. The parents were white and they wanted to adopt a white baby. In fact, they met the mother, who was white.

When she was one month old the parents noticed she was a mulatto and the rejection, although never admitted, came to be very strong, mainly because one year later her adopted mother became pregnant with a white girl.

When the adopted parents noticed that Maria had dark skin, they understood immediately that the biological father was black.

The adopted father was often absent; he used to work very hard and have many love affairs. Maria grew up being rejected by the mother and ignored by the father. The mother was always telling her how much she loved her but at the same time trying to take her for plastic surgery and making all sorts of efforts to *whiten* her persona – making her nose thinner, her hair straight, and so on.

Maria developed the persona of a 'nice, friendly and funny woman'. But she would not let intimate relationships become real and, of course, she would also run away from men and have no real friends to count on. According to the analyst's impression she was a borderline patient.

When she was already two years in analysis, she made this statue in ceramics where we can see her lying with her head on Paula's lap. This sculpture shows the positive transference at the time.

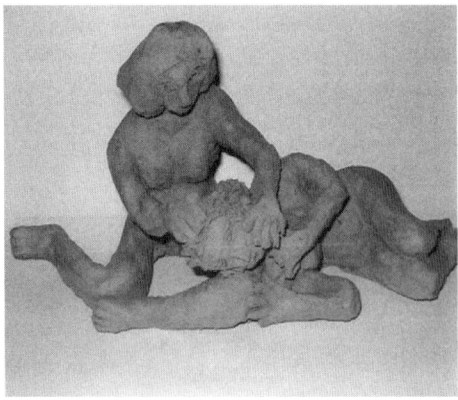

Figure 1

Later on, after more three years of analysis, she made another ceramic statue.

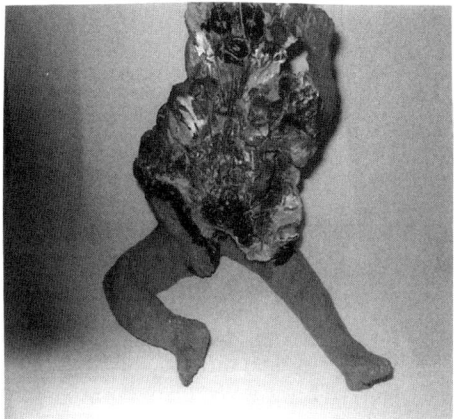

Figure 2

At that time, facing the prejudice hidden in the double-bind affirmations of the parents (Bateson 1956), she said she felt she had to take away her skin to become a new person. The figure in the sculpture is tearing away the skin from the vagina to the head, with both hands. This new person would be accepted, in her fantasy, by the family and society.

By then she was very anxious, feeling the racial prejudice as the biggest problem she had. One can easily recognize how destructive was her relationship with her nuclear family and how its prejudice led her to become psychologically disturbed. Also in the milieu she lived – very high social class – it was rare to find somebody with dark skin.

The last sculpture is very impressive. The skin is represented all in blue; the edges of the skin to the inside of the body are black, as well as the face. The viscera come out very colourful but they look cut like a huge wound.

The hands in the vagina and in the head show, as she said, the places where she feels she suffers more. At this moment of the therapy, Maria almost underwent a psychotic crisis. Taking away the skin would not solve the internal problems. She would have to cure the wound first, and then take care of the skin, that is, *the persona*. She could only survive if she herself accepted her black condition.

We think this extraodinary image has much more to say about her and her inner psyche. First of all, the colour symbolism is very strong. The blue portrays an alchemical symbolism, as *unio mentalis*, the passage from the *nigredo* to the *albedo*, the white, the totality of all colours.[1] Blue has an intense complexity of associations, but here we have it connected to the black (of the face and of the edges of the body). James Hillman[2] wrote about many of these alchemical associations, also in relation to the music of the black culture in the United States, the blues. Generally, in fact, blue is associated with black in African cultures and with white in Caucasian cultures. Hillman also reminds us, quoting Cézanne, that blue may give depth to other colours[3].

Concerning the culture unconscious of Brazil and its stereotypes, blue in general has a connection to happiness, to light, to white. In colloquial language people may say something like: 'Is everything *blue* with you?' meaning, 'Is everything all right?' Or: 'I'll dress myself in blue to bring me luck', and so on. Certainly, the colour blue of her skin represented her *persona*, the false impression she tried to give everybody that she was a happy woman, a very lucky one. Of course it is a very false gaiety and the colour blue keeps all its ambiguity of the false lightness of the exterior and the deep heavy suffering of the soul.

The skin being dressed out shows the multi-coloured potentialities that are coming out like a flood, invading her conscious ego. Everything looks horribly mixed. Will she be able to hold this excruciating tension? The body, which represents the limits of the ego, is torn apart. The analyst must be very present in this situation, as a positive mother (to compensate the destructive unconscious mother), and help the patient mend her wounded identity.

This case, because of its severity and damage to the self identity, showed itself to be a very difficult one, a long term case that developed involving a maternal transference that was necessary to build up parts of the self that were split up.

We see here three main points we would like to discuss:

1. There are a large number of mestizos or mulattos in the Brazilian population and their contribution to our culture is a fact generally not recognized. (The patient is a mulatto who is and feels rejected on account of her colour. She also rejects her own identity.)

2. The importance in a multicultural society like Brazil of the definition of an entity we call *racial persona*. As you know Jung defines persona in a synthetic way:

> *The persona is a complicated system of relations between individual consciousness and society, fittingly enough a kind of mask, designed on the one hand to make a definite impression upon others, and, on the other, to conceal the true nature of the individual.*
>
> (Jung 1928, para. 305)

---

1 See on symbolism of the colour blue, Hillman: *Alchemical Blue and the Unio Mentalis*, 1982

2 Hillman, op. cit.

3 See Hillman, op. cit, p. 41: 'Cézanne wrote: 'Blue gives other colors their vibration, so one must bring a certain amount of blue into a painting'.

The *racial persona* is a derivative of the concept of persona; it encompasses the totality of racial traits that delineates the external appearance of the individual, that is, the colour of the skin, the texture of the hair and other racial features.

3. Also we should always take into account the *cultural unconscious* (Henderson 1990) of a country or region, with its *stereotypes and stereotypical images* (Vannoy-Adams 1996). We will try to describe the stereotypical images in this clinical case, as they play a crucial role in the relationship of the patient with her family and the social environment.

I use the expression *cultural unconscious* following Joseph Henderson, as the segment of the collective unconscious belonging to a nation, or a culture (Henderson 1990). I think this concept is central in anthropological and ethnological studies. We use the concepts of *stereotypes* and *stereotypical images* as conceived by Michael Vannoy-Adams. This author understands the cultural unconscious as the part of the collective unconscious that contains stereotypes and stereotypical images of a particular culture or ethnic group (Adams 1996, 2005).

The Role of Crossbreeding in the Build up of the Brazilian Identity

Maria should not feel strange or awkward for not being white. In Brazil since colonial times the population has been formed by crossbreeding of different races. The history of Brazil is a saga of various journeys and multiple encounters of different peoples and races, from the time of its discovery in 1500 by the Portuguese, who were allegedly white and had come from Iberia. The intermixture of races has gone on and increased throughout the history of Brazil.

Contrary to what occurred in North America, for instance, the Portuguese ships of Pedro Álvares Cabral that laid anchor in 1500 on the shores of Bahia, did not carry stable Calvinistic families, as was the case of the *Mayflower*, who arrived in North America to populate the Brave New World. In fact, there were very few women accompanying the first Portuguese who arrived on the Brazilian coasts. Duly organized families did not arrive initially on the Brazilian continent, but rather solitary men, men who saw no professional opportunities any longer in Portugal or elsewhere in Europe, and many of whom had undergone hard experiences in prison. They were truly outcasts *(degradados),* so much so, that the intermixture with the local, the natives has prevailed since the start of colonial times in Brazil. The first mother of all Brazilians is a native woman, a great Indian mother, the great mother archetype of all Brazilians.

Since the beginning of colonial times the crossbreeding with natives reflected itself even in the language spoken in our green paradise of forests, enormous and generous rivers and sandy white shores: Portuguese was not the language of the colony, but a strange mixture of Portuguese with the local dialects of the Indians, the *nheengatu* in the north and *abanheém* in the south region of Brazil. These Indian dialects remained present and used throughout Brazil till the end of the XVIIIth century! *The strong, unbiased admixture of races evidenced itself even as a form of speech* (Costa e Silva, personal communication).

For as long as the Portuguese needed more hands for labour they tried to enslave the Indians; this however proved to be very difficult. Many natives fled to the interior of the Amazon forest and other unknown parts of inland Brazil. Many died in the midst of the tremendous and cruel hard work imposed by the Portuguese masters or by disease brought by the white man with whom they were having contact for the first time.

Thus began the traffic of human beings from various countries of Africa to work as slaves in the sugar cane plantations in the northeastern region, and in the gold mines of central Brazil. A more organized, systematic importation of slaves from Africa started at the end of the XVIth century, and only stopped in 1853! In fact, slavery was abolished by decree only in 1888 in Brazil, making it the last country in the civilized western world to have slavery abolished.

The role of the mestizos in the development of Brazil is generally disregarded. But the influence of the Indian mestizos and mulattos – should not be disregarded in the composition of the ethnic identity of the new country.

And this is crucial in explaining why Brazil has a special kind of racial prejudice, quite different from Anglo-Saxon racism. We could even postulate two kinds of racism: Anglo-Saxon racism and Latin racism. Anglo-Saxon racism has a more defined character, it separates places and races; the word apartheid means segregation. In the USA Martin Luther King had to face segregated places in buses for whites and blacks. In Brazil the shadow of a strong racial prejudice appears in disguise, so much in disguise that some optimistic writers have come to assert that in Brazil there is *racial democracy*, which is not at all true. *In fact, Brazilian racial prejudice appears in disguise, hand in hand with a social prejudice,* as we shall see now. The basic, distinctive character of Brazilian racism is that it is not based on the racial origin of the person, but on the colour of his or her skin. *This turns racism into a central element in the collective shadow of Brazil.*

Racism of the Past, Racism of Today

Darci Ribeiro brings the old slavery to our present day Brazil with a challenging psychological interpretation; I would say a Jungian interpretation that tells us about the *cultural unconscious* of Brazil:

> No people that go through this [the slavery period] as its daily routine through the centuries would get out of it without being indelibly imprinted with it. All of us, Brazilians, are the same flesh as those tortured blacks and Indians. All of us Brazilians are, in an equal way, the possessed hand that tortured them. The tenderness, sweetness and the most atrocious cruelty conjugated themselves here to make us the suffering and sorrowful people that we are and the insensible and brutal people that we also are. Descendants of slaves and masters of slaves, we will always be servants to the malignancy distillated and sowed in us ... The most terrible aspect of our heritage is to always carry with us the scar of the torturer printed in our souls, ready to explode in its characteristic and racist brutality.
>
> (Darci Ribeiro 1995, p. 120, free translation)

This is indeed a very psychological interpretation of the permanence of the slavery period in the cultural unconscious of Brazil, after almost three hundred years of slavery and more than a century after its abolition. While working with sociological and anthropological concepts, Darci Ribeiro is also suggesting a psychological image. The images of the sadistic master and the suffering slave must be considered as an important archetypal image in the cultural unconscious of Brazil, and also in the make up of its very stratified social classes.

Maria has inside her the master, but also the suffering slave. She carries inside her the sadness of her biological mother who gave her for adoption because although this woman was white, she got pregnant by a black man. Maria carries the suffered prejudice of this black natural father, but she also acquired, through adoption, the opportunity of belonging to a higher class, and by accepting the plastic surgeries that transform her racial characteristics, she becomes one of those who reject blackness.

The daily paper *Folha de S. Paulo* conducted a very sensitive and detailed research on the prevalence of racial prejudice in Brazil. Carried out among the general population, this research demonstrated to what extent racial prejudice exists in Brazilian society. It included all races, whites, blacks, Indians, mulattos, *morenos* or *mestizos* of all strata of education and people at all levels of income: the richer classes, the middle class and destitute people. This important research came out in a small book called *Cordial Racism* (*Follha de S. Paulo*, Datafolha, 1998).

This curious name given to the Brazilian form of racism was based on the notions of *Brazilian cordiality* as defined by the historian Sergio Buarque de Holanda[1]. According to Holanda,

> Brazil's contribution to civilization will be cordiality. We will give to the world *the cordial man*. The affability in dealing with other people, hospitality, generosity, virtues so praised by foreigners who visit us, represent, in effect, a defined feature of the Brazilian character, to the extent, at least, that patterns of human sociability formed within the rural and patriarchal milieux.
>
> (Holanda 1936/1999, pp. 146, ff.; free translation)

But Holanda reminds us that it would be a mistake to understand this cordiality as mere good manners, as civility. According to him the word *cordial* should be understood in its precise and etymological sense. Holanda affirms that the Brazilian is far from having a ritualistic notion of life, being cordial and putting the private above the collective. 'Our way of sociability is just the opposite of politeness', writes Sérgio Buarque de Holanda.

> it may deceive in appearance – this is explained by the fact that the attitude of politeness consists precisely of a kind of deliberate mimic of manifestations which are spontaneous in the 'cordial man': it is the natural and vivid way to behave that translates itself into a formula. Besides that, politeness is, in a certain way, the organization of defences in society. It stops at the exterior, involving only the skin-deep part of the individual, even serving, when necessary, as a peaceful form of resistance. It is the equivalent of a disguise that allows each one to keep one's sensibility and emotions intact.
>
> (Holanda, op. cit., p. 147; free translation)

This text written by Sergio Buarque de Hollanda in 1936 pertains to his book *Raízes do Brasil* (Roots of Brasil); it is one of the most famous works about Brazilian cultural history, today *a must* for Brazilianists, anthropologists and sociologists specializing in Latin American culture. In it we can find examples of cultural stereotypes, precious psychological gems in texts not dealing specifically with the psychology of the unconscious, for Holanda gives us a precise and vivid description of the archetype of the persona working within the collective psyche of present-day Brazilian society.

Now we can understand the reasons why *Folha de S. Paulo* named its research *Cordial Racism*. Knowing the implications and contradistinctions that Holanda meant by *cordial, we can have a better idea of the disguise for violence, rejection, hate, superior attitude, and mainly, the lack*

---

1 Sérgio Buarque de Holanda-Raízes do Brasil., S. Paulo: Companhia das Letras, 1936/1999, 26th edn.

of openness to equality in opportunities for jobs with better salary and better education in universities for blacks, mulattos and Indians in Brazil.

Our patient Maria is *cordial* in her persona, seemingly nice to others, both in her family and her social milieu. But, at the same time, she doesn't believe in her own feelings and she pretends friendship because she doesn't believe in the other people's affection. Maria does not believe in the feelings of her white sister and rejects her. Once Maria brought to analysis a complaint about her sister – who accused her of rejecting everybody and did not let her enter her room to try on her clothes and jewels. (She rejects the sister but *seems cordial* to the rest of the world).

Social Class and Racial Prejudice in Brazil

It is usually extremely difficult for a black person to acquire a higher standard of life in Brazil. When this happens, it is like a miracle; *the black man becomes white*, or, to express it more clearly, *he is considered white and even perceives himself to be white ... There is a strong connection between the colour of the skin and social class in Brazil, or between racial prejudice and class prejudice.*

The very stratified social system, in which a social position has much to do with the colour of the skin, has its origins from the very time of the abolition of slavery. At that time, Brazil had a predominantly agrarian economy. The masters of the slaves were the landowners and they knew that the abolition would not change social relations deeply and that they would go on keeping their power. (Contrary to the abolitionists, who were more naïve in this respect and sought deep social transformations). The white masters of slaves, also landowners, had the monopoly of power, political, economic and social. The lower levels of the populations were mostly composed of recently freed men of colour, Indians and some poor whites; they were expected just to obey and follow orders. So, the stratified social system that existed in colonial times already obeyed a rigid ethnic pattern. Even after the abolition of slavery, as in colonial times, the stratified system did not depend on slavery to continue to exist[1].

The half million slaves who were freed in 1888 entered a complex multi-racial social system in which *the archetype of the persona* acquired a particular bias which we will call *the racial persona*. This *racial persona* is of central importance for the *social placement of the individual*. One must remember that Brazil from the start was never a bi-racial society like the United States or South Africa. One must remember that from that beginning the population was mixed, as mentioned before. The

---

1   See T. Skidmore, *Preto no branco*. Rio de Janeiro: Paz e Terra, 1989, 2ª ed., pp. 54, 55. [*Black into White. Race and Nationality in Brazilian Thought*. Oxford University Press, 1974].

vast majority of the population had Indian or black blood. From the point of view of phenotype, the multi-racial society allowed all kinds of shades of colour between the white European and the black Afro-Brazilian. The colour of the skin, the texture of the hair and other physical features, that is, his *racial persona*, would help to a great extent the efforts of an individual to rise up in the social scale. In this social mobility the mulattos or mestizos have a racial persona that makes them especially able to change places in the social scale. As a cynic Brazilian saying goes: 'money turns things white' (Skidmore, op.cit., p. 55). As a person acquires money and he or she is able to go up in the social scale, *his or her skin, as if it were by miracle, clears up.*

This is also true for Maria, now 36 years old, who still lives in her parents' apartment. She is kept paralysed in a double bind situation; although she knows some people accept her (falsely/hypocritically) only because of her social position, she still prefers this false acceptance to trying to go and live by herself and having to face more directly the social rejection.

Considering the *racial persona* of a middle-class Brazilian we could say that the mulattos and mestizos are responsible for the so-called racial democracy in Brazil. The capacity of mobility in the social scale *depends largely on the colour of the skin.* Those with a racial persona that sums up more traces of pure black have less chances of mobility in the social scale.

In Brazil, in fact, it is a very surprising and confusing factor to perceive the large extent to which the ethnic group is an attribute of a social class, more than of the colour of the skin! Recently the well-known football player Ronaldo was interviewed by a magazine in Brazil about the constant racist occurrences in football games in Europe and South America. Ronaldo responded that he was quite sad about those incidents, *but,* in his words, '*as he was a white man*' he was *not directly subject to these racists attacks, although he 'could quite understand the suffering of his friends*'.[1] Ronaldo is a dark-skinned mulatto. In his case the very common phenomenon in Brazil has happened: the perception of the colour of the skin goes hand in hand with the social class. Surely Ronaldo Nazário would have admitted being a mulatto before, when he was a very poor boy in the district of Bento Ribeiro in the suburbs of Rio de Janeiro. But after having defended Brazil's soccer team in the World Cup games in 1994 in the United States, he became a world champion when he was only 18 years old. Playing since then in professional teams in Italy and Spain, he became a multi-millionaire. He is not a mulatto any more; people won't call him so, and it seems he believes them!

Another interesting example of this mixture of social class and

---

1 Ronaldo Nazário, in *Veja* Magazine, on line, June 1st, 2005.

colour of the skin is reported by Meira Penna[1], showing that this attitude dates a long way back:

Henry Koster, an English traveller in Brazil in the XIXth century, was surprised to see a mulatto occupying the high rank of chief-captain; he then heard the following explanation: '*Yes, he was originally a mestizo, but now as a chief-captain, he must be no other person than a white man*'.

The Whitening of the Race

The peculiar racial prejudice in Brazil involves a powerful fantasy of the *whitening of the race*. According to American Brazilianist Thomas Skidmore (1974/1989) the Brazilian intellectual élite was greatly influenced by European racist ideas and wanted a *whitening of the race* as far back as around the end of the XIXth century.[2] But surely one can say about colour in modern society Brazil that in fact the number of *mestizos, mulattos and morenos got higher,* and not only by a *whitening of the blacks* but also by a *darkening of the whites*....

The *whitening* thesis maintained that through repeated crossbreeding the white genes, being stronger, would predominate over black or Indian genes, coming to produce a white generation after various generations of mestizos. Brazil would thus reach ethnic purity through miscegenation! These racist ideas are understandable in the sense that Brazil's intellectual élite was looking at European and North American ideas predominant at the time.

This ideal led to the fantasy, particular to part of the Brazilian élite in the years between 1889 to 1930, *of a theory of whitening the race not by separation or exclusion, but, surprisingly enough, by crossbreeding.* This theory has been specific to Brazil and deserves to be discussed in its symbolic aspects. It has many times been presented as a scientific formula but it has never been adopted anywhere else.[3] The first ethnologist to present this idea was Joao Batista de Lacerda, during the 1st Universal Congress of Races in London, 1911.[4]

The *alchemical idea* of the whitening of the race was counter-opposed by another theoretical movement that started in the '30s in Brazil: the movement of cultural anthropology and cultural syncretism led by Gilberto Freire and some other important scholars. Freire attacked these ideas strongly. Since cultural anthropology argued that environment and culture were the main thing, the races were in themselves less important as etiological phenomena. From the 1930 on, with the rise of Nazi-fascism in Europe with its fanatic overvaluation

---

1 J.O. de Meira Penna, *Psicologia do Subdesenvolvimento*. Rio de Janeiro: APEC, 1972, 2nd print.
2 See Thomas Skidmore: *Black into White: Race and Nationality in Brazilian Thought*. Oxford University Press, 1974.
3 On whitening, see Skidmore, op. cit., pp. 81 ff.
4 João Batista de Lacerda, see T. Skidmore, op. cit. pp. 81 ff.

of the race factor, the social approach of Freire's with its emphasis on environment proved to be the right one. The old ideas of whitening of the race disappeared in Brazil; theories of scientific racism became an anachronism. This also happened in the whole of South America. *But the idea of the inferiority of non-white groups still remained in the cultural unconscious*: the idea that blacks may come to a social realization only in sports or in music, not through an academic profession.

Final Conclusions

We must conclude from all that has been said before that crossbreeding in Brazil did not constellate a racial democracy as many important ethnologists and anthropologists came wrongly to conclude, among them Gilberto Freire. Brazil is indeed a *racist society* because of the social class implications within the ethnic groups.

Darci Ribeiro comments on the Brazilian forms of racism, arguing that they are better anyway than the classical forms of racism which I call here Anglo-Saxon racism, that is, the racial prejudice that promotes separateness, not crossbreeding.

But there is a danger in the racial assimilation of Brazilian society: *the leadership* among the blacks is non-existent and one is led to think that social inferiority is a natural phenomenon and should be accepted naturally. In Anglo-Saxon racism, where the races are kept separated, black leadership is kept intact and solidarity also becomes greater, as opposed to the situation that appears to be more integrative, but is quite oppressive in reality. Anyway, *one can have racial democracy only when there is complete social democracy for all,* something that Brazilian society is still far from attaining.

One should also emphasize that the essence of the racial prejudice in Brazil *leads to an integrative force that predominates over a segregating force.* The Brazilian generally sees the lighter-coloured mulatto as a white man; this attitude leads to miscegenation.

In the cultural unconscious of Brazil one can see a situation that analytical psychology has always pointed out as most dangerous: *the dissociation of psychic contents.* In the case of Brazil the racial prejudice itself is dissociated and repressed. In cultures where there was open racism in the past, at least they had significant leaders, like Martin Luther King in the United States and Nelson Mandela in South Africa. These strong and meaningful leaderships led the repressed groups on their way to finding meaningful existence in society.

But in Brazil, as sociologist Florestan Fernandes said, 'the Brazilian is ashamed of having [racial] prejudice', or we would say, from the psychological point of view: *the Brazilian has enormous difficulties in becoming conscious of his racial prejudice because it is deeply dissociated in the cultural unconscious.* The result of this dissociation is a tremendous energy between the sophisticated persona of the so-called *cordial man* and his *cordial racism*, a shadow of anger and superior attitude and a subtle scorn toward those of the ethnic groups down below in the social pyramid.

Going back to the clinical case we dealt with here, Maria introjected the rejection she suffered early in childhood from the mother (the most significant), also the father and later in school. So she herself developed a process of not accepting her own ethnic identity, resulting in a deep conflict with her own selfhood. It is up to the analysis to show her how to meet her true self, with its true colours (they appear in the sculpture as a multi-coloured inside world). That will not happen without great suffering.

We know that the archetype of the shadow shows its destructive aspects not only in projection, but also in the collective phenomena, we are dealing with here; the shadow has *a great capacity of contamination*. In large urban areas of Brazil riots of violence and destruction have occurred recently, mainly in the larger cities of Rio de Janeiro and Sao Paulo. Many explanations are offered for these outbreaks of violence. They centre on the trafficking of drugs. Surely the phenomenon of international drug trafficking is the main cause, but the violence will not be controlled unless other problems present in this very complex, multi-racial society which is Brazilian society can be dealt with, including the racial problem deeply connected to social class differences.

Maria has recently graduated in psychology, and this was very important for her self-esteem. She started social work with children in the Rio slums. As a trained psychologist she thinks she has a lot to do to help those kids and to feel accepted by society. She said that she is now living in a world that makes sense for her; the world she also belongs to.

References

Adams, M.V. (1996). *The Multicultural Imagination. 'Race', Color, and the Unconscious*. London & New York: Routledge.

— (2005) *The Islamic Unconscious in the Dreams of a Contemporary Muslim Man*. Paper presented at 2nd International Academic Conference of Analytical Psychology and Jungian Studies. Texas University, 2005. Website: www.jungnewyork.com

Bateson, G., Jackson, D., Haley, J. & Weakland, J. (1956). 'Towards a theory of schizophrenia'. *Behavioral Science*, 1, 251-64.

Bomfim, M. (2005). *A América Latina*. Rio de Janeiro: Topbooks.

Buarque De Holanda, S. (1936). *Raízes do Brasil*. S. Paulo: Companhia das Letras, 1999, 26th edn.

Cardoso, F.H. (1962). *Capitalismo e escravidão no Brasil meridional*. São Paulo: Difel.

Costa e Silva, A. (2004). *Francisco Felix de Sousa, mercador de escravos*. Rio de Janeiro: Eduerj.

Fernandes, F. (1964). *A integração do negro na sociedade de massas*. São Paulo.

Folha De S. Paulo/ DataFolha (1998). *Racismo cordial. S. Paulo*: Ática, 2nd edn.

Henderson, J. (1984). *Cultural Attitudes in Psychological Perspective*. Toronto: Inner City Books.

– (1990). 'The cultural unconscious'. In: *Shadow and Self. Selected Papers in Analytical Psychology*. Wilmette, Il: Chiron Publications, 103-13.

Hillman, J. (1982). 'Alchemical blue and the unio mentalis'. In *Spring: an Annual of Archetypal Psychology and Jungian Thought*, 33- 50.

Jung, C.G. (1928). 'The relations between the ego and the unconscious'. *CW* 7, 1975.

Kamel, A. (2006). *Não somos racistas*. Rio de Janeiro: Nova Fronteira.

Meira Penna, J.O (1972). *A Psicologia do sub-desenvolvimento*. Rio de Janeiro: Editora APEC.

Revista Veja, 'Veja on-line', June 1st, 2005. Quotation by Ronaldo about racism in European football teams.

Ribeiro, D. (1995). *O povo brasileiro*. S. Paulo: Companhia das Letras.

Skidmore, T. (1989). *Preto no branco*. Rio de Janeiro: Paz e Terra, 2nd edn. [*Black into White. Race and Nationality in Brazilian Thought*. Oxford: Oxford University Press, 1974].

The Stranger in the Therapeutic Space[1]

Uwe Langendorf
Germany (DGAP)

Abstract

There is nothing like a stranger. Every unknown person is not a stranger at first, but becomes a stranger as a product of a psycho-sociological process. Every group needs the stranger to defend its identity. If they cannot find one, they must invent him. The stranger is our object of shame. He is like a person without skin. His will always become violated. The group refuses to understand anything of his difficult position and demands his consent to deny his violation.

However, it is not always the stranger himself who threatens the group. It is enough that he is available for this particular function. The development of the ghetto of Venice is an excellent historical example. The frontier of the ghetto is stabilized from both sides. You will find inhabitants of different ghettos all over the world: Jews in Europe, Armenians in Turkey, black people in the USA. Everywhere the blemish of shame is attached to them.

Before therapy begins to heal that big wound, first we have to admit that the wound exists at all. Now the therapist himself begins to be ashamed. Later the stranger has to be liberated from his exotic state. At last he recognizes himself as an individual. Now both patient and therapist recognize that they cannot tolerate each other. Then – and not earlier – the space is given to heal the wound.

Inside the therapeutic space you have to find three skins. The skin of the stranger. It must grow and become coherent and strong. The skin of the therapist. It must be strong and permeable. And at last the common skin of the therapeutic room. This room should be neither too narrow nor too wide.

In today's globalization, the question of the treatment of strangers becomes more and more important.

* * *

When I began my training as an analyst, therapy for people from other cultures did not feature. How one should work analytically with people from foreign cultures, was simply not asked, and I heard

---

1 Translated from the German by Professor Paul Bishop, Department of German, University of Glasgow. We very much appreciate his generosity.

nothing about it. Nor did there seem to be a need for it. People from other cultures apparently did not turn up in analysts' waiting rooms.

In the meantime this has all changed. In our country around 16% of the population is from another culture, and the figure is set to rise (Machleid 2005, p. 77). In some schools in Berlin up to 80% of children are the children of migrants. The problems of migrants are enormous, and their need of psychotherapy can hardly be overestimated. Many migrants live in ghetto-like circumstances, of which someone from outside has little knowledge. In my own analytical practice around a quarter of my patients are foreigners. In short, there is good reason for me to concern myself with this problem.

But I also have a quite personal reason for doing so. I believe my interest derives in part from the fact that, due to my personal appearance, I have, since my childhood, often been taken to come from southern Europe or the Mediterranean. All nationalities have been ascribed to me, from Syria to Senegal; no one would believe I am German. Probably, and unconsciously, a second self-image has been built up in me, that of someone from the South, whom I never wanted to be. Perhaps I am, in secret, on the search for that Other in me …

But then, I could only be disappointed. Foreigners never correspond to the image that one has of them. Whatever I impute to them, I will never actually find in them what I am looking for. Perhaps I will learn above all to set aside my own prejudices, layer by layer, like an onion. And, just as when one does that, one begins to cry.

Half of the problem lies in the countertransference. When I was formulating the theme of this lecture, a space for therapy floated before my eyes, in which the strangeness of other people could unfold. Unnoticed, I had placed myself in the role of the observer. But it should be about the relatedness in which I must perceive my own countertransference.

A Frau Meyer has an appointment. I meet a beautiful, dark-skinned woman. She speaks perfect German, as she has been working for many years in Berlin. I feel uncertain, I have difficulty in controlling my confusion, in suppressing the rising prejudices that I find embarrassing, and, I admit it, my sexual curiosity. For her part, Frau Meyer knows this. This is how Germans react to her, she lets me know, they only see the coloured woman, not the person.

Her story sounds quite bad. Because her mother had no more children after her, her father sent her back to her family and married another woman, who bore him more children. Frau Meyer quickly stops my pity. (She knows this, too.) 'That is our culture', she says, with pride in her voice. I have the feeling that my analytic standards are not sufficient. Of course it must be bad enough for a small girl when her mother is sent away. But when this is part of the culture which she identifies with?

Of course there are societies which traumatize their children through their cultural upbringing. But should I be using European standards to judge? At any rate, I cannot interpret the cultural moment as traumatic, without attacking the cultural identity of the woman. And, in my interpretation, is there not a touch of the secret feeling of superiority of the white man?

In working with people from different cultures I do not feel well prepared by analytical theories, whether they are Freudian or Jungian. When they examine foreign cultures, they all peer through European glasses. In an unreflected way, they set the European individual as the standard. All psychoanalytic schools begin with the development of individuals from their drive-based or archetypal starting-point that must negotiate with an environment that says 'yes' or 'no'. Of course there are general, human, fundamental structures that one must always consider. But as a rule analytical theories neglect the identity of the large groups into which the child is born. These collective patterns already exist when the child is born, and form his or her group-identity. Kakar has described how, right from the start, an Indian child grows up into an identity as a Hindu or a Muslim (Kakar 1997, p. 55). In this way typical, national characters arise. These different structures are, as I see it, based less in archetypal, inherited dispositions than in the cultural memory of the nations which mediates these collective identities (Assmann 1992, p. 48). When the analyst and the patient belong to the same group, these collective identities are not so noticeable. But if each is a stranger to the other, then these alienating differences appear. So I regularly hear people from other cultures saying: 'We do things differently, you don't understand!'

Such differences are also in evidence in daily life. Our technical standards, our rules of professional distance, our 'technical neutrality' (Kernberg 1978, p. 69) are designed for Europeans. But what might be valid for us can be entirely false for peoples from other cultures. Kakar speaks of the 'guru model', 'according to which the therapist should display pity, interest, warmth and responsibility much more openly that is possible or desirable in psychoanalytic treatment' (Kakar 1995, p. 197). Gressot describes the Bantu healer, who enters into such an intensive dialogue with the patient that the limits of the identity of each become blurred and a quasi-psychotic level is reached (Gressot 1957, p. 726). Kawada writes about the attitude of Japanese therapists, for example in Morita therapy, which responds to the needs of the patient for dependency in a way far greater than we would consider acceptable (Kawada 1977 p. 276).

Just as I would not wish to apply our standards in a schematic way to people from other cultures, nor would I wish to imitate such foreign attitudes. I, too, have made mistakes. For example, I had to learn that with clients from oriental countries I should not see too much in the opening question, 'How are you today, *Herr Doktor?*', but should respond with the corresponding question, 'I'm well, thank you, and how are you?' Without this introductory ritual, the conversation does not take off. It would be wrong to see this ritual in terms of resistance (Ardjomandi 1993, p. 67). I have also learnt to give up the usual reserve with East Asian patients and to take a much more direct personal attitude towards them. With such individuals, silence can have a traumatizing effect.

Nevertheless, I wish to desist from making general rules. Even between two people, each of whom comes from different cultures, there can be major differences. I have the feeling of entering new territory where I have to find a path that leads forwards. But it is usually not quite so simple. Occasionally I discover negative reactions in myself, and in such moments I wish this or that person to go to hell! The feeling of strangeness crops up again; I feel I am back at the beginning, and perhaps into this frustration there creeps an unconscious hatred towards the countertransference. Perhaps I then start to idealize my patients, or to think of them as particularly disturbed and myself an exceptionally self-sacrificing therapist. The 'hatred in the countertransference' (Winnicott 1983, p. 77) must be carefully considered in work with people from other cultures. At the same time, it should be remembered that, in such work, one's own identity is constantly under subtle forms of attack. I begin to discover the limits of my own empathy, and this cannot happen without disappointment.

But being foreign or a stranger is not itself the real problem. It's not about a 'clash of civilizations' (Huntington 2006, p. 11). In our work we are dealing with migrants. These people have usually fled intolerable conditions, have come to us with great expectations, and now discover that they are not really accepted. They cannot put down roots here and remain outsiders forever because, for one thing, they sense our reserve, and for another, they cannot identify themselves with us, without giving up their own identity. For all these reasons their new home must seem to them to be a cold, inhospitable country.

An Iranian once told me how, after his arrival in Berlin, he had stood in the cold on the platform, seen the train-driver sitting in his train – and profoundly envied him: 'He can sit in the warm, he has a job and a home; but I'm standing out here in the cold and have nothing', he thought.

A female Korean student was part of a work-group with three Germans. At the end the four women decided to go for a coffee. In front of the café the three German women turned to her and said goodbye.

Migrants do not feel themselves to be accepted in their new environment. But nor do they feel they any longer belong to their old homeland. Turkish people, who have lived for a long time in

Germany, are called back in Turkey *almanci*, a derogatory expression. A Korean woman, who has lived in Germany for over 30 years, has never overcome her feeling of being abandoned. Every day, on waking up, she thinks: What am I doing here? But in Korea, she no longer feels at home, either. In fact, she has nowhere on earth she could call her home.

In addition to the feelings of abandonment and loss comes the guilt at having left family and one's own country in the lurch. The greatest suffering, however, stems from a sense of shame. In the foreign environment migrants feel uncertain, exposed, and vulnerable. They have no right to be here. The deepest shame stems from the disappointment of their desire to be accepted (Tisseron 2000, p. 43). They feel themselves to be considered exotic specimens, not valued as individuals. They live as if wrapped in shame. 'Do I smell or something?', an Asian woman once asked me. In this sort of way foreigners are marginalized and excluded by the xenophobia around them. They live in an invisible ghetto of shame.

Xenophobia is the projection of strangeness, or foreignness, onto the object. Yet strangeness is not a property of an object, but it resides in a relation, it arises in an interpersonal dimension. There is no such thing as the essence of strangeness, of strangeness-in-itself. We encounter something unknown and identify it with a complex of pre-existent expectations. So this is why I think of strangeness as a construct. As far as I know, all human societies have formed certain ideas about strangeness, foreignness, and how to engage with foreign people. As an example one might mention the Akan of modern Ghana. They have three types of stranger: Ohoho, a stranger from another tribe of the Akan; Ntafo, a non-Akan, who comes to them as a trader or a Muslim preacher; and Odonko, a non-Akan who comes from the steppes, and who can be used as a slave. In each case a different set of rules applies. But the stranger stands fundamentally outside the law: 'The stranger cannot break a law' (Kramer 1987, p. 15).

Each society attributes to the stranger precisely the function it requires him or her to have. Sometimes the stranger is idealized, like those Asian wisdom-teachers, who enjoy such popularity; sometimes the stranger is despised and driven out, like the boat-refugees from Senegal on the shores of Europe. Very often the stranger becomes a container for those feelings of guilt and shame from which society wishes to rid itself. I should like to demonstrate this process using the example of the history of the ghetto in Venice (Sennett 1997, p. 267).

Ever since the Lateran Council of 1179, the cities in Christendom have always tried to isolate the Jews in defined ghettoes. But the very first ghetto was, thanks to its position as an island, created in Venice. Ghetto derives from the word for 'foundry', and this is the name of an island on the outskirts of the city. At the end of the fifteenth century the foundries were turned into dockyards, the arsenal. Because the ghetto that arose only had two entrances, it could easily be sealed off and observed.

Around 1500 Venice was without doubt the richest, most powerful, and most modern city in the world at that time. It dominated the trade between East and West, the Mediterranean, the financial trade, and a large part of the northern Italian mainland. In terms of luxury and sexual freedom, Venice far exceeded anything in the past. Young, homosexual men went around in gondolas, naked apart from women's jewellery. The prostitutes were so rich that they had to wear a yellow shawl so they could be distinguished from the honest women in the city. In short, the Venice of 1500 was the most outstanding city in Europe.

Ten years later, its splendour was a thing of the past. The Turks had conquered the eastern Mediterranean, the Portuguese had taken over the trade between East and West via the sea-route to Africa, an alliance of enemies had pushed the Venetian army back to the coast of Mestre. Only her superiority on the seas prevented the worse. And if that was not enough, the syphilis that had come into the city from America took a large toll of victims.

The people of Venice attributed their distress to their collapse in morality, and pushed the blame onto the Jews. It was the Jews who were said to have brought in the syphilitic infection, and they were held to have been responsible for the swift spread of the disease. A Jew's very body was regarded as a source of infection, and one took care to avoid touching it. Likewise, the Jews were associated with sexual immorality and prostitution, and the lending of money was regarded as in some way an act of impropriety. Even the rituals of purification made by the Jews were seen as evidence of their dirty condition. The pious Christian of the time never washed, and gave off an 'odour of sanctity', *olor de sandidad* (Wurmser 2001, p. 113), whereas the Jew, who took hygienic measures, smelt different, smelt foreign. In other words: the Jews represented everything the city wished to rid itself of.

The Signoria took various precautions to limit the Jewish 'danger'. They could not be driven out because they were needed to support trade. So it was decided that each Jewish man or woman should wear a piece of yellow clothing, to make themselves visible, just as the prostitutes were. Moreover, all the Jews had to move into the ghetto that stood empty. In the evening all Jews had to be back there, the doors of the ghetto were closed from the outside, and the entrances placed under watch. On Christian feast days, when the monks preached their sermons against the murderers of Christ, and the Christian mob bayed for blood, the doors of the ghetto remained closed, a sort of preventive detention.

And so it came about that the Jews were isolated and exposed to contempt.

The most effective way in which the ghetto had an isolating effect lay in the creation of a sense of shame, not for something one had done, but for something one was: a Jew, the wearer of a yellow sign, as someone (or something) dirty, infectious, and disgusting, despised, and regarded as on the same level as prostitutes. Thus Venice found a container for its own sense of humiliation. As the ghetto demonstrates, shame delimits in two ways: those who have been outlawed have a sense of shame in front of other people, and those who are 'pure' are ashamed to come into contact with those who are outlaws.

I said that migrants today live in an invisible ghetto … What is it like to live in a ghetto? Can we who live around, but not in, the ghetto imagine what it is like?

Frau Kim has been living and working in Germany for half her life. She speaks perfect German. Now, she has been living together for five years with a German man: they share the rent, their table, their bed. But sometimes the man says: 'This is my flat'. That upsets her. He has a son; she has a daughter, both from previous marriages. The son visits the father almost every day, but he does not greet Frau Kim, and ignores her. Her daughter lives abroad and only comes to visit occasionally. When he first met her, the young German man said to the girl from Korea: 'That's funny, you don't smell like a dog'. And, in a way, that is a funny remark, because the girl was in fact treated by the two Germans no better than a dog would be, or at least a foreign dog, and in the end the man ended up forbidding the daughter from visiting 'his flat' at all. Frau Kim cannot understand why she cannot welcome her daughter there. Does she have fewer rights, because she is a foreigner? Is this the way the Germans are? In Korea one tries to be hospitable. At work, too, she feels time and again with German colleagues, even the women, that she is not one of them. She is a stranger. Why are we rejected? she asks. Do we smell? Every morning she wakes up with a feeling of abandonment.

When I hear her talking like this, I feel ashamed to be a German. The unspoken question hangs in the air: 'You're a German, too. Why are you all like that?' Perhaps it is this unspoken assumption: that an Asian woman could never feel at home with a German man, that preserves a barely noticeable sense of distance. I have learnt a lot from her. In the course of her analysis, something very moving has happened. But she always behaves as if she could leave at any moment. A sense of reservation on her part; on mine, a feeling of shame. In fact, on both sides there is a sense of shame, since being excluded (when one wants to be included) induces shame, and the subtler the form of exclusion, the deeper, the more refined the sense of shame. This is the ghetto.

The story of Frau Kim underscores my thesis: foreignness is a construct. For it is how other people think an Asian woman should be that turns her into a foreigner. If one believes that people from Korea smell like dogs, then that's that, and when one perceives something different, the prejudice remains, uncorrected. At this point I should like to cite a few lines from a song (here in its English version):

In the musical 'South Pacific', by Rodgers and Hammerstein, we hear:

> You have to be taught before it is to late,
> before you are six or seven or eight,
> to hate the people your relatives hate,
> you have to be carefully taught …
> you have to be afraid of people,
> whose eyes are oddly made,
> of people whose skin is a different shade,
> you have to be carefully taught.
>
> (Wurmser 2001, p. 10)

Work with migrants is, to an unusual degree, work on the countertransference. In the process this work is effected by something I have not yet mentioned, namely the experience of violence and terror. Most migrants – and all those I have seen – bring it with them from their land of origin and from their families. The same applies to the children of migrants, to whom the traumatic experiences of their parents are passed on.

I saw a young female student from Vietnam. She was two years old when her parents had come to Germany. The family had experienced the entry of the Vietcong into Saigon. Her father, an official under the Diem régime, had been taken to a particularly hard re-education camp. Thanks to money from relatives the family succeeded in leaving the country as boat refugees. In Germany the family lived almost entirely cut-off, more Vietnamese than the Vietnamese, full of guilt and shame towards the other members of the family they had left behind and exposed to reprisals. The mother was beyond help; the father was depressive, occasionally suicidal. The daughter had to cope with the task of learning to live in German society, but at the same time she had to represent for her parents the homeland they had lost.

Our initial encounters worked very well: I was looking forward to our work together, when the young woman explained – with a friendly smile, which she always had – that she would prefer to have her therapy with a female colleague. And left me feeling disappointed. As I later discovered, this therapy never actually took place. But I do know that from the outset I had became inwardly reserved towards her, because I was shocked by the cruelty of what she had experienced, and in our first session I had hesitated when the woman had demanded that I respond directly to her problems. Perhaps, precisely in the moment I hesitated, the opportunity had been lost.

Maybe you will shake your heads about my assertion that the majority of migrants have been traumatized by terrorist violence. But wherever my patients come from, terror and violence have dominated – or continue to dominate – their country. In many countries, democratic forms of government have replaced military dictatorships, but the terrorization still goes on at the familial or social level. Those who have been traumatized still experience exclusion and violence as terror and further traumatization when they are with us.

Let me introduce you to Pedro from Latin America, the son of a plantation owner. His father was a violent man, who used to hit his son with an iron bar, and insult him: 'Nothing good will ever come of you!' This father had been responsible for the illness, even death, of several children. He had become infected with syphilis from prostitutes and had refused treatment. When a child was born damaged, he said it was because of the worms. So medication against worms was supplied, which of course did not help. Pedro became a journalist and reported in the newspapers about the police. Although the military dictatorship was over, there was still terror in the form of the war between the police and bandits. Pedro uncovered the methods of torture used by the police and some questionable deaths. As a result, he himself was observed, spied upon, and threatened by the police. His life was in danger, he had to make sure he was always accompanied; he had to sit in cafés with his back to the wall, keep an eye on the door, watch out for cars, sleep somewhere else than in his own flat, and so on. He went to Germany, but could not get used to the place, and he is terribly homesick: he misses his own country. He paints a lot. His pictures show his native countryside – or distorted faces. One night, two oriental men beat him up on the street – it just happened. Ever since he has been suffering from anxieties, from insomnia; he does not dare go out of the house, he cannot travel on the underground. Thanks to his therapy, his anxiety has improved somewhat. His attackers live in his neighbourhood, and they could still be a threat to him. He hides away at home; he can no longer paint and write; it is an immense effort for him to come to his therapeutic sessions. Even I, too, become his persecutor, if I ask him to do something to reduce his anxiety. He sits in front of me as if he were on trial, his answers are quiet and hesitant. 'I don't know, I can't go on'. The more I try to 'deal with' his anxiety, the worse it gets. Only when I ask him about the story of his father does he become more lively, and something of his potentially murderous anger becomes evident. Pedro is not an isolated case, and his problem is not a purely familial drama. As he describes it, his homeland is full of violence and terror, the arbitrariness of the police is just part of all that. One of his brothers, as strong as an ox, has joined the bandits and been shot by one of his 'colleagues'. Pedro bears within him the terror from which he has suffered. When I first saw him, I thought: a guerrillero, a Che Guevara-type.

An example of continuous, 'cumulative' terror is offered by Korean history. From 1910 to 1945 Korea was a Japanese colony and was brutally suppressed. After its liberation, Korea was devastated in the war of 1950-1953, at the end of which a hard-line, Stalinist dictatorship was established in the North, while from 1960 until 1987 a similarly harsh dictatorship governed the South. Since then South Korea has been a democracy, but the remnants of terror persist ... (Kern 2005, p. 182).

Another example is Iran. I have spoken with a man who was persecuted by the Shah's secret service, then by the Khomeini régime. The methods were the same, he said, and in some cases the same people were involved. In humiliating circumstances he managed to escape and build up a new existence in Germany. Yet he remained damaged by the traumatizing experiences he had undergone.

A young Iranian was able to free himself from his nightmarish burden with the help of therapy. Even his childhood and his family have been affected by violence. When he was fourteen, his eighteen-year-old sister was arrested, because she had taken part in demonstrations against the Khomeini régime. The parent and his father visited her in prison, they were maltreated by the guards, her father had to humble himself in front of the mullah, the girl was finally executed. She was given an anonymous grave, a concrete block without a name. The revolutionary guards destroyed even this and her father was beaten up in the graveyard. Her brother succeeded in fleeing, but he was threatened by the person who helped him escape with homosexual rape, which he only narrowly avoided. In Germany he had built up an enormous system of defence-mechanisms. He let nothing become close to him, he only maintained superficial contact with other people, the kind he could easily drop, he presented a façade of polite charm through which nothing could pass. It was important for him to be able to leave at any moment. In his daydreams he pursued his fantasies of revenge.

In the course of therapy he managed to lower some of his defences and he described some of his horrific experiences. This made him physically ill, but afterwards he felt better, he became approachable and was able to embark on a relationship with a German woman, that to this day continues to lift a weight from his shoulders.

At that time I was feeling bad as well, I could barely cope with the horror of the terror and I felt utterly helpless. Sometimes I felt tempted to simply brush the story away from me, on the basis that 'because it ought not to happen, it didn't happen'. But I managed to stay with it, without flipping my lid.

Yet I still ask myself whether the terror-induced trauma is a major motivation for resistance in the countertransference. To put it concretely: do we analysts perhaps try not to notice the traumatizing effect of collective terror, and instead withdraw to an individualistic point-of view?

Many parts of the world are still dominated by terror, in some places to an increasing extent. Perhaps we Germans have a particularly strong resistance to noticing this because we do not wish to be reminded of the time when Germany itself was a land of terror ...

If we really wish, however, to understand the psychological problems of migrants, then we have to come to terms with the nature of terror. The word terror derives from Latin, and means fright or horror, to be distinguished from anxiety, or *pavor*. Terror takes hold of the whole of the individual in his or her most vital aspects; it begins genetically much earlier than anxiety, it cannot be objectified and it knows no distance. It reaches into the earliest, pre-linguistic levels of the psyche. Terror through collective violence threatens the individual, both from without and from within, with a nameless fear. Because terror aims to destroy the human being's identity, to empty the individual of any narcissistic satisfaction. The victims of terror are filled with an all-embracing sense of shame and disgust with themselves. Under the influence of terror an inner representative of it takes shape, which represents the demands of terror and exercises a tyrannical domination over the psyche. Amigorena talks about a tyrannical agency (Amigorena 1979, p. 610). Thus there arises an insoluble conflict between the structures that already exist, the super-ego and the ego-ideal as well the newly-formed parts that have split off, and a part of the real ego, that has to accept compromises and, in part, becomes an accomplice to the terror. The ego terrorizes itself, and at the same time it condemns and despises itself for doing this. The dreams collected in Charlotte Berad's *The Third Reich of the Dream* [*Das Dritte Reich des Traums*] gives an idea of the inner violence to which terror can give rise (Berad 1981, p. 11). The victims of terrorist violence free themselves from it despite sustained resistance and seem to hold on from within to what is destroying them.

I can summarize what has been said so far by sketching an outline of the complex of the migrant's trauma. It consists of:

- a feeling of abandonment, anxiety about losing the good inner objects

- anxiety about the loss of identity

- the guilt at having abandoned the good objects one has left behind

- guilt-anxiety arising from a conflict of loyalty and an anxiety about having betrayed one's good objects

- anxiety about shame arising from the disappointed narcissistic wish to be accepted in the new home country
- a splitting between the old and the new identity
- the inability to put down roots in one's old country as well as in the new 'motherland'
- traumatization as a result of terrorist violence and its consequences
- the key factors are mourning and shame.

Let me tell you about Frau Li. She, too, comes from Korea, has been working on a piece of research for over ten years in Germany, in order to obtain an academic qualification she needs in her home country. Persistent physical complaints make it difficult for her to finish this work. She suffers from attacks of conjunctivitis, rhinitis, and breathing difficulties, so that, despite making a huge effort, she achieves very little. Her permission to stay depends on this piece of work and on the support of her academic supervisor, who is, however, disappointed by her slow progress.

This is the second round of therapy. She felt treated by my predecessor as if she was an exotic specimen, and attacked by the interpretations offered: for example, 'you are using your symptoms to take revenge on your father'. In general, she felt no one believed her. The doctors never found a suitable explanation and said it was all psychological.

Her analysis begins with an immense idealization of me as a person. She relates traumatic moments from the story of her life in a moving way, she talks through connections, she expresses positive as well as negative feelings towards me: but the symptom remains unchanged. Over a long period I became identified with her goal of finishing her research. I was able to read part of her work and was impressed. Eventually she gave me an overview of her situation. As if scales fell from my eyes, I suddenly saw that the completion of her work was something she would never achieve. Her prospects appeared in a dismal light: a return to her home without a qualification, all her efforts in vain, her parents' money squandered, poor job prospects, nothing but shame. In her home country she could simply rot away.

Her life story is this: Her mother appears to have had nothing but hatred for her from the outset because she had wanted a boy, after giving birth to her sister: what a disgrace! Her father had beaten her in choleric fits of anger with a cane until she was bleeding and humiliated. Her mother had also hit her, but slowly, systematically, justifying this by what she said was the recalcitrant character of the child. A child such as her deserved the blows she received. In addition, her sister consistently received preferential treatment, an innate privilege expressed by being given bigger presents and being offered undeserved praise. My patient had been the better child at school, but this was something that could not be admitted, because it would have upset the superiority of the older sister. Even in school she was regularly beaten. Whilst she was a student, her father still exercised strict control and would hit her at the slightest wrongdoing. Contact with young men was completely forbidden.

The pressure of the military dictatorship influenced the social atmosphere. On the campus students were regularly spied upon, arrested, men with truncheons were paid to be always ready to beat up student demonstrations, the smell of teargas frequently drifted across the university site.

Her family itself was under political pressure. During the time of Japanese colonial rule two uncles had been arrested and treated brutally. After the Korean War one of the uncles had gone to North Korea. As a result my patient's family was under police observation, their house was searched, the uncle's name could never be mentioned, the children were not even allowed to know of his existence. Even the professional position of her father became compromised. Her parents could only try to raise their children so as to make them examples of industriousness and good behaviour, in order to demonstrate that they were beyond reproach.

My patient became caught in an insoluble dilemma. On the one hand she felt herself full of anger and rebellion, because of her parents' cruelty towards her: she desired revenge. On the other hand she had internalized the Confucian ideal of the dutiful child: the child has to show respect and gratitude to its parents throughout its life, so however the parents behave, it is not permitted to criticize them.

Her failure filled my patient with shame and self-hatred. To identify her inhibition to work as psychogenic would have filled her with mortal shame. She would have preferred to have been diagnosed with terminal cancer. Among Germans she felt rejected and not accepted, she had experienced the hurtful feeling of not belonging. Even I, she felt, did not understand her. But equally, she could not return to the society of her home country with its tight control; she felt she would suffocate. The mistreatment to which she had been helplessly exposed had left a vast sense of shame and done profound damage to her feeling of self-worth, wounds that would not quickly heal.

For a certain period of time I was infected by our mutual idealization, carried away by the feeling of being able to work with an unusual patient, with whom I would form an unusual therapeutic couple. The more the traumatization of my patient came to light, the more my image of her became one of an unusually difficult case, but even then we could still form an unusual duo. Perhaps I was also occasionally tempted to make the impossible possible. But because, despite all my efforts, the complex of complaints remained, I increasingly became an unusually unsuccessful analyst. When I finally realized that the great goals would never be reached, I had to lower my ambitions considerably. I feared she would be hugely disappointed, or even break off the treatment, but instead my patient appeared relieved. Perhaps it even did her good when I realized her goals were unachievable.

In fact, I had been expecting for some time that her negative father-transference with strong emotions would eventually manifest itself against me, and I was ready to go through this experience with her. But this did not happen. I remained someone who was good, if powerless. As a result of this therapy, I did actually feel that I was powerless when faced with the judgmental violence of the judge within. My patient had penetrated deep within me, and yet she retained her negative father-complex. My dilemma may well be typical of work with migrants. I identified with her rebellious, freedom-loving side and I believed I could understand her sense of upset and her traumatization, even if their extent filled with me with dismay. But inwardly I can barely begin to understand what power the tradition of the 'dutiful child' had over her. I have no way of gaining access to her inner judge. Perhaps I would have had to excavate my own history to recover the feelings of resentment from the time when in Germany itself terror, crime, and racial hatred were dominant.

As a spark of hope my patient described a dream she had recently had: She is led by a German man downstairs to a room, where she is to be forced to drink a glass of poison. The compulsion is irresistible. The man simply has to try and find a quiet place where she can drink the poison. She goes along willingly, she does not try to resist. Finally they come in the basement to a hospital ward. She hopes that here she can draw attention to herself, so that the man cannot carry out his intention and she does not drink.

Has the therapy failed? In my view, one should not think in terms of success or failure. Perhaps I was simply able to act as and remain a container for unbearable contents. My patient has asked if, even after her return as a failure to her home country, she can remain in touch with me via the Internet. I have agreed to this.

Strangers in the Therapeutic Space

As I said in my introduction, work with migrants is becoming increasingly important in today's world of globalization. The process of globalization is revolutionizing the world we live in as only the Industrial Revolution before it did. The new world economic order has been on an unstoppable upward trajectory since 1994, when the founding of the World Trade Organization introduced a worldwide liberalization of economic and cultural relations. Since then, the exchange between individuals and nations has been becoming more intense and faster. But this does not mean that people understand each other better. At the same time, the dangers from international terrorism have also increased. A fraternal relationship between all human beings seems a long way off.

Seen superficially, some people believe that the various civilizations are coming together. Life styles, patterns of consumption, working practices are becoming increasingly similar. English appears to be the universal language. The reverse side of this development lies in the levelling-out and the loss of diversity of human cultures. For economists, this development is a good thing, because it should make economic relations more efficient and bring more prosperity for all. Bill Clinton spoke of the 'rising tide that lifts all boats' (Mander 2002, p. 10). This promise is dubious. It seems to me to be the case that, in the global game, there will be winners and losers. In any event, what will be lost is the diversity of cultures. Cultural forms, mythologies, and languages are disappearing more quickly than one can save them. This impoverishment of diversity goes along with a reduction in natural species, with desertification, and with the spread of monocultures. Globalization has the effect, it strikes me, of establishing a single, Western styled civilization. The loss of cultural diversity should give us, I think, just as much a pause for thought as the disappearance of biological species. Does not the demand for efficiency in economic-therapeutic terms herald a unification of our different psychotherapeutic techniques? Kakar talks of the 'Western cultural (and moral) imagination which, because of the predominance of America and Europe in psychoanalytic discourse, has the tendency to disguise its moral sermons about health and maturity under the cloak of general psychoanalytic concepts' (Kakar 1995, p. 207). This, too, is part of the global monoculture. Some people regard this development as inevitable.

Instead, however, we can see the diversity of cultures as a precious resource and as an opportunity for humankind, just as the biologists are discovering a richness in the diversity in the various life forms of nature. This requires, first of all, respect for difference and a shift away from the monoculture of Eurocentrism in our sciences, too. Kakar again:

> A conscious perception of the cultural context of psychoanalysis would contribute to extending knowledge and tolerance of our common discipline in the interest of the broad spectrum of human possibilities and a greater cautiousness when dealing with such concepts as pathology and deviance.
>
> (Kakar 1995, p. 207)

Let me bring these considerations to a close with a text by a

Lakondo Indian (Rätsch 1984, p. 283). The Lakondo Indians are an ethnic group facing extinction in southern Mexico. Missionaries and civilization have all but nearly extinguished their culture. I would like to quote from a prophecy handed down in their traditions:

> The end of the world will come. As we have been told, so we say. Our end will come, when there are no more trees, then, when they are all chopped down, when there are humans everywhere, when there are no more forests. As it is said, so we say, thus our fathers said. They said: let it be so, for it is true, it is said, when the entire forest is full of people, when the entire forest is full of people who live close together, and all the trees are chopped down, when there are no more mahogany trees, when all the trees have gone, been chopped down and there are only mountains, then the end of the world will come. Not quite yet, but it will be soon. Then the end will have been reached. As we say. There will remain nothing for us.
>
> We say this, but we do not exactly know whether there will be a storm or not, whether the sun will scorch us. Perhaps there will be a huge chill or something else. But our true lord, Hachäkym, will have our blood.
>
> This time, this time no one will be spared, there will remain nothing left, no animals, nothing. There will be nothing there, the earth will be empty.
>
> For, when the end of all speaking, the end of the world comes, then, my dear children, there will be nothing there.
>
> Then it will all be over. Thus spoke the gods. In Yaxchilan they wrote it on the stones. They wrote, they said when our end should come. We say that it was Hachäkym, a true lord, who commanded the red storm and the end of all speaking.

I consider it important for us to become more alert to the signs of the levelling-out that is taking place in the process of globalization. For this development is not inevitable. It is becoming increasingly clear that the brave new world of a single culture, economic efficiency, and megacities is not capable of surviving. Instead, we have to learn to respect diversity. And this begins in *our* work with a respect for the diversity in which each and every single human being is a small universe.

References

Amigorena, H., Vignar, M. (1979). 'Zwischen Außen und Innen. Die tyrannische Instanz' ('Between outer and inner. The tyrannical situation'). *Psyche*, 7, 610-19.

Ardjomandi, M. (1993). 'Die fremde Kultur der Schiiten' ('The foreign culture of the Shiites'. In *Das Fremde in der Psychoanalyse* (*The Stranger in Psychoanalysis*) by Streeck Ulrich. München: Pfeiffer.

Assmann, J. (1992). *Das kulturelle Gedächtnis. Schrift, Erinnerung und politische Identität in frühen Hochkulturen* (*The Cultural Context. Writing, Memories, Political Identity in the Earlier History*). München: Beck.

Berad, C. (1981). *Das Dritte Reich des Traums* (*The Third Reich of the Dream*). München: Suhrkamp.

Gressot, M. (1957). 'Übertragungsphänomene in der Medizin der Primitiven' (Phenomena in the medicine of the primitive). *Psyche*, 10, 714-32.

Huntington, S. (2006). *Kampf der Kulturen* (Culture Clash). Hamburg: Spiegel.

Kakar S (1995). *Klinische Arbeit und Kulturelle Imagination* (*Clinical work and cultural imagination*).

– (1997). *Die Gewalt der Frommen. Psychologie religiöser und ethnischer Konflikte* (*The Violence of the Believers. Psychology of Religious and Ethnic Conflicts*). München: Beck.

Peter, R. Apsel (1995). *Interkulturelle psychoanalytische Therapie* (*Intercultural Psychoanalytical Therapy*). Frankfurt/M: Brand & Apsel.

Kern, T., P. Köllner (2005). *Südkorea und Nordkorea* (*South and North Korea*). Frankfurt/M: Campus.

Kawada, A. (1977). 'Die Psychoanalyse in Japan' ('Psychoanalysis in Japan'). *Psyche*, 3, 272-85.

Kernberg, O. (1978). 'Borderline-Störungen und pathologischer Narzissmus' (*Borderline Conditions and Pathological Narcissism*, 1975). Frankfurt/M: Suhrkamp.

Machleidt, W., Callies, I.T. (2005). 'Transkulturelle Psychiatrie und Migrationpsychische Erkrankungen aus ethnischer Sicht Z' ('Transcultural psychiatry and psychotic illnesses among immigrants from an ethnic viewpoint'). *Die Psychiatrie*, 2, 77-84.

Mander, J., Goldsmith, E. (2002). *Schwarzbuch Globalisierung* (*The Case against the Global Economy*). München: Riemann.

Rätsch, C., Maax, K. (1984). *Ein Kosmos im Regenwald. Mythen und Visionen der Lakandonenindianer* (*The cosmology, myths and philosophy of the Lakondo Indians*). Köln: Diederichs.

Sennett, R. (2000). *Fleisch und Stein* (*Flesh and Stone*). Frankfurt/M: Suhrkamp.

Tisseron, S. (2000). *Phänomen Scham* (*Shame Phenomenon*). München: Reinhard.

Winnicott, D.W. (1983). *Von der Kinderheilkunde zur Psychoanalyse* (*Paediatrics and Psychoanalysis*). Hamburg: Fischer.

Wurmser, L. (2001). *Ideen und Wertewelt des Judentums* (*Ideas and Values in Jewish Culture*). Göttingen: Vandenhoeck & Ruprecht.

Wednesday, 15 August 2007

My Heart Is on My Tongue – The Untranslated Self in a Translated World

Antjie Krog
South Africa

Abstract: The South African Truth and Reconciliation Commission (TRC) was the first body to provide translation in all the languages of the country, setting people free from groping around with distorted tongues, unable to see, talk or hear one another … After three centuries of silence South Africans could daily hear the black voice talking and being translated; for the first time white South Africans could hear and listen. Through translation we could access our deepest emotions and feelings.

But among the two thousand testimonies there were some that were incomprehensible, that confirmed every racial stereotype built up over many years of apartheid. What does one do with these 'untranslatable' narratives? This paper looks at one TRC testimony and one Bushman story, both of them translated from indigenous languages and both posing enormous moral dilemmas. Read in a particular way, the Bushmen story seems to say that they had no sense of responsibility. I will look at the story in its cultural context as revealed through translation to see if another conclusion is possible. In the TRC testimony, I and two colleagues looked at the slippages between the original Xhosa testimony and the interpreted version and explore the consequences thereof.

I want to make the point that a narrative can be experienced as discriminatory and ethically problematic when read through a particular, in this case a western, perspective. But the moment there is an attempt to interpret the narrative via its embeddedness in an indigenous worldview, it becomes breathtakingly ethical, fair and logical.

* * *

I want to address two points. The first, and easiest, is the absolute necessity of interpretation and translation if health, healing and transformation are at stake. Secondly, I want to explore some of the possibilities and conditions for interpreting and translation in South Africa.

Let me start with a literary example. With the rise of feminism and feminist critiques, it was said that the famous female characters in literature, such as Anna Karenina, Madame Bovary, Lady Chatterley were mostly the products of the male fantasies of their male authors in male dominated literature. They were not like women; they were men's version of women. Today one seldom hears that accusation any more because, since then, there has been a worldwide explosion of female narratives that has put enough ways of being a woman forward that male (and perhaps also female) writers can successfully imagine a female character.

I want to suggest that the same analogy holds for black and white during apartheid South Africa. The dominating narrative for three hundred years in South Africa had been white. The official sound of the country was white. Black people were written about, imagined, recorded, filmed in the way white people thought black people were. Authentic black voices often had to carry the burden of resisting this white noise instead of experiencing the freedom of simply being.

The Truth Commission, within two years, in one concerted effort, suddenly put two thousand black narratives out on air. These were no longer merely the voices of educated, urban men, or of liberation heroes, poets, and journalists, but a variety of black voices ranging from a tea woman to a shepherd to a girl who survived a necklace attempt. The theme was devastating. But the scale of the variety of accents, rhythms, cultural markers, vocabularies, was breathtaking. This could only happen because for the first time in the history of South Africa, an official body provided translation from any mother tongue as part of its mandate to restore the human dignity of people. It meant that a survivor could say 'She stood there, her chest a furnace' instead of 'she burnt'.

Why is it important to describe what happened as accurately as possible?

Appearing before the TRC, a victim who survived a massacre testified how his wife's upper body fell on to his lap and how he saw a butterfly, a red, growing butterfly on her blouse. I was fascinated by the choice of the word butterfly to describe the fatal wound. In an interview afterwards with his psychologist, I was told that it took the man four years to arrive at that word, and that, at that moment, he made his first step to healing.

Thus, in order to start the process of healing, one needs to find words for one's experience. It seems that the closer the words are to the experience, the better the handles to get hold of the experience and take control of it (Scarry 1985, p. 33; Danieli 1998, p. 673). Testifiers before the TRC could access, through translation, their deepest emotions, wisdom and feelings and it did not end somewhere in a cul-de-sac of gender, area, politics, language or culture. More importantly, testifiers could access their victims and perpetrators.

How crucial translation was for any kind of change, such as reconciliation, to take place, became remarkably clear during the TRC hearings of the St. James massacre. On the video footage available at the hearing, one could see the three young black men who applied for amnesty for this incident, sitting quite arrogantly behind their table when the hearings started – sneering and sniggering when a question was asked. One of the members of the congregation, who lost his wife on that day, asked the amnesty seekers to turn around because he wanted to ask them something. All of this was translated. They turned around and he asked them, directly but with great difficulty, whether the one who had shot his wife could remember her – she was wearing a blue coat and was sitting near the door. This interaction visibly shook the young men. Later in the hearing they asked permission to speak to the man and then asked him for forgiveness, their face expressions changed, their sneering tone gone. The man was crying by then, saying that in all these years since his wife died, he had never cried.

When emotional and mental health is at stake, translation is clearly important. But what are the conditions for translation and interpreting?

During a recent poetry festival, I had to select an *imbongi* (Xhosa praise singer). Several local *imbongi* sent examples of their work. Based on the following translation, made by the praise singer himself, the following poet seemed a possibility.

Version One

> I ask you to be quiet, for the imbongi from Xhalanga to speak.
> Let the weak ones be quiet
> I am speaking of important matters.
> I shall show the lies in good Xhosa
> The liars will be shaking,
> I will talk clearly in opposition.
>
> Iimbongi, lend me two opportunities
> I will use them both.
> Young men lend me two opportunities
> I will use them inside as well as outside.
> Young men, lend me two opportunities
> I will use them to look after the aged.
> Young men, lend me two opportunities.
> I will use them both to protect us.
> Young men, lend me two opportunities.
> I will respect the elders and be brave.
> Women, lend me words for healing.

I requested Koos Oosthuyzen, who did Xhosa translations for me, to retranslate the poem. He grew up as the child of a missionary in the Eastern Cape, speaks classic Xhosa and is intimately familiar with rural customs and culture. Being a minister himself, his Afrikaans is also classically elegant. He made the following translation which he calls a more literal translation:

Version Two

Silence please, for the imbongi of Vulture hill is bellowing.
Those who trudge along like wasted livestock
    will be speechless for a change
because I am going to say things that weigh heavily
I am going to say them in deep Xhosa from Xhosaland
My words will let some people fall about frightened like liars,
They will jump around like rattling red rhebuck in a rapid wind.
I will sing clear and solid like a songbird on a stony mountain.

Iimbongi, lend me two bush tiger capes
With one I shall gird myself and with the other sweep
    the way clear.

Boys, lend me two fighting sticks.
The one I will take to meetings
    and with the other one hack away weed.

Initiates, lend me two curved hilt knives.
With the one I will slaughter for the ancestors
    and with the other cut strips for the grey headed.

Men, lend me two wild olive tree staffs.
With one I will tame animals and with the other
    chase the thunder away.

Young men, lend me two dancing canes.
One I will give to the cranefeather heads
    and with the other loudly beat my shield.

Women, lend me a long row of words.
I shall call out restoration from the abundance thereof
    and praise *Qamata* with the rest.

I do not want to talk about the merit of the translation strategy used by Koos Oosthuyzen, that is another debate. I only want to make the point that a translator needs to understand intimately the source language he is translating from as well as be proficient in the target language that he translates into. This translation enabled me to distinguish between an ordinary poet and an exceptional one.

Read against the background of discrimination that we are emerging from in South Africa, a translation like this, from what is regarded as just one of several oral poets living in Gugulethu, challenges two myths: that oral poetry does not really work on paper and that poetry in indigenous languages is of inferior quality to the work written in English. So again, if one hopes to transform a country into a place that respect and value one another, good translation is essential.

But what happens when the translation and interpretation are good, but there is an underlying culture in the source text that neither the target audience nor the translator is aware of? What if it is not possible for elements of that culture to cross the translation or interpretation bridge intact?

As an example of this, here is an extract from a Bushmen narrative. It was faithfully recorded and, by all evidence, brilliantly translated by linguist Wilhelm Bleek and Lucy Lloyd between 13 April and 19 September 1872 (Lewis-Williams 2000, p. 58).

Death on the Hunting Ground

13 April

Another man shoots a man while they are shooting springbok. The man is wounded. All the other men leave the springbok and run to him as he sits in pain weeping, they stand over him. 'What is this thing here which shot our brother?' they ask. The other man answers: 'I did not mean to shoot him, I was busy shooting springbok. Our brother was wounded when he was behind the springbok's back.

15 April

'I did not mean to shoot our brother. I was shooting at the springbok. The arrow went into the springbok's dust. Our brother was near and did not see. He could not avoid it because he was looking at the springbok. He did not see the arrow. I weep for our brother because he is our friend. He is not a stranger who is different, he is our friend. So I worry about our brother, my heart cries for our brother, my heart is not happy about our brother'.

One of them says to him:

'It seems to me, you did not think of our brother's children, you shot him among the springbok when he could not see because of the dust. You did not wait to shoot the springbok as it passed by this side – so that you could shoot the springbok in this place. I saw how you came near to our brother. I saw our brother and I saw you both stooping as you approached each other while the springbok moved between you (*16 April*) you did not seem to see our brother'. The other man says: 'I did not see our brother, the dust had shut in for the springbok were many'.

The wounded man says: 'Our brother is angry with you, but I am the one who did not see well because of the dust. The dust was dense, for the springbok were many. I am wounded because I was watching the springbok. I did not look carefully on that side, for, if I had, I should have avoided the arrow. You scold our brother as if the arrow did not come in through the dust but that is how it was: I did not see the arrow. I could have avoided it and prevented our brother's pain. Lift me up and carry me away to my house. I do not feel as if I can walk. I am in great pain. I must go to lie by myself in pain at the house. Leave the springbok. You will shoot another day. My blood is out. I was wounded early that is why I cannot see well, although it is early. The shade is great, the shade of the tree. The springboks' dust shut my eyes. We did not see each other'.

'We know we are right', says one of the other. (*17 April*) 'Our brother did not see you. We said: 'that man sitting far over there looks as if he is wounded. Over there another man is running to him as he sits. The other man helps him to sit yonder; he looks at the other man. He turns him over so that he can look at the wound. They are both sitting, let us go and see (*18 April*) because the man over there beckons, he knows there is much blood. We must be correct when we talk to the people at home, when the women question us. The women will not speak nicely. They will ask things. The wound seems to be large for the arrow point is still on the shaft – so the wound is deep'.

The other man says: 'The wound is like that. We must run very fast to see so that we can speak nicely to the women. As we speak making their hearts stand still'. (*19 April*) They run strongly; they run fast.

The wounded man tells them to speak gently, not angrily to the man who shot him. 'Remember that it was the arrow's fault. The arrow hit me of its own accord. Our brother here speaks the truth. He did not shoot me. We say truly, we did not see each other. (*20 April*) If I had looked I might have seen him coming, then stooping I should have gone round and sat down, for we approached each other in a direct line. The springbok ran through between us. The dust was dense. The springbok were in the dust; the dust of the springboks' feet was dense. I sat drawing the bow. I was completely still while I waited, because I did not shoot'.

The people carry him to the house. His wife cries, the other women cry. They ask: 'You others, your friend seems to have been fighting: you have shot your friend'.

The men say to the women: 'We did not do it on purpose. It was a false shooting; a false shot's arrow it was. You did not tell the children to play away from the house, that is why the man accidentally shot the other man'. 'My wife is stupid', says one (*22 April*). 'She does not listen when I speak to her. She does not behave in the way her father and mother taught her'.

The other man says: 'My wife is doing foolish things, but I want her to see that it was a false shot's wound. This is how it happened. It is ugly. The wound makes people afraid. I might also have been wounded because she did not say to my boys: "Go out of the house". Dust covered my bed when I returned. My house was as if she has gone away'.

If one does not know much about the Bushmen, how would one understand this extract? It seems that by retelling the incident in a specific way, the Bushmen *shifted the blame* every time smoothly from one to the other. The proverbial buck had thus been passed from:

the killer –> the wounded –> women –> children

Blame moved from the most powerful to the most vulnerable. Could one say that, for their survival, they *needed* to remove the blame from the grownups in order to continue their mutual co-existence and dependence? In other words, what one would simply regard as an abdication of responsibility could actually be explained as its opposite: a pragmatic execution of responsibility in the interdependent context of hunter-gatherers? But what are the ethical implications of always blaming the women and children?

I will come back to this narrative. Let me take a few steps back. A South African theologian and philosopher, Gabriel Setiloane, wrote a book in which he wanted to know why his mother, who was the third generation of being Christian, nevertheless set out food for the ancestors every evening. Even more pertinent: why did it not bother him even though he was a Minister in the Methodist church?

In his seminal work on the image of God among the Sotho-Tswana, Setiloane puts forward the hypothesis that 'the Christian faith held, expressed and practised by the Sotho-Tswana today is a faith which, while passing all the orthodox criteria to make it 'Christian' is nevertheless understood within the assumptions of the '*mekgwa ya bo-rra rona*' (customs, beliefs and ways of life) (Setiloane 1976, p. 161). Willoughby says that 'Bantu life is essentially religious … Religion so pervades the life of the people that it regulates their doing and governs their leisure to an extent that it is hard for Europeans to imagine' (Willoughby in Setiloane 1976, p. 224). This pervasive spirituality was described by missionaries who complained that they had to change their missionary tactics because they found that the black people of Southern Africa did not conform to their idea of heathens: they had a spirituality that had nothing to do with visible totems or altars.

According to Jean and John Comaroff, Moffat complained that there were 'no idols to shatter, no altars to seize, no fetishes to smash' among the Sotho-Tswana' (Comaroff 1992, p. 271). For Setiloane, Christianity is embedded and therefore more than just 'linked' to an indigenous Southern African view of the world. This worldview is not simply a pagan add-on to Christianity, but is in fact the *foundation* of it.

So, if the black people of Southern Africa have a 'different' kind of spirituality, is it not possible that the Bushmen with their sophisticated cosmology played an important role in the formation of the Southern African worldview? With this as a possibility, let us rethink the Bushmen narrative, but this time as if it is embedded in a worldview of interconnectedness. Let us see how a philosophy that says all things are interrelated in a dynamic process of transmitting life, changes the perception of the ethics in this narrative.

Suddenly the narrative becomes highly moral. One realizes that through the retelling, the Bushmen did not *remove* or *shift* the blame, but in fact *distributed* it. In terms of interconnectedness towards wholeness, the death of the hunter became everybody's business. Everybody, even the youngest woman and child, was responsible when somebody died. Every death affects us all. We have to care about everybody who dies, to feel affected by every bit of spilt blood on earth, because we are all interconnected-towards-wholeness.

The point I want to make here is that even a well translated narrative can be experienced as discriminatory and ethically problematic when read through a particular, in this case a western, perspective. But the moment there is an attempt to interpret the narrative via its embeddedness in an indigenous worldview, it becomes breathtakingly ethical and fair. One also realizes the impossibility of having any reciprocal meaningful interaction when the philosophy underpinning a narrative is not known or understood by one of the parties.

One needs interpretation in most health care sectors, but in the area of mental health, one needs much more.

One of the most incoherent testimonies I heard during the two years of reporting on the Truth Commission was that of Mrs Konile. Mrs Konile's son, Zabonke, was murdered by the Security Police in an incident that became known as the Gugulethu Seven. Her testimony stayed with me for many years as a sharp reminder of how I, as a white person, at times seem to have no other tools but racist stereotyping to make sense of the actions of a black person. Most of the TRC testimonies powerfully undermined the racial stereotypes that have been built over centuries of colonialism and apartheid, yet this testimony seemed so confused and closed to me that I remember thinking that if I did a normal reporting job of Mrs Konile's narrative on radio, it would only strengthen racist views. At the same time, I suspected that her testimony was important, precisely because it was different from the others and that, perhaps, one needed other tools to make sense of it, because bearing witness, as Terrence Des Pres (1977) says, is not just a linguistic, but also an existential stance.

It was however clearly not only I who had problems with her testimony. On the video footage of the TRC hearing into the incident (Day 2 Tape 6B) one could see how restless and uncomfortable the other mothers became when Mrs Konile testified. Some of the Commissioners also seemed to look puzzled.

So what was my problem with the testimony given in Xhosa and interpreted into English?

With the TRC part of the new and open South Africa I was very conscious how the testimonies were ripping several apartheid lies to pieces. Judging from the letters and remarks from conservative elements of the South African community, however, it was clear that there was resistance to give up these beneficial myths. In over-simplifying and over-emphasizing a possible racist reading of Mrs Konile's testimony, I hope to explain my discomfort with the 'strangeness' of her testimony.

One of the racist myths one had been raised with was that black people were not able to see or think three dimensionally (Mbembe 2001). That was why they failed their driving tests and covered the bed with a bedspread the wrong side up. Mrs Konile seemed to have no sense of geographical space.

> But I never thought that because Peza was usually coming to Cape Town I am not – I don't even know Cape Town and now we went on to the pensions.

Mrs Konile talked about Cape Town right through her testimony, but she seemed never to be sure whether she was indeed in Cape Town. People living on the Cape Flats (the sprawling townships around Cape Town) often felt cut off from Cape Town proper and would only refer to the name of the township where they live, but Mrs Konile's geographical instability was in sharp contrast to the other Cape Town women who testified with her and who accurately moved their testimonies between townships, city, mortuaries and linking roads.

Another racist myth was that black people were not really unhappy with apartheid, but were incited by the communists to protest. And indeed the spatial incoherence of Mrs Konile's testimony is later joined by a political confusion when Mrs Konile said: 'The ANC is a comrade in Cape Town'. To Mrs Konile the ANC was one single comrade living in Cape Town. In the next paragraph she suggested that the ANC not only lived in Cape Town, but that the ANC WAS in fact Cape Town. Does one accept that it was possible to live in one of the most highly politicized areas on the Cape Flats during the mid-eighties with one's child recruited for military action for the ANC's military wing, while at the same time not having a clue what the ANC was? Not even when thousands of comrades marched with the cortege to the graveyard on the day of the funeral? Later in her testimony Mrs Konile seemed to confirm this by asking: 'What is ANC? What is ANC?'

Yet another racist myth was that black people do not really care about their children, that was why they so easily stayed in white people's backyards and looked after white people's children. Instead of talking about her son, Mrs Konile talked about a goat.

> We went and came back from getting our pensions. I said oh! I had a very – a very scary period, there was this – this was this goat looking up, this one next to me said oh! Having a dream like that with a goat looking up is a very bad dream.

Who or what was this goat? Was it a real goat she saw that day which she simply made part of her TRC narrative? Was she living in a world where goats and people alternate? Was the goat her son? Was Mrs Konile known for daydreaming or 'seeing' things? Was she using it as a psychological image to enable her to bring the unconscious to the conscious? Was superstition a word to be used in this context? Should the goat be regarded in terms of universal symbolism such as abundant virility, creative energy, superiority (Cooper 1995, p. 74)? In Christian symbolism the goat signifies the devil, the sinner, the scapegoat.

After two paragraphs about her son, Mrs Konile continues about a rock which pinned her down as she was digging for coals (digging for coals in Cape Town?), how she fainted or regained consciousness, hospitals and injections, thirst and cold. Her testimony seemed to drift from one surrealist scenario to the next; most of her testimony had nothing to do with her son but was describing her own personal suffering in a highly confused way – leaving the impression that her son's main value for her was monetary and that she was never really aware who or what he was fighting for or what was happening around her. She also seemed to have no idea what to ask of the perpetrators or the Commission.

The question remained: what would make it possible for a white person to ever understand and empathize with Mrs Konile as an interconnected fellow human being (or to report her testimony in such a way that both its power and integrity stay intact? Or to treat her mental health if she so wished?)

Ten years ago I didn't have an answer. However, after having joined the University of the Western Cape, I ordered the original Xhosa audio version of the testimony from the South African Archives (tape: 08) and formed an association with two colleagues: Nosisi Mpolweni-Zantsi from the Xhosa department and Professor Kopano Ratele from the Psychology department. Mpolweni-Zantsi transcribed the original Xhosa from the tape and retranslated it together with Ratele.

Despite my suspicion that it was the interpretation that failed Mrs Konile, it seemed remarkably accurate. As we moved deeper into the analysis we realized that Mrs Konile was not only narrating coherently within particular frameworks, she was also resisting other frameworks imposed on her. Many of the discoveries were only uncovered by our study of the original version so that we have come to the conclusion that the meta-codes that could have transmitted her shared reality with many South Africans were somehow hamstrung, either by her interpreter or the transcriber of the testimony on the website. Although these slippages seem small they often lead to major confusions.

The first clarification was one of pronunciation. Reading the reports on the Gugulethu incident, as well as detail about her second appearance before the TRC, we realized that the TRC official website misspelt her surname: she was Mrs Konile and not Mrs Khonele as the website suggested.

The second clarification was spatial. When we listened to the original Xhosa on the cassette, Nosisi Mpolweni- Zantsi (2007) picked up that Mrs Konile was pronouncing the Xhosa for 'mortuary' and 'comrade' in a way that was peculiar to rural Transkei. The TRC hearing where Mrs Konile was testifying was held in Cape Town, the Gugulethu incident happened in Cape Town, all the other mothers who testified, lived in Cape Town, Mrs Konile herself mentioned Cape Town repeatedly, so we assumed that she was also from Cape Town.

The official version on the TRC website however starts as follows: 'I am Ms Khonele (sic) from [*indistinct*] I have three children […] etc'. What word was indicated by '*indistinct*'? We assumed that the '[*indistinct*]' word(s) was Cape Town. We returned to the beginning of the testimony where Mrs Konile was saying: I am Ms Konile from and the word 'Indwe' was then recognized. 'I am Mrs Konile from Indwe. It was correctly interpreted, but the TRC transcriber, perhaps not being familiar with this small hamlet near Queenstown, could not distinguish the word. (The word 'Indwe' as well as her surname was correctly transcribed after Mrs Konile's second appearance before the TRC some months later.)

Suddenly a lot of things made perfect sense. Although one cannot dig coal in Cape Town, Indwe is famous for its shallow coal deposits and several coal diggers experienced rock falls. But it is absolutely the poorest of the extremely poor who dig for coal in Indwe. Through the cultural and geographical knowledge of my colleague Nosisi Mpolweni-Zantsi, Mrs Konile emerged as a woman caught in dire poverty and loneliness in a harsh and remote part of the Eastern Cape after her son's death.

Through Nosisi's retranslation we learned that Mrs Konile didn't SEE the goat, she dreamt about the goat. The word 'dream' was omitted in the translation itself. As a Xhosa cultural sacrifice, the goat was an indicator of the bad news to come. Kopano Ratele explored the notion of interconnectedness and wrote in a subsequent paper (2007) about the goat dream:

> On the deeper philosophical level I interpret the dream as telling Mrs Konile about a wholeness being threatened, because she is *not an individual*, not in the way it is defined in the dominant frameworks of psychology. Rather the dream reveals that she is still whole in that she is part of a world where she is in contact with the living and the living-dead.
>
> There is little existential loneliness here. It is only later, on learning of the death of her son, that her wholeness is ruptured, that she feels she is becoming an individual in a terrible way. Her son's death introduces her to a deep loneliness. She experiences it as being cut off from the community. She is sighing because she has become an individual through the death of her son, selected as it were to become an individual. She is saying: 'I am suffering, because I had been forced to become an individual. All the other mothers are together here in Gugulethu, they talk and support each other, but I am outside of it all'.
>
> The word 'I' is actually not talking about her real psychological individuality. Mrs Konile is using 'I' as a form of complaint, She is saying: 'I don't want to be I. I want to be us, but the killing of my son, made me into an I. This deed has removed me and I can't get back to where I belong. The last time I was whole, was when the goat spoke to me, since then I had been simply removed, cut off'.
>
> So to understand Mrs Konile, to get to a psychological comprehensibility, our approach needs to be founded on her reality, her notion of her position in a universe of people, animals and things, and her thoughts and feeling of how she relates to others and the environment. In other words, meaning systems undergird the possibility of being understood by others.

Conclusion

In his book *Culture and Mental Health*, Leslie Swartz (1998) underlines the importance of translation and interpretation in the area of health. And let me repeat that I find it incomprehensible that interpreting is not available on a significant scale in health care sectors, that every single doctor, even those from Cuba and India who cannot speak an indigenous language, does not have an interpreter he or she regularly works with. Swartz suggests that, because of globalization and forced displacement, it is also true for many other countries. He explores four views of the interpreter's role: the invisible interpreter, the interpreter as culture broker, the interpreter as junior colleague and the interpreter as client advocate. He also explores several problems that could arise in such a relationship (Swartz 1998, pp. 36-45).

Let us take a look at the invisible interpreter. Of course the interpreter is never invisible and, as Christine Anthonissen points out in a recent paper (2007) on interpreters, brings their own individual world to the process. I would suggest that the interpreters during the TRC process were as close to being invisible as possible. Because they were in separate booths, the victim would look directly at Tutu or Mary Burton. The only indication that translation was happening was the headphones. Although some victims had problems with the fact that Mary Burton speaks to them but they hear a man's voice over the headphone, it seems that if the interpreter is physically not present, it can create an important sense of direct communication.

I would suggest that the interpreter should also be the culture broker in a discussion afterwards because it is only when the interviewer brings his or her own questions and assumptions, often underpinned by colonial, racist, gender or religious notions, that the possibility of real understanding opens up. I would also suggest that a strong sense of hierarchy could easily freeze the proper exploration of cultural and psychological possibilities. I found the alliance that developed between Nosisi Mpolweni-Zantsi and Kopano Ratele immensely fruitful, and more and more I was useful only as the person with some questions. The lessening of my role did not matter because the comprehension of Mrs Konile's testimony grew.

I am therefore suggesting that in a country where unemployment is high, where many people have very good understanding of several languages, they should be trained to interpret specifically in health matters. Doctors, hospitals, clinics should have interpreters and over time individual roles, ways of securing confidentiality, checks and balances will develop.

Let me end with the title of this paper. In a country trying to move out of a past of discrimination and a highly uneven spread of skills, translation is a crucial strategy for survival – not only for all the untranslated narratives, but to free us from those who assume that they can translate the untranslated through their own perspectives, or worse, those who believe untranslated means not worthy of the trouble of translation.

Translation creates space for one's heart in a language. Who you are, what you yearn for, does not simply die in a cul-de-sac of a power-less language. Translation lets the osmosis of human knowledge take place between cultures. Translation ensures that all kinds of concepts are being brought into one's language for which one has to discover equivalents which, in turn, leads to a more perceptive and empathetic patient, doctor and interpreter.

Translation always brings empowerment with it. In one's mother tongue one has access to the entire majestic pipe-organ of one's body and brain and all its registers of emotion and observation; in the dominating language, one often tries to express oneself on a toy piano. Allow the patient to use everything she has, and allow the doctor to have a nuanced conversation with her client.

But benefits are also extended to the powerful language. The challenge is that at times in the translation process things will come up that strike one with their difficulty, complexity and inability to fit into the resources one's language and culture use to make sense of the world. These things – from lexical items through speech acts up to the cultural behaviour patterns of translators – will be different from one's own culture and one will have to find resources and touch-stones in one's own culture. This will keep the powerful language fit enough to be tolerant.

Translation is essential for us to live in respect of each other. We have to translate each other to ourselves, to transform our behaviour into living a life acknowledging that to be human is to be vulnerable. And to be vulnerable is to be fully human.

References

Anthonissen, C. (2007). *On Interpreting the Interpreter – Experiences of Language Practitioners Mediating for the TRC* (still to be published in a special issue of the *Journal of Multicultural Discourses*).

Comaroff, J. & J. (1992). *Ethnography and the Historical Imagination*. Boulder, San Francisco: Oxford Westview Press.

Cooper, J.C. (1995). *An Illustrated Encyclopedia of Traditional Symbols*. London: Thames & Hudson.

Danieli, Y. (ed.) (1998). *International Handbook of Multigenerational Legacies of Trauma*. New York: Kluwer.

Des Pres, T. (1977). *The Survivor – Anatomy of Life in the Death Camps*. New York: Pocket Books.

Lewis-Williams, J.D. (ed.) (2000). *Stories that Float from Afar*. Cape Town: David Philip.

Mbembe, A. (2001). *On the Postcolony*. Berkeley, Los Angeles, London: University of California Press.

Mpolweni-Zantsi, N. (2007). *The Importance of the Original: Challenges in Interpreting a Xhosa Testimony Before the South African TRC* (still to be published in a special issue of the *Journal of Multicultural Discourses*).

Ratele K. (2007). *The South African Truth and Reconciliation Commission* (TRC): *Ways of Knowing Mrs Konile* (still to be published in the *International Handbook on Indigenous Methodologies*).

Scarry, E. (1985). *The Body in Pain – The Making and Unmaking of the World*. New York: Oxford University Press.

Swartz, L. (1998). *Culture and Mental Health – A Southern African View*. Cape Town: Oxford University Press.

TRC Video Tapes (1996). Cape Town Day 2, Tape 6B
TRC Cassette Tapes (Mrs Konile's testimony from tape 08)
First TRC Testimony of Mrs Konile:
www.doj.gov.za/trc/hrvtrans/heide/ct00100.htm

Panel: A Passage to Africa
Part II, Contemporary Perspectives on
'Jung's Journey to Africa'

John Beebe
USA (CGJISF)

Introductory Remarks

The trouble we who weren't actually born here have in coming to Africa is that we think we know so much about this continent. For when in our lives have we not heard about Africa? In my own childhood, the Tarzan movies, with their inevitable crocodiles suggesting the whole array of primitive childhood fears; in my teens, a big Hollywood film, *The Snows of Kilimanjaro* (adapted from a Hemingway story), in which Gregory Peck tells Susan Hayward he has come to Africa to 'get the fat off his soul'; with a college, audience, a grainy print of *Cry, the Beloved Country*, from the novel by Alan Paton; after medical school, Doris Lessing's *Children of Violence* novels; in my midlife years, the televised release of Nelson Mandela from prison (that I set my alarm in California for 4 a.m. to be sure to see) – each time these images have given me the sense that I knew Africa.

It's hard to believe, though his own education was not quite so media-driven, that Jung didn't bring the same assumption when he assayed the 'dark' continent for himself in 1925. Yet if his experience was at all like mine, the problem for him was *not* that the continent of Africa was dark but that it had already been lit for him by the glare of unconscious complexes. For instance, Jung reports in *Memories, Dreams, Reflections* that the only time a black man appeared in his dreams during the entire African sojourn, was in a nightmare involving a dark-skinned barber trying, with a terrifying hot curling iron, to kink his hair. Jung eventually realized that the model for this dream figure was the barber who had cut his hair in Chattanooga, Tennessee, thirteen years before. He had imported a figure from another culture to Africa.

Jung says in *MDR* that at the time of the dream, he thought it was compensatory to his conscious attempts to subject himself to an African influence by undertaking the journey. Michael Vannoy Adams in a now-classic discussion of this dream[1] has argued that this is an

---

1 Adams, Michael Vannoy (1996). *The Multicultural Imagination: 'Race,' Color, and the Unconscious.* London & New York, Routledge, pp. 74-80. My interpretation of Jung's dream builds on his.

ego-defensive interpretation that continues to cover Jung's evident fear of really accepting any true African influence on his thinking (the hair growing from his head), which remained rigidly European, resisting the impact of African culture. My own view is that there may indeed have been a heavy influence on Jung's thinking while in Africa that Jung's unconscious was worrying about (the kinking of his hair, which he clearly did not want in the dream) but that it wasn't coming from Africa, but rather from the influence of what Sam Kimbles would call a *cultural complex* that was twisting the way Jung was thinking about Africans. I am referring to the category mistake of thinking about Africa on the basis of a limited experience with African descendants in America, an experience shaped by early twentieth century American cultural assumptions and projections, which would have made the barber himself all but invisible[1] to Jung. The fantasy figure that emerged to replace him in Jung's psyche, a carrier of dangerous hot emotionality (the outsize curling iron), whatever else he may have come to signify for Jung personally or archetypally, was historically the introjective identification of collective American fantasies about blacks, an inappropriate model to use in organizing a European man's thoughts about the consciousness of Africans.

Jung's dream suggests to me that given the frighteningly inductive power of cultural complexes around race, a more reliable way to help our psyches accomplish the passage to Africa would be to look not at our preconceived images of Africans but instead at the images we carry of people from non-African backgrounds who have come to Africa. I suspect we all have at least one especially vivid image of someone who has come to Africa from another part of the world. For many of us here, Jung provides that image, but do we really know what he was seeking by coming here?

It might help, in trying to answer that question, to summon other images of Western journeyers to Africa; images that I know have shaped my own expectations of what may be found here.

I would like to start with the image of the central character in a classic American film. I want to recall for you the image of Katharine Hepburn in *The African Queen*, playing the role of Rose Sayer. Rose and her brother are English missionaries in German East Africa in 1914. When the war breaks out, their African village is burned by the Germans, and when her brother protests, he is beaten by a German

---

1 Kimbles, Samuel (2000). 'The Cultural Complex and the myth of invisibility'. In *The Vision Thing*, ed. Thomas Singer. London & New York: Routledge. See also Kimbles, Samuel (1999), 'Poisons and panaceas in analytic training'. In *Destruction and Creation: Personal and Cultural Transformations*, Proceedings of the 14th International Congress for Analytical Psychology, Florence, 1998, ed. Mary Ann Mattoon. Einsiedeln: Daimon Verlag, pp. 431-435; and Singer, Thomas & Kimbles, Samuel (Eds.) (2004). *The Cultural Complex: Contemporary Jungian Perspectives on Psyche and Society*. Hove & New York: Brunner-Routledge.

soldier and left to die. Rose conceives a proper British revenge. She decides to go by river in a mail and supply boat, the *African Queen*, captained by the Canadian Charlie Allnut, played by a grimy, dyspeptic Humphrey Bogart, to the lake where the German gunboat, the *Empress Louisa*, is controlling the flow of arms and men, effectively blocking any English counterattack. She wants to turn the *African Queen*, which carries dynamite, into a torpedo that will blow up the *Louisa*. Rose's problem is to get Allnut, a distinctly unheroic single man, to rise to her heroic task.

In this film, Africa is the stage for a heroic scenario, and Katharine Hepburn is the image of a distinctly feminine hero. She is an Anglicized Athena. But the title of the film – taken from the name of the boat – suggests that her character, Rose, is inspired by a more African mother goddess, while it is the *Louisa* that suggests the patriarchal anima from Europe that Rose's eruption of feminine agency is meant to overcome. The African environment provides a whole set of complicated obstacles; the effect is to test the resolve of the partners. In the end they discover that they love each other. This is finally a triumph not of the masculine will but of the feminine heart. The idea Rose embodies for us is that *Africa is a place to stage a hero myth in which the feminine can finally triumph.*

Let me offer you a second image. This is from the follow-up to the most popular television series of thirty years ago in the United States, *Roots*, which described how Africans came to America by tracing the history of a particular family descended from a West African man named Kunta Kinte, who was captured and brought to the North American continent as a slave. The episodes in the series revealed what happened to this man and his descendants, right up to the Civil War. Two years later, a second series, *Roots: the Next Generations*, took the story into the present. The image I want to summon is from that second series, which shows the author, Alex Haley, who got the idea for the book on which *Roots* was based. He is collecting genealogical information from his old female relatives in Tennessee. The information leads him to visit Africa, where he encounters an oral historian who tediously recites everything that has happened to the tribe over many generations. When Haley is nearly asleep from the hours-long recitation, he suddenly hears the name Kunta Kinte and learns for the first time what Africa remembered of the man who had disappeared from its history in the eighteenth century. Here is the ultimate 'root' of his identity as an African American. The joy on Haley's face, as conveyed by the great actor James Earl Jones, suggests the pleasure we all get when we can match our life experience to an archetypal root. The implication is that *we can find in Africa the pure, uncontaminated roots of our identities as humans, before the corruptions of civilization have set in.*

A different kind of emotional image of what people from the West often expect to find by coming to this continent is portrayed in the film *Out of Africa*. This 1985 film is about the transformation of the animus as exemplified in the life of Karen Blixen, the Danish baroness who became the writer Isak Dinesen as a direct consequence of her time in Africa. The emergence of a writer from a frustrated woman is a tricky metamorphosis to portray, but it is played to perfection by Meryl Streep. Her character's story begins in much the same imperial time as *The African Queen*, around 1913, when the headstrong Karen decides to come to Africa to marry, in hopes of being able to realize herself in ways that are closed for her in her native Denmark. In Africa, Karen feels she can shape her life as she pleases, and she starts to do so through a series of acts of extraordinary will: marrying a man she has proposed to, managing a farm, leading a supply expedition to bring food to the men at the front after the war has broken out and her husband joins the British forces. These are extraverted thinking feats of the Katharine Hepburn type, but Karen Blixen's African story contrasts with Rose Sayer's triumphant passage through Africa in *The African Queen*, by emphasizing the *defeats* involved. Karen Blixen's trip to the front results in her contracting syphilis from her husband; she cannot have children; the man who accepts her as a lover will not marry her; her coffee plantation eventually fails; her lover dies.

Along the way, the writer's animus is softened by tragedy, and opens her up to the Self's perspective on life. This is symbolized by the African landscape as seen by the plane that Karen's lover pilots, a plane that gives Karen, as she says, 'a glimpse of the world through God's eye'. The pilot/lover, the legendary Denys Finch Hatton, is played with only limited success by Robert Redford, and it is a bit embarrassing that this ivory hunter is, at best, an enlightened colonial, in one of those sentimental movies where the servants of colour love their good white masters and only despise the bad ones. But Meryl Streep succeeds in conveying a sense of expanding consciousness in the midst of personal defeat, and Redford gets across the softening effect introverted feeling can have on the animus by fostering a love for life as it is. One gets the feeling that the blossoming of Karen Blixen as the wise teller of tales Isak Dinesen was one that only African soil could have nourished.

I think of Karen Blixen as a bit like Ruth Bailey, a woman who came to Africa for a wedding and was led to discover a very different kind of *coniunctio* – an encounter with the greater personality through her meeting with C.G. Jung. I see Jung as her Finch Hatton, the man to recognize a courageous woman, and connect her to a wider possibility, by letting her join his own journey through Africa, in the context of a limited relationship. To amplify Ruth Bailey's role in Jung's journey to Africa through the Hollywood image of Meryl Streep playing Karen

Blixen is not to rewrite, or be overly suggestive of, the history that we do know about the nurse, around thirty, from England who later said, 'I am not sure whether I picked C.G. up or he picked me up' at the fancy dress party in the hotel in Mombasa, shortly after their boat from Southampton had docked and she came upon Jung in the lounge, studying the maps for his journey to Mt. Elgon. [1] Rather, it is to help us see the romance involved in anyone's finding Africa in company with another non-African. That can come perilously close to colonialism, but it is the position most of us are in here, and that she was in when Jung invited her to join his party's journey. Ruth Bailey didn't know then that she would become Jung's housekeeper at the end of his life, that she would become his final companion, the one chosen to 'see him out', on his final journey to a place he hadn't been before. Perhaps 'romance' will seem to many of you a misleading metaphor for their exchange, since no one has ever suggested a love relationship between these two. But to those who can understand the romance in friendship without needing to look for evidence of an affair that cannot be found, I will say that Meryl Streep's Karen Blixen in *Out of Africa* conveys, for me, why Jung's anima wanted to have Ruth Bailey with him on his trip to Mt. Elgon. She had captured the projection of his own desire to live more fully in the moment. I think Ruth Bailey modelled for Jung a way to use his extraverted sensation to see more simply and more objectively – that is, with greater freedom from intuitive presuppositions about what the archetypes of experience are supposed to be. *Out of Africa* has helped me to understand the role of Africa in fostering Jung's unlikely friendship with Ruth Bailey, for the central idea of the film is that *Africa is a place where attending to the real is welcome.*

Applying these projected images to what the journey to Africa may have meant to Jung is of course to confess my own expectations of this time in Africa, a continent so infinitely more various than any projections we can bring to it. So let me own those expectations as mine as I state what they are. Perhaps they will accord with some of yours. I expect this African stage to give me room to assert my own point of view, even if it humbles me in the process. I expect to get closer, here, to my identity as a human being. And I expect to be led to a more realistic place if I try too rigidly to apply European and American cultural standards to the way I think, observe, and travel on in Africa.

---

1   Glin Bennet, 'Domestic Life with C.G. Jung: Tape-recorded Conversations with Ruth Bailey', *Spring* (1986), p. 177-189. This quote is on p. 178. Ruth Bailey's recollection of Jung in old age, asking her to 'see me out' appears on p. 186 of this article.

Life and Soul

Karina Turok
South Africa

As someone born in Cape Town, South Africa, I have been asked to share with you a little bit of my journey as a photographer, photographing in an African context. My first exploration into social documentary began with a study of my own community, my roots in Cape Town. I called this group of photographs 'Jews on the tip of Africa' and it formed the final year's work towards a degree in fine art. The work is a series of rather quirky and sometimes ironic photographs of a community of people, in a sense, out of context. I struggled to make reference to the African context in which we live and began becoming painfully aware that these pictures could have been taken in almost any part of the world and that, in many ways, is really a reflection of life for many people of European descent living in South Africa. For many, living in Africa was and, indeed still is, a vague background to the daily experience of life. A hair cutting ceremony of a three year old boy; a watchmaker in Long Street, Cape Town; a brother and his two sisters, shop owners in a suburb called Woodstock in Cape Town.

My thesis for my Masters and Fine Art degree forms the main subject of this talk. It is entitled 'Social Skin' and looked at the rituals and initiations of adolescent women across a wide range of experience including religious and secular groups. I narrowed my focus down to four very different young South African women as they approached their adult identity and specifically focused on those initiations that involved the transformation of the physical body. Some of the processes involved permanent alteration of the body and others were temporary changes. I also wanted to address issues pertaining to the medium of photography and the role of the photographer. In particular, I wanted to acknowledge my outsider status in the lives of the people being photographed and to diffuse this precarious and ethically charged position by giving cameras to the women I worked with so that they could control and photograph themselves as well as photographing me.

Tania Leroux, who was 17 when I met her, lives in a community called Rocklands in Mitchells Plain, and this community had practised tooth extraction. These are Tania's words:

I have no dreams. I don't know what I want. Most of my friends have had pulled out four, six teeth. I want to experience it myself. People think it's sexy to have the gold in the false teeth. People admire that fashion in Mitchells Plain. Most of the gangsters have false teeth with gold in. I would like to have a plain set and a set with gold in. I prefer a boy without teeth. The way he smiles, he looks sexier without his teeth. It's much better for kissing; it looks cute and the guys like us more without teeth. I was fifteen when I knew I was going to do it. Most girls do it at fourteen; most boys do it at eighteen.

Tania's mother, Katy, in the photograph, had her teeth out when she was fourteen and both Tania's late grandparents had all their teeth out when they were young teenagers. In here is Tania re-enacting her mother's identity. She peers at herself, at her reflection in the mirror.

The origin of tooth extraction is not clear. Some say it's for oral sex. Heterosexual men in prison extract their teeth. Slave owners in the Cape would mark their slaves by extracting their teeth and many slaves were from Malaysia and some from Indonesia where the filing of front teeth was practised. Another theory was to do with tetanus at this time which gave people lockjaw and so they extracted teeth to survive.

I must say that, after Tania had gone through this process, when she was re-integrated into her work community, she exuded this confidence that I hadn't seen in her prior to it.

I displayed the initiates' images in little books which I prepared and placed their photographs over mine in the books. I enjoyed playing with notions of authority and the inversion of the question of authorship. The exciting part was seeing striking images produced by a couple of the women in particular. The two who were least likely to have ever held a camera before, let alone use one, and it certainly made me question my role as a producer of images.

I played around with the notion of the extreme inside perspective and the extreme outside perspective. This is an electron microscope photograph of Tania's tooth and an aerial perspective of the community of Rocklands, Mitchell Plain where she lived. [See following page]

The initiations are all very different with the common link being that they are conventionally seen as being on the margins of mainstream. My thesis questions the notion of what, if anything, is mainstream or normal.

The *intonjane* is a traditional ritual to mark the rite of passage in the Xhosa community to denote maturity. Currently, due to western religious and educational influences, this tradition has become lost in many areas. I was taken to a village in the Transkei where the *intonjane* was held in seclusion and had a public meeting with the elders of the village including the fathers and uncles and, on the outskirts, the mothers of the initiates. Through interpreters, we established an understanding and ultimately we were welcomed with incredible hospitality and pride in the sharing of Xhosa tradition. I stayed with the Chief, Chief Samela's family, during both periods in the village.

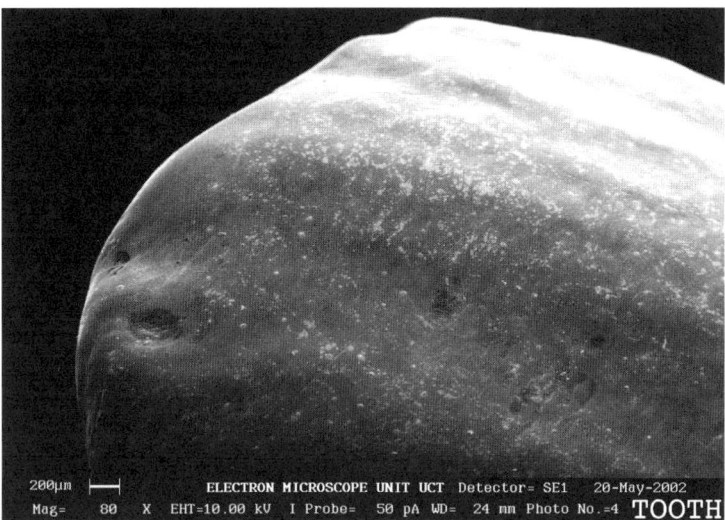

Tooth

Aerial Photo

The details of the customs may vary according to each family and their tribal influence. Some common aspects are that the young women are separated from the general community and put into isolation in a rural hut for a period of approximately 10 days. They are not allowed to emerge or be seen out of the confines of the hut. As a woman enters into the process of her *intonjane*, her hair may be shaved by her father or a senior woman of the community. Her face and body are painted white. The *intonjane* uses imbola, a special traditional mask, to hide her face and she also wears a black scarf to hide her face. She is committed to quiet contemplation and may only talk in whispers. During this time she is not called by her name but by a ritual name, *intonjane*, and she speaks softly, she does not raise her voice. Usually, a group of women, anything from two to 10, will go through the process together. Each group of young women are usually sisters from within the same family or relatives. They are usually teenagers or in their twenties but girls as young as 7 and women as old as 40 have been known to go through the process. Older women are encouraged to go through the *intonjane* if they are experiencing difficulties in their lives. These problems are often attributed to the fact that they have not yet gone through the initiation. The young women are expected to remain behind a woven reed curtain at all times. This curtain is attached at various high points on the wall on one side of the rondavel and stretches down to the floor and is about 8 metres wide. Here they are peering through the gaps in the curtain. The next photograph was taken by myself as I looked into the window of the rondavel and the second one was taken by one of the girls as she looked out of that same window.

The letting of blood is symbolic of the cleansing and bonding with ancestors. A goat is slaughtered at the beginning to appease the ancestors. On the day of communal celebration for the *intonjane*, a sheep is slaughtered, and a cow is slaughtered for each initiate and each one, in turn, eats the meat of her specific cow. She must be accompanied at all times by a nurse ikhankhata. This is the person who looks after her needs, cooks, washes and feeds her. The braaied meat is eaten off a woven reed place mat with a stick which is whittled into a sharp point resembling a pencil.

In some communities the party can occur during the two-week confinement period or after the period has ended and then it marks the coming out of the initiates. On this day they perform various symbolic rituals. The initiates emerge from seclusion naked above the waist and covered in an ochre coloured paint. They walk in a line down towards the river, with the eldest holding the family spears. Additional girls join the parade in solidarity with the main initiates. At a point near the river, one of the women in charge shouts the signal for the girls to run.

Social skin – Intonjane insider/outsider

ept the Intonjane
day of the party,
... They braai it.
eight days we go
friends allowed.

because I was not sick. I didn't feel bad. I do that Intonjane because we must its our custom, but
other people can be sick she can't get right, but when she make Intonjane she feel good. The
hardest thing about the Intonjane process is to make everything organised, to buy goats, sheep,
cattle and all the food, and also the clothes, we must wear new blankets, the mats, all that must

Once at the river, the initiates wash themselves or are washed by the women in charge. The ochre is removed and the girls huddle together to preserve any warmth. In winter months, I should add, the temperatures often dropped to below zero. The party then proceeds to the next stage of the coming out which involves each initiate being adorned in a particular reed head-dress, the same adorns their arms, waist and ankles. Once they are finally dressed, they return to the centre of the celebration and present themselves to the patriarch of the family, kneeling before him, returning the family spears in front of him, at his feet. They respectfully look at the ground while he delivers a message to them.

Finally, the initiates and their entourage return to the huts to change into their final outfit which includes a black scarf, a shirt, shawl and skirt. They can now be seen and they dress themselves beautifully with new clothes, clothes they have never worn before.

Until I arrived at this village and actually engaged with the girls, I didn't know whether female circumcision was involved in this ritual or not and after being there I realized that it was not. There is so much secrecy and rumour about it that, until faced with the reality, I was not to know. On arriving, when I first met the girls in the hut and they were huddled in the freezing cold with a blanket around them, they were obviously quite intimidated because I was together with the chief and parents. One initiate suddenly reaches into her blanket: her cell phone's ringing!

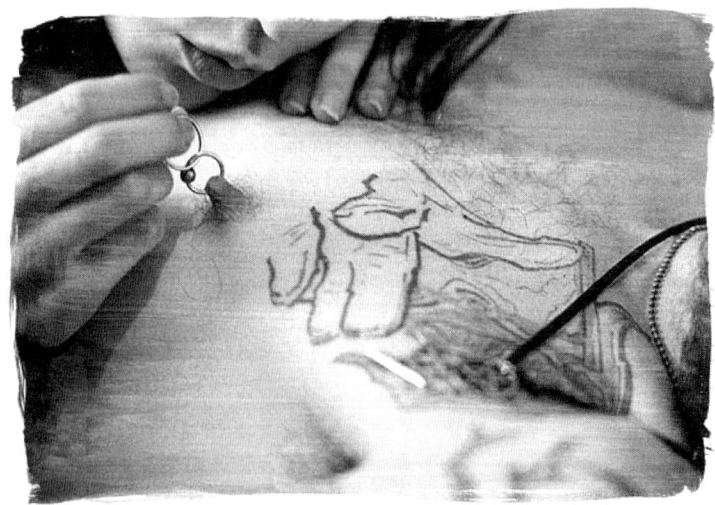

Piercing

Piercing and Tattooing

Nerissa is the daughter of an Afrikaans family. Her father was a former ambassador of the previous regime and she spent years in Europe and in the US. People who are pierced or tattooed whom I interviewed carried diverse motivations for pursuing the practice. For many pierced and tattooed people, the moments of being pierced as well as the often private knowledge of the piercing are invested with symbolic power capable of reclaiming previous experiences of powerlessness or even abuse. For others it is about a sense of self projected into a public space whereby the reflection of being noticed by others reaffirms the individual's desire to be seen. For example, the obvious exhibitionism of facial piercing or the navel ring. Some feel positive and empowered by their bodies for the first time. Most find it adds to sexual stimulation and titillation. Some use the activity of piercing to mark significant events in their lives, both as celebrations of joy or commitment to partners as well as icons to memorialize pain and loss. It is interesting to note how the markers of the body, the signs of identity, particularly within this social group, enter into the construction of social relations.

My work attempts to address the body as signifier of self perception and self deception in which silence and repression, domesticity and confinement, vulnerability and retreat simultaneously resonate and contradict. Invoked through skin, hair and teeth, putting the female body in a social and personal context.

Hair Covering

In Jewish law, a sheitel, a wig, is used to cover a woman's hair from the time she is married. Some rabbis allow the woman to wear a wig made of her own hair. There are those who state that a woman is not allowed to reveal even one hair, even the hair at the temples. In the privacy of her own home, provided no men are present, a married woman is not obligated to cover her hair in the presence of her husband and children, however, it is considered a blessing, a mitzvah, if she undertakes to cover her hair at all times so that it is not exposed, even to the walls, the rafters or the beams of her house. The notion of being able to achieve a higher level of spirituality is attached to a woman who follows this dogma. To cover their hair in public is considered a biblical commandment from Moses, to cover their hair in private is a law of rabbinical authority, a lower level of authority and therefore is open to interpretation and the practices of the local community.

Thank you very much.

The Sable Venus on the Middle Passage: Images of the Transatlantic Slave Trade

Michael Vannoy Adams
USA (JPA)

Among all archetypes, the journey is perhaps the most universal. Of course, there are always variations on themes. There is the external journey, and there is the internal journey. There are personal journeys, and there are collective journeys. There is the journey as quest, but there is also the journey as conquest. There are journeys of heroes, journeys of villains, journeys of victims, and journeys of survivors. There are journeys of exploration and journeys of exploitation. Not every journey is a journey of individuation.

There is the journey to Africa – for example, the journeys of Jung to North Africa in 1920 and to East Africa in 1925-26, as well as the journey of Jungians to South Africa in 2007. There is also the journey from Africa. Of journeys from Africa, the most universal is the journey of all humanity from Africa, as the evidence of mitochondrial DNA has conclusively proved, but there is also another journey from Africa, not of all humanity, but the journey of Africans in the transatlantic slave trade – the 'night sea journey' of the Middle Passage to the Americas.

The passengers on the ships of the Middle Passage were not immigrants but 'imports'. They were slaves. As James A. Rawley says, a slave was a 'commodity', and the slave trade was a 'business' (1981, p. 7). Rawley estimates the imports of slaves into the Americas, 1451-1870, at 11,345,000 (ibid., p. 428).

The most notorious image of those ships is the diagram of the *Brookes*. Abolitionists published the diagram in 1788, when a law that would restrict that ship to 454 slaves was under consideration in the British Parliament. One witness testified that in 1783 the ship had carried approximately 600 slaves, of whom 70, or 11.6%, had died on the journey. 'It was calculated', Rawley says, 'that if every man slave was allowed six feet by one foot four inches, platform space, every woman five feet ten by one foot four, every boy five feet by one foot two, and every girl four feet six by one foot, the *Brookes* could hold 451 slaves' (ibid., p. 283).

These are, of course, merely the physical dimensions of the journey – not the psychic dimensions, which Rawley aptly calls the 'trauma of the Middle Passage'. It was not just that Africans were traumatized when they were enslaved. They were also traumatized when they were, as Rawley says, 'confined on a ship that would sail into the alien sea for an unknown destination and unknown purposes' (p. 290).

Hardly any personal accounts of the journey exist, but one by Olaudah Equiano describes an initial experience of the ship. 'I was now', he says, 'persuaded that I had gotten into a world of bad spirits and that they were going to kill me'. On the ship he saw 'a large furnace or copper', and he had a fantasy that the white men on the ship were going to boil him. He fainted. When he recovered, he asked other slaves on the ship 'if we were not to be eaten by those white men with horrible looks, red faces, and long hair' (Gates 1987, p. 33). There is, of course, a certain irony to all this, for one of the fantasies of Europeans was that Africans were cannibals who would boil them and eat them. Equiano was reassured that he was not going to be boiled and eaten, that he was not going to be killed, but he was still convinced that the world of white men that he had got into on the ship was a world of 'bad spirits' – and that was, in fact, an accurate description of the psychic reality of the situation. The white men *were* bad spirits.

'The psychological impact', Rawley says, of the Middle Passage upon the involuntary passengers was noted by contemporaries'. For example, a doctor reported that one ship had carried 602 slaves, of whom 155, or 25.7%, had died on the journey. He estimated that two-thirds of those deaths had been the result of melancholy. The doctor, Rawley says, 'could cure none who had the melancholy (1981, p. 291). Diagnostically, the trauma of the transatlantic slave trade was an incurable depression.

The archetype of the journey comprises three stages: separation, initiation, and return (Campbell 1968, p. 30). As a journey, however, the transatlantic slave trade included only two stages: separation and initiation – or separation and trauma. In a sense, of course, every initiation is a trauma, and every trauma is an initiation. Also, every journey is a journey toward an unknown destination for unknown purposes. The slave trade was hardly exceptional in that respect. Every journey is a journey of the ego into the unconscious.

As an initiatory experience, however, the slave trade was an especially traumatic experience. It was a journey with no return. On a beach in Dahomey (now Benin), there is the 'Gate of No Return'. It symbolizes, Henry Louis Gates, Jr., says, that 'the spirits of slaves, the dead, are welcome home through this gate' (1999, p. 226). Of course, it is one thing to return dead and in spirit, another to return alive and in body.

What so depressed Equiano was the realization that 'I now saw myself deprived of all chance of returning to my native country' (Gates 1987, p. 33). The result was often, if not insanity, suicide. The captain of one ship reported that slaves committed suicide because 'tis their belief that when they die they return home to their own country and friends again' (Mannix 1962, pp. 117-18). A doctor on another ship also reported that slaves 'wished to die on an idea that they should then get back to their own country'. The captain of that ship devised an ingenious solution to the problem – to behead the dead in order to prevent any idea of suicide. 'The captain in order to obviate this idea', the doctor said, 'thought of an expedient, viz. to cut off the heads of those who died intimating to them' – that is, to the slaves – 'that if determined to go, they must return without heads' (ibid., p. 118). From a psychoanalytic perspective, decapitation is dissociation. To return without a head would be to return without spirit – or without psyche. To sever the head from the body was to sever the slave from Africa spiritually or psychically.

Of course, some contemporary descendants of slaves do return to Africa – for example, to Gorée Island off the coast of Senegal. This is not just the slave trade, in an ironic reversal, as a tourist trade, a mere exercise in nostalgia or sentimentality. It is a return to the scene of the trauma, as if such a journey might be a curative experience.

Perhaps the most egregiously perverse image of the transatlantic slave trade is the Sable Venus. 'Venus' is, of course, the proper name of a goddess, but it is also a generic name, or epithet, for a woman. The most famous 'Venus' from Africa is not the Sable Venus but the Hottentot Venus.

The Hottentot Venus was a real woman, Saartjie Baartman. In 1810, she was transported from South Africa to Europe, where she was exhibited as a curiosity in England and France. Europeans were fascinated by her body, which was caricatured with a Cupid on her buttocks. After her death in 1815, her body was dissected by Cuvier, and her skeleton, brain, and genitals were preserved and displayed at the *Musée de l'Homme* in Paris until 1974. Her remains were finally interred in South Africa in 2002.

In contrast to the Hottentot Venus, the Sable Venus was not a real woman but an imaginal woman. A book, *The History, Civil and Commercial, of the British Colonies in the West Indies*, by Bryan Edwards includes a poem, 'The Sable Venus: An Ode', by Isaac Teale. The poem compares the Sable Venus to the Venus of Botticelli [Slide #8]:

> The loveliest limbs her form compose,
> Such as her sister VENUS chose,
> > In FLORENCE, where she's seen;
> Both just alike, except the white,
> No difference, no – none at night,
> > The beauteous dames between.
>
> (Edwards 1801, pp. 34-5)

Sable Venus

The second volume of the third edition of the book in 1801 includes both the poem and an image. The image is 'The Voyage of the Sable Venus from Angola to the West Indies' by Thomas Stothard, Esquire, of the Royal Academy. If any image is obscene, this is it. It is iconography as pornography. 'No more preposterous misinterpretation was ever perpetrated of the "Middle Passage", Hugh Honour says, than the

Sable Venus'. Honour remarks that neither the poem nor the image 'so much as alludes to slavery: the theme of both is the physical charm of the black woman' (1989, p. 33).

Daniel P. Mannix notes that 'a wealth of classical details' embellishes the image (1962, p. 113). In this image, there is no African goddess, and there are no African gods. The goddess and the gods are all Roman – and although the goddess is black, all the gods are white. The image 'Romanizes' and 'whitens' the slave trade. There are twelve figures in the image. Eleven of the figures are white – only one of the figures is black. The Sable Venus rides on a scallop shell and sits on a velvet throne. In the sky are six cherubs. Two cherubs fan the Sable Venus with ostrich plumes while one cherub holds a peacock feather. In the sea, two dolphins, with two cherubs, pull the scallop shell, while to the right Triton blows a horn. On the left Cupid draws a bow and aims an arrow at Neptune, who holds not a trident but a flag, the Union Jack. The Sable Venus eyes the reins and holds them as she guides the dolphins, as if the journey from Africa to the Americas were entirely voluntary – as if it were not a journey by force but a journey by choice.

The Sable Venus is virtually nude. 'Except for bracelets, anklets, and a collar of pearls', Mannix says, 'she wears nothing but a narrow embroidered girdle' (ibid., p. 112). The obscenity of the image is not the virtual nudity. The perversity of the image is the audacity of the mythological amplification. Roman myth is utterly inappropriate and inapplicable as a parallel to the slave trade. This is not just an incompetent amplification – a comparison for which there is no basis. It is a radically disingenuous amplification. The amplification is a euphemism that represses the enormity of the slave trade and conveniently excuses it.

The image reveals even as it conceals. It is obviously not an image that accurately depicts the psychic reality of black African men and women in the transatlantic slave trade. The value of the image is that it accurately depicts the psychic reality of white European men. The image is not a slave narrative but a master narrative. It is a projection, a cultural imposition that serves a quite specific purpose for white European men. The image is an example of how Africa has provided Europe with an opportunity for what Gates calls 'the projection of fantasies from its collective unconscious' (1999, pp. 16-17) – or, more accurately, from its cultural unconscious.

The image is not so much a cultural complex as it is a cultural duplex. It is a duplicitous image, an image that, even as it represses what Hugh Thomas calls the 'iniquity' of the slave trade (1997, p. 11), expresses the duplicity of white European men. The image is a certain variety of anima that a certain variety of ego imposes culturally on a scene. It is the exotic, erotic anima of an imperialistic, psychopathic ego. In this image, which is both racist and sexist, the slave is a woman

– and not just any woman but a woman no man coerces because she always consents. As a woman, the slave never resists.

The function of the image is aesthetic. The image stylizes an ugly, coercive experience, the slave trade, and revises it into a beautiful, consensual – and sensual – experience. Slavery is lovely. In this stylization and revision, Britain waves the flag, and, like Neptune, rules the waves – and, by Cupid, loves the slave as a woman. The image implies that slaves are like women who, like Venus, just love it. Slaves, however, were not goddesses enthroned on shells. They were women and men, girls and boys, confined on ships. They did not wear bracelets, anklets, and collars of pearls. They wore chains. In the slave trade there were flags – among them, the Union Jack and the Stars and Stripes – but there were no cherubs, dolphins, Triton, Cupid, and Neptune, and there was no Venus. What Marcus Wood calls 'the ludicrous panoply of Gods and putti' (2000, p. 54) is not just the use of an image. It is the abuse of an image.

On the journey of the Sable Venus, there are no white men with horrible looks, red faces, and long hair. There are no bad spirits. There are only white gods. There are no black slaves – much less 600 black slaves. There is only one black goddess – and she is not a black African goddess but a black European goddess. The wealth of classical details does not just embellish the image to demonstrate the erudition of the artist. The mythological amplification converts an atrocity into art. It does not just normalize the slave trade. It idealizes it. It is all royally academic. This is not truth and reconciliation. It is lie and rationalization.

References

Campbell, J. (1968). *The Hero with a Thousand Faces*. Princeton, NJ: Princeton University Press.

Edwards, B. (1801). *The History, Civil and Commercial, of the British West Indies*. London: John Stockdale, 3rd ed., vol. 2.

Gates, Jr., H.L. (ed.) (1987). *The Classic Slave Narratives*. New York: Mentor.

– (1999). *Wonders of the African World*. New York: Alfred A. Knopf.

Honour, H. (1989). *The Image of the Black in Western Art*. Cambridge, MA & London: Oxford University Press, vol. 4, part 1.

Mannix, D.P., with Cowley, M. (1962). *Black Cargoes: A History of the Atlantic Slave Trade, 1518-1865*. New York: Viking Press.

Rawley, J.A. (1981). *The Transatlantic Slave Trade: A History*. New York & London: W.W. Norton.

Thomas, H. (1997). *The Slave Trade: The Story of the Atlantic Slave Trade: 1440-1870*. New York: Simon & Schuster.

Wood, M. (2000). *Blind Memory: Visual Representations of Slavery in England and America, 1780-1865*. New York: Routledge.

The Journey to Africa:
Cultural Melancholia in Black and White

Samuel Kimbles
USA (CGJISF)

An evolution and development of his theory and a 'mature expression of it' followed Jung's return to Africa at age 50. What Jung found was his raison d'être, his myth or the purpose of human life and his life as the creation of consciousness. Within the colonial relationship of the early 20th century, Jung was to characterize his lost world as follows:

> Through scientific understanding, our world has become dehumanized. Man feels himself isolated in the cosmos. He is no longer involved in nature and has lost his emotional participation in natural events, which hitherto had a symbolic meaning for him. Thunder is no longer the voice of a god, nor is lightning his avenging missile. No river contains a spirit, no tree means a man's life, no snake is the embodiment of wisdom, and no mountain still harbours a great demon. Neither do things speak to him nor can he speak to things, like stones, springs, plants, and animals. He no longer has a bush-soul identifying him with a wild animal. His immediate communication with nature is gone forever, and the emotional energy it generated has sunk into the unconscious.
>
> (*CW* 8, para. 585)

One can hear in Jung's description a longing for a lost and by-gone world. In other words one can hear Jung's cultural melancholia.

The European national self as described by psychoanalysis and analytical psychology of the early 20th century was structured as a modern counterpart of the primitive and colonized other. The idea of this colonized other expressed a fantasy of an uncivilized, primitive, timeless people on a dark continent. Following psychoanalysis, though Jung chooses the internal over the political as a point of focus for his sense of that lost connection, he did see it as a collective loss also. The internal focus on the individual however, as Zaretsky describes, is the idea of a historically specific experience of singularity and interiority, sociologically grounded in modern processes of industrialization and urbanization and in the history of the family (2004, p. 5). However, the relationship between an individual's social condition and his or her subjectivity was *undertheorized*. The internal focus obscured the political, economic, and cultural preconditions necessary for the flourishing of an internal life.

The earlier colonial inheritances of Africa that existed at the time of Jung's 1925 trip to Africa still exist today as a cultural complex in the collective consciousness of many. In a short paper by Binyavanga Wainaina, entitled 'How to Write About Africa', she gives a few guidelines:

- Always use the word 'Africa' or 'Darkness' or 'Safari' in your titles.
- You can use the subtitle Congo, the Shadow, etc.
- Never have a picture of a well-adjusted African
- In your text, treat Africa as if it were one country, and make sure you show how Africans have music and rhythm deep in their souls.
- Display taboo subjects: ordinary domestic scenes, love between Africans.
- Your African characters may include naked warriors, loyal servants, diviners and seers, ancient wise men living in hermitic splendor. Or corrupt politicians, inept polygamous travel-guides.
- Always include The Starving African, who wanders the refugee camp nearly naked, and waits for the benevolence of the West. Her children have flies on their eyelids and potbellies, and her breasts are flat and empty.
- Bad western characters may include children of Tory cabinet ministers, Afrikaners.
- Animals must be treated as well rounded, complex characters.
- Readers will be put off if you don't mention the light in Africa … and sunsets. There is always a big sky. Wide-open spaces/ Africa is the place of Wide Empty Spaces.
- Always end your book with Nelson Mandela saying something about rainbows or renaissances.

I propose that Jung's journey to Africa was motivated primarily by his relationship to longing and nostalgia – his connection primarily with loss, both personally and culturally, and expressed his relationship to cultural melancholia. Melancholy is an emotional situation in which loss is unassimilated with the consequent return of the thing lost into psychic life. To situate Jung's longing as reflecting an underlying melancholia allows me to draw out a continuation of the experience of loss in our current relationship to Africa.

Turning to the relationship of loss to Black American consciousness, in contrast, to the lost experienced and expressed by Jung reveals quite a different image of the journey. Two different ways of relating to loss. Two different melancholies. One black, one white.

August Wilson, a black playwright, in his play *Gem of the Ocean*, writes about black life in an American urban setting at the turn of the twentieth century. The central character is a 285-year old, fiery matriarch, Aunt Ester, who carries the memory of the trip from Africa on the slave ships, up to and including life in America in the twentieth century. The action of the play ultimately centres on a journey of redemption for a man Citizen Barlow (named as such by his mother after the emancipation of slaves). Aunt Ester, her aids Eli, Black Mary and Solly two names: David and Solomon takes Citizen Barlow on a journey to a place that will wash his soul clean. This shamanic journey is to the city of bones. Wilson, describes the city as:

> It's only a half mile by a half mile but that's a city. It's made of bones. Pearly white bones. All the buildings and everything's made of bones. I seen it. I been there. My mother live there. I got an aunt and three uncles live down there in the city made of bones. That's the center of the world. In time it will all come to light … the people made a kingdom out of nothing. They were the people that didn't make it across the water. They sat down right here, they say, "let's make a kingdom. Let's make a city of bones."
>
> (2006, p. 52)

The city of bones is the place where the unredeemed live; 'those soul aspects, those souls who didn't make it between the two pharaohs on both sides of the blood-red waters' (Garnet 1843). One can hear the sound from the city of bones, as Cornel West says in 'the urtext of black culture. Neither a word nor a book, not an architectural monument or a legal brief. Instead, it is a guttural cry and a wrenching moan – a cry not so much for help as for home, a moan less out of complaint than for recognition – John Coltrane's saxophone solos, Billie Holiday's vocal leaps, Baldwin's poignant essays transform and transfigure in artistic form this cry and moan' (p. 81). Wilson, in *The Gem of the Ocean*, has Aunt Ester say, 'the people got a burning tongue … their mouths are on fire with song. That water can't put it out' (p. 53). The journey to the city of bones is not an abstraction, but a daily journey to redeem individuality, diversity, heterogeneity, and human dignity for the invisible ones of Ralph Ellison's novel the *Invisible Man*. Those who suffer the rootlessness; homelessness and namelessness are always on the way to or trying to find their way to the city of bones. This is melancholia in black.

Since, Freud's paper 'Mourning and Melancholia' (1917), successful mourning means that the ego is freed up from its former attachments and is thus able to attach to new objects and form a new life. Losses can include a person, an ideal, a country, one's liberty, one's identity and have, of course, in this time of frequent relocations, one's culture. Looking at loss and mourning or the failure to mourn at the group level or the individual level of the group psyche is inevitably linked to cultural melancholia. For Jung it was his lost connection to the primitive layer of his psyche, the two million year old man that activated his journey to Africa. For Blacks and many other groups, the lost objects of families, ancestors, homelands, places, and ideals *occasion* the activation of the journey. Such losses, and the traumatic events that make them happen, become part of the group's character and structure individual psychology, through *participation mystique*, that is the unconscious consequence of belonging to a group. These continued attachments, not detachment of libido, carry demands for recognition, restitution or reparation and are important parts of the group and individual's healing process. This is the telos involved in the journey to the city of bones.

To end or to begin with a few lines from the Black spiritual 'Nobody Knows the Trouble I've Seen' is to give/present a way of holding and expressing the journey that for me is the quintessential product of the journey, both for black and white and a transformation of melancholia into liberation:

> Nobody knows the trouble I've seen
> Nobody knows but Jesus
> Nobody knows the trouble I've seen
> Glory hallelujah!

References

Freud, S. (1917). *Mourning and Melancholia. SE* 14.
Garnet, H.H. (1843/1970). 'An Address to the Slaves of the United States of America of 1843'. In *Black Nationalism in America*, eds. John Bracey, August Meier & Elliot Rudwick. Indianapolis: Bobbs-Merrill, p. 73
Gates, H.L. Jr. & West, C. (1997). *The Future of the Race/* London, New York: Vintage Books.
Jung, C.G. (1976). 'Healing the split'. In *The Symbolic Life. CW* 18, 253-64.
Wainaina, B. (2005). 'How to write about Africa'. *Granta 92*, 91-97.
Wilson, A. (2006). *The Gem of the Ocean.* New York: Theatre Communications Group.
Zaretsky, E. (2004). *Secrets of the Soul.* London, New York: Vintage Books.

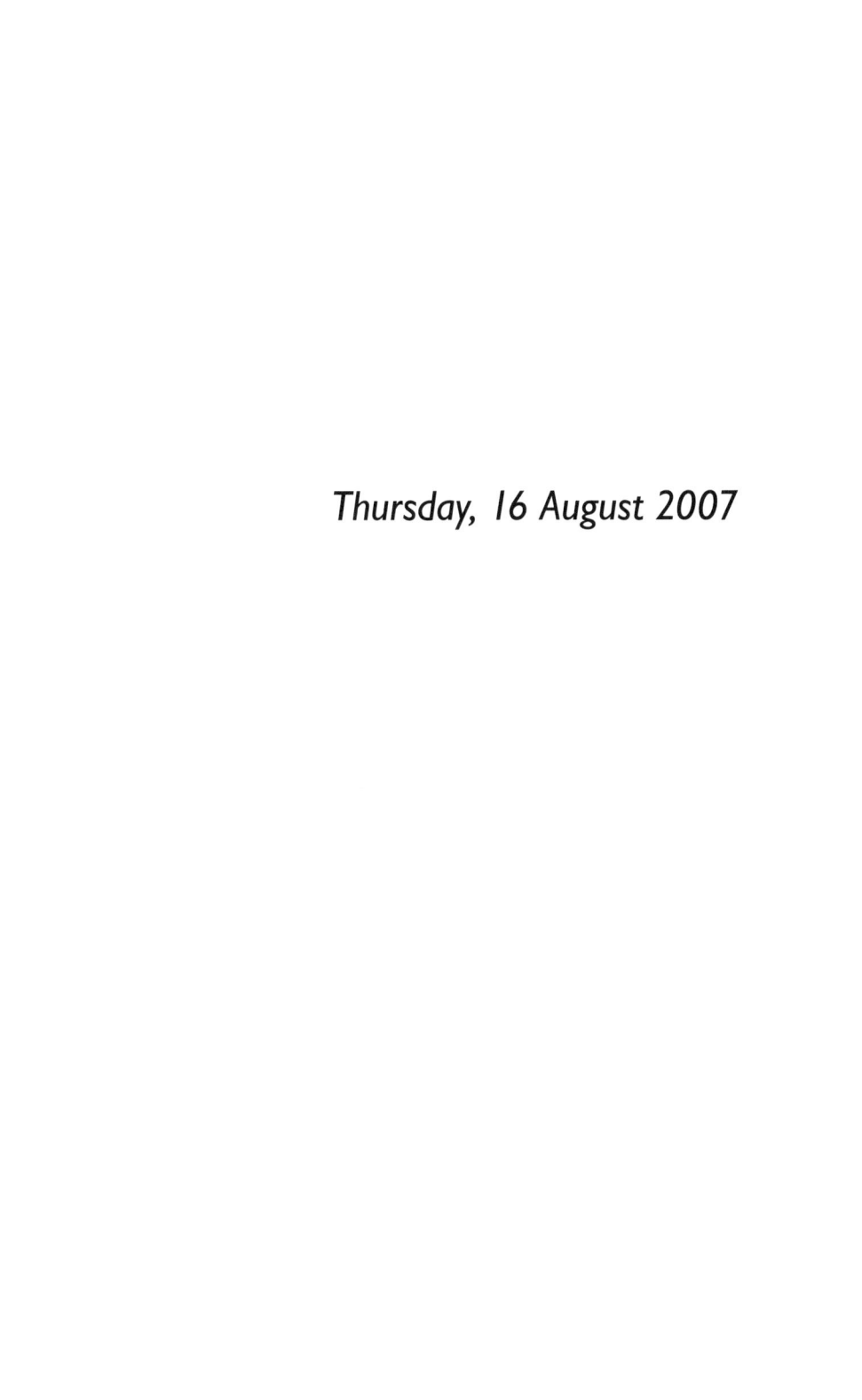

Thursday, 16 August 2007

The Containing Function of the Transference[1]

François Martin-Vallas
France (SFPA)

Abstract

The author offers a personal account of the way the transference in its archetypal dimension can weave a truly psychic neo-reality between the analyst and his analysand, such that it is common to both and yet quite different for both of them. Around a dozen years ago, he had described this neo-reality as a transferential chimera, before discovering that a French Freudian, Michel de M'Uzan (1994), had already coined this expression some time before. Having contacted the latter, he realized that what each had independently so named, stood for the same clinical reality. He was naturally encouraged to delve further into this theme and published the essence of his work in two articles which appeared in the *Journal of Analytical Psychology*, first, a clinical paper (Martin-Vallas 2006), followed by a theoretical paper in (2008). The burden of the present argument is already outlined in those two earlier papers, and the focus here is on the idea that the transferential chimera represents a genuine psychic container within which some of the processes of transformation inherent to the analytic relationship can take place. He begins with several clinical vignettes, goes on to develop a series of hypotheses about the containing function of the transference and concludes with framing those hypotheses against the previously described clinical situations.

* * *

Clinical Situations

Nymphéa

The first clinical example concerns a patient I have called *Nymphéa* – a detailed clinical exposé of the case appeared in the *Journal of Analytical Psychology* (Martin-Vallas 2002). She is a woman who first consulted me twenty years ago, presenting an enormous shapeless figure, completely destructured within herself and whom I received in face to face psychotherapy which rapidly moved to twice weekly sessions. One peculiarity she had was intolerable for me at the time: she would stare straight into my eyes, and I had the feeling of being totally vacuumed up, of being unable to think, of being melted down and

---

1 In the Programme this presentation went under the title of 'About the Transferential Chimera'

feeling to all intents and purposes, dead inside myself. I did not really understand what was happening, other than it was difficult for me to bear, and it lasted for about two and a half years. She spoke of things that were doubtless interesting, but the content of what she told me was of no importance to me. I was so caught up in this invasive sense of being absorbed by her, that I was quite powerless to do anything. Then, after a time, I told myself that maybe, if she went on the couch, I would feel more protected. We discussed this at some length, she eventually relented and to my intense relief, she announced: 'I'll do it'.

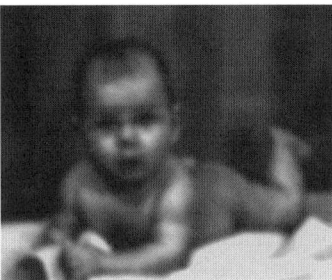

She made a dash for the couch, lay flat on her belly with her eyes gazing straight into mine and I suddenly had a flash of inspiration. It brought to mind those photos of babies lying on their stomach, eyes glued to the lens and I said to myself that I was in fact her only lens! Only then, was I able to ask myself what was going on; I had no solution, but I recovered my capacity to think. Eventually, this woman got better. She is still in analysis with me – I will refrain from telling you about what ensued in our work as space does not allow for it.

Helen

The next clinical situation to which I wish to refer is much more recent, but it too has challenged me greatly. It concerns a woman in her early twenties whom I have called Helen. The first time she came to see me, I had barely opened the door to my consulting room that I knew I did not want to work with her. She presented all the classic symptoms of an impending schizophrenic breakdown. She had very bizarre facial expressions; her speech interrupted in mid-sentence or mid-word and would start up again as if she had not uttered anything before. She scared me a great deal, to such an extent that if we started work she would likely disintegrate, destructure and swiftly finish up in a psychiatric ward. At the same time, I felt I could say little in the face of the hopes she had already placed in me, without even knowing me, before she even got to my consulting room. I had to help her, that is what she was telling me.

Thus, she quickly recounted her life and I noted that in the preceding three years she had more or less destroyed all that she had managed to achieve beforehand. She was socially unstable despite living with a man, but one who abused her in a variety of ways from what I could surmise. She had lost her network of friends, having completed studies and obtained a qualification she had abandoned any professional connections. There was nothing left for her. As our first encounter proceeded, a kind of scheme formed in my mind, which struck me as diabolical, but which at the same time was a compromise which at least had a chance of perhaps letting me lead her out of the morass without utterly destroying her; my chief anxiety was how not to compound the destruction.

Towards the end I told her I did not think it was possible for her to begin psychotherapeutic treatment at this point, given that it was unwise to start building up something on one hand when there was so much destruction on the other. So I suggested to her, not without feeling totally hypocritical, that I would be entirely at her disposal, once she had dumped her boyfriend, found some accommodation and got a job. I might as well have asked her to sort herself out on her own and only come back then. I really thought it was not feasible. It ended there. I convinced myself that I would never see her again, even if I was not proud of myself. In the aftermath, I recalled that while I was telling her all this, she was watching me attentively, and nodding.

She returned some six months later, she had left her boyfriend, a female friend had agreed to put her up, she had resumed her friend-ships and had found a job. I was completely stunned and I wondered how she had managed all this, what must have happened. In any event I had no choice, I had to stick to my bargain. So here we are now three years into our work together.

Claire

The third clinical vignette is about a woman I shall call Claire. She originally came to see me after her husband had gone off with his secretary and she could not get over the separation. For five years we pursued a face to face psychotherapy during which I supported her while she mourned her husband, found a new lover who became her partner and now her second husband. In the meantime, her children had had to be allowed to grow up, leave the nest and make their own lives; it was not easy for her to let them go. Evidently these were the tasks she had come to me with at the start, she had managed to sort the work and to get on with it and it was a while already that I was wondering why she still came, especially as she showed no sign of being ready to leave. I did nevertheless have an inkling as to why this was. Often, I would sense a deep suffering, it had no words for it, it was difficult to name, something which made me think of what

Winnicott terms agony. I felt it, but it was impossible to broach the subject and I had no wish to push her towards it in any way, since I could tell that everything she had achieved was of great import to her and if she herself had no desire to go there, all the more reason to let it go. I sensed there was something deeply painful, terribly brittle even, behind it.

Then there was, to me, a very surprising session. She arrived and, as was her wont, remained silent. Only this time the silence lasted ten minutes according to my watch, and notably during the entire silence her eyes remained dipped into mine without it being in the least disagreeable for me. At one point she stirred, that gave me the cue to enquire of her what was happening, and she said:

> It's odd. It's as if I could stay like this forever. Then, it's as if I were madly in love with you, with your gaze, but it was strange. It's as if I were somewhere else. I was going to say, it was not me. Also, it's as though nothing mattered anymore. And then something was coming to me. But all right, this is not going to help me solve my problems ...

The session continued, but she had really stumbled across something she had never met inside herself before, and the character of subsequent sessions has been profoundly altered since.

Mothers' Day

The final clinical example I want to mention is one I call 'Mothers' Day'. It occurred three years ago and it was admittedly the very first time a patient had wished me a Happy Mother's Day!

Naturally, she had not realized this. It concerns a woman in analysis on the couch, who initially began in therapy and then decided to explore what was really going on at base. She is one of those analysands who fortunately let us think that they really desire to get down to work. One day she came to her session, lay down and began to thank me warmly for all the help I was giving her to the extent that I remained present for her and offered her my support. It is true she was at a juncture where she had important professional decisions to make, that she told me all about it and drew comfort from my attention, yet all the same I questioned why she was telling me all this at that point. She is not in the habit of voicing such things; rather she is more prone to going straight into more intimate preoccupations inside herself.

Then she started up about the happy mother's day her seven year old daughter had wished her and describing how touched she had been by the little poem she had written for her and by the way she had made this present. There again I was puzzled as I failed to grasp any association to the thread which was leading her to speak in this way.

Then she said, 'Oh, yes!' and continued to describe what had occurred in relation to her daughter the previous day. She had been driving her daughter to some activity or other, when suddenly the little girl burst into tears, telling her mother how upset she was with daddy because he paid much much more attention to her little brother. Of course she did try to be with them, to play ball with them so she could be with daddy, but really ball games were not her thing. She would like it if they could all do things together, or just her and daddy … At some stage my patient told her: 'You will have to tell Daddy about this'. At which the child retorted 'How could I dare do that?' My patient went on: 'OK, this evening I shall play with your little brother and you can meanwhile talk to Daddy on your own. Only don't leave it to the last minute, when it's time to go to bed, as you know it would not work then'. Which she managed to do. She continued and told me when in the evening she went to her daughter to give her a goodnight kiss, the little girl said to her:

> Oh Mummy, thank you. It was really good that you could be there and help me to talk to Daddy, because I know I could not do it by myself.

That was for me the clincher for the whole session, as more than anything, I was able to sense the emotion as if she were wishing me a happy mother's day, I felt the same emotion as she had described arising between her and her daughter. I had at once the feeling of being entirely immersed in the alchemy of the transference.

Theoretical Reflexions

What of the transference? First of all I think there is something particularly important in the Jungian approach to the transference. For Jung the transference is truly a means of picking up the thread of incest.

Incest

When he states, '*its specific content, [is] commonly called incest*' (Jung 1946, para. 362), to my mind he is saying something really very powerful. Yet what does he mean there by incest?

Obviously he is referring to incest with mother and I love the illustration of it by William Blake which featured on the cover of an issue of the *Cahiers jungiens de psychanalyse*. It is incest with mother and in the Metamorphoses Jung uses a phrase, which I find quite remarkable, where he lists a number of very important elements which in his view constitute maternal incest, 'Life is a constant struggle against extinction, a violent yet fleeting deliverance from ever-lurking night. This death is no external enemy, it is his own inner longing for the stillness and profound peace of all-knowing non-existence, for all-seeing sleep in the ocean of coming-to-be and passing away' (Jung 1956, para. 553) – 'his own inner longing for the stillness and profound peace of all-knowing non-existence' – we are here in the vicinity of something which approximates to the death instinct. As with 'the [ocean] of passing away'. But in the case of 'the ocean of coming-to-be' we find ourselves on the other side. I shall not here discuss the death instinct. I think it is a very complicated point, but I am left wondering all the same whether it is not a vestige, of necessity a vestige, of that incestuous drive towards the mother, and a vestige in the form of a tendency towards pure destructiveness.

Incest

Thus, for Jung incest is something which tends towards re-birth, but only tends towards it and which is obviously just as apt to be destructive. So starting from here, my question is: what could prevent it from becoming destructive? What makes it prone to coming-to-be and not just to passing away? What makes it possible for life to sustain itself? In a word, what will contain, what will be the vessel, the uterus of this tale?

The Quaternio

The first thing that occurred to me is that it had to rest on the *quaternio* (Jung 1946, para. 422) that is, the archetypal structure which organizes the transference, that is to say something which is allied to incest, but not the same incest as there it is brother-sister incest. Brother-sister incest implies that on one hand there is a gender difference, on the other it is a generational issue. Given there is a brother and a sister, there must also be parents and children and people of different sexes. Whereas in the case of maternal incest, it is not about sex; rather it is and it is not about sex, it is completely undifferentiated.

At the level of the *quaternio* Jung states there is: 'quartering [which] comes about through the crossing of the matrilineal by a patrilineal line of division' (Jung 1946, para. 422), which means that there is here something of the father. I think in fact there needs to be something of the father for there 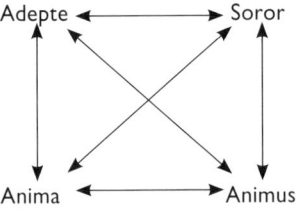 to be a differentiation of gender and of generation. Moreover, Jung says something else that I find quite salient: '*incest, as an endogamous relationship, is an expression of the libido which serves to hold the family together*' (Jung 1946, para. 431). In  other words he posits here a containing function and from it he garners a dynamic concept since he goes on to say: '*two forms together hold each other in check*' (Jung 1946, para. 431). This is not the Freudian bastion nor any fixed bastion; instead these are the reciprocal dynamics of two opposing forces which make for an equilibrium.

So from this I have sketched the outline of a preliminary container, one containing the *quaternio*, a double chambered container to represent the fact that here is a two-person relationship, and perhaps even more so to represent the fact that this is a dynamic of two opposites, the endogamous libido and the exogamous libido, and finally, that it is the dynamic itself that constitutes the container.

Some Epistemological Observations

Now I want to make a few digressions about methodology and the sketches I am proposing to you.

A Dynamic Container

In the first place there is the provenance of the container. Physics offers us a model I find useful in the representation of what might be the dynamic of containment.

Control Rods
different rates of fission reaction

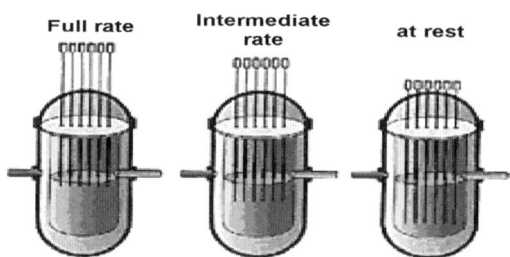

Full rate   Intermediate rate   at rest

It is the way an atomic energy cell functions. In the red field you can see a radioactive mass in a state of fission. Above it there are graphite rods, graphite having the property of absorbing the radiation emanating from the nuclear fission to such an extent that if you lower the rods into the centre of the nuclear reactor, the graphite will absorb part of the radiation, which in turn will reduce the intensity of the nuclear reaction. If you lower the bars to the very bottom, you will stop the reactor functioning entirely.

I believe something akin to this happens in the transference, and we all experience during occasional sessions the extent to which we absorb some of the libidinal energy emanating from our patients. We also experience those times when we need to stop absorbing it and cease to be the equivalent of graphite rods, so that the work might continue without the patient becoming engulfed by what we could designate as the Great Mother. It is a dynamic equilibrium which self-regulates, where we do, after all, consciously intervene to some small degree, but which on the whole self-regulates in the space between the two persons.

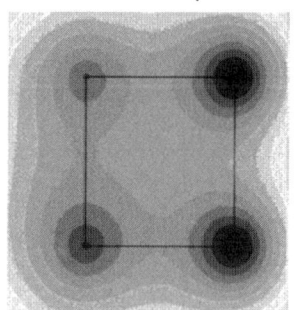

A Quantum Representation

There is a further example, this time from quantum physics I want to call to mind. We know about Jung's affinity with Pauli; we therefore know he was familiar with the field of quantum physics. The model I propose to you now is static; it represents something which exists in stasis.

To follow the analogy of quantum mechanics, this is what my next model would be like: Take a field of probability, probability that something might occur, that something will be represented. The field of probability, with the aid of its palette of different greys, simply indicates that occurrences will follow this path rather than that. That is all it shows.

Now I stumbled upon yet another aspect of quantum mechanics in a sentence of Jung's, and it is this:

> Everything unconscious is undifferentiated, and everything that happens unconsciously proceeds on the basis of non-differentiation – that is to say, there is no determining whether it belongs or does not belong to the self.
>
> (1953, para. 329)

I take this to mean that a content of the unconscious, given that it is in the unconscious, and there I believe he is referring to the collective unconscious – is not a repressed content. So an unconscious content, given that it is unconscious and given that it has not manifested itself, nobody can tell if it belongs to the subject, nor whether it does not belong to the subject so long as its manifestation has not taken place. This is not because we cannot know this; it is because its attribute of belonging or not belonging to the subject does not yet exist.

In truth, it is a very difficult thing to imagine, but I am fond of these questions which challenge us to step away from too neat a representation. If, for instance, you take an electron, an electron we know is a particle and a particle necessarily has a mass, a position and speed. Yet particle physicists will disagree with you and say this is not so. If you want to know the speed of a particle, you have to measure it, find it, but it is your very action of measuring that will cause the particle to have a speed at that particular moment, whereas immediately prior to measuring it, it only possessed the probability of speed. The same goes for its positioning; and it is not just a matter of saying: 'before determining the position of my particle I did not know where it was'. I think it is more accurate to say, 'before determining the position of the particle, it did not have one; all it had was the probability of a position in this or other place in the space/time continuum'. If we transpose this thinking to a clinical context and follow what Jung said about the contents of the unconscious, it really removes us from all presuppositions, from any *a priori* knowledge of what might occur in each of our patients or in ourselves.

Quantum Teleportation

Returning to my idea of the *quaternio*, I want to make a final digression into recent developments in quantum mechanics which I have found utterly fascinating. It concerns teleportation [telekinesis] – it is voguish in the realm of science fiction – by teleportation I mean I de-materialize here and immediately, I re-materialize at the other end of the universe.

What quantum mechanics has revealed recently is that teleportation exists and moreover, it works! It all began with a very odd story: Einstein and two colleagues, Podolski and Rosen, discovered what is now referred to as the EPR Paradox, named after their initials. Having discovered the paradox, Einstein thought he had established that quantum mechanics was merely a tool and not an accurate representation of reality, because quantum mechanics anticipated the impossible. Something we now call the absurd proof.

Here is what is involved: starting with one particle, out of it we create twin particles, [for the purpose of this discussion, let us call one P, the other P'] which in all respects are identical, except that they are exactly inverted in relation to one another, something like the inversion obtained between the left and the right when an object is observed together with its mirror image.

Now if you make an alteration to the yellow particle, the same change will immediately appear in the blue particle, irrespective of the distance separating the two particles. *A priori*, such an occurrence is unfeasible in the world we know since it would suppose transmitting information at an infinite speed. Einstein took this to mean that he was at the frontier of quantum mechanics and that a different explanation more in accord with reality would need to be found. The trouble is that in the 1980s a Frenchman was able to demonstrate that this is what actually happened! It really is what happens. Thus in the following decade this phenomenon has been put to use in teleportation.

Now let us imagine two scientists, say Julie and Jules, each in possession of one of these twin particles. Julie is in the USA and Jules

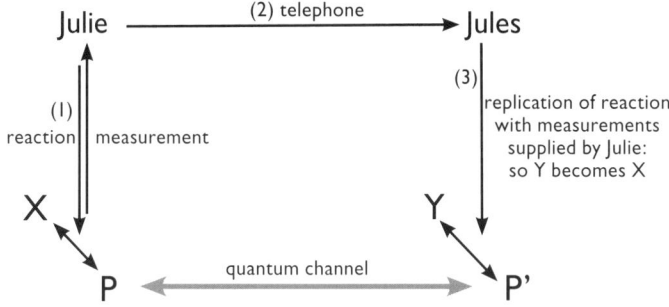

is in Japan. Julie has an atom called Atom X which she would like to measure, but she does not have the measuring device, it is with Jules in Japan.

Julie will create a reaction between Atom X and the particle P, with the result that the change of particle P will be instantaneously transferred to the twinned particle P' in Japan; on account of their twinning if one changes so does the other. This is the level of the quantum channel, a means of communication apparently out with the constraints of time and space.

At this stage, Julie calls Jules and tells him exactly what she has done. Jules will do the same thing with the Atom Y he has, which is the same Atom as X, but in an indifferenciated state, and will discover he is in possession of Atom X in Japan. In other words, all the attributes of Atom X have been teleported onto Atom Y which has become Atom X.

What greatly interested me in this model is that there are two communication channels, one an instantaneous quantum channel, which is absolute, outside time and space but which of itself is insufficient. There is also the need for a classic method of communication, like a fax, a telephone, or anything one could wish for, to transmit consciously information in the real world. Is this not precisely the situation where we find ourselves? There are things that occur in the immediacy of the respective unconscious of analyst and analysand, but none of it makes sense without a conscious relationship.

Projections

Again, returning to my idea of the *quaternio*, which, I think the reader will now see, is just my model for an extremely complicated reality of which we are able to represent only certain elements, only a few dimensions. The question which arises for me is this: what is it that allows the quaternio itself to be contained, to be differentiated, humanized, since we find ourselves at a purely archetypal level, which as Jung tells us is inhuman?

He tells us furthermore, '*the very word transference is closely akin to projection*' (1946, para. 359). And then he goes on to state: 'the unconscious infection brings with it the therapeutic possibility – which should not be underestimated – of the illness being transferred to the doctor' (1946, para. 365). Moreover, throughout his life he emphasizes the fact that the transference is an unconscious phenomenon both in the analysand and in the analyst.

He then notes that the content of transference projections is entirely non-specific (1946, para. 361). Yet he began by telling us that the specific content of the transference was incest, and now he is telling us that the content is entirely non specific, that at the level of projections there are no specific contents, which necessitates the existence of different levels. I think therefore that the level to which he is referring now is not archetypal, rather it is the level of ego defence mechanisms as described by Freud.

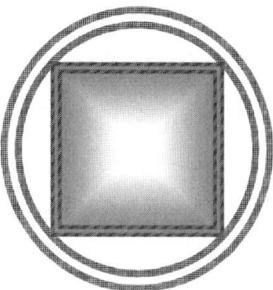

Figure 1

This led me to draw up a second model (Fig. 1), with a second external container which I imagine as the network of transferential and countertransferential projections. It is where I believe resides the importance of unconscious communication, the importance of *participation mystique*, of psychic infection, because it is where we find the interstices of the analyst's and analysand's projections, thus creating a projective container, a human, in contrast to an archetypal, container.

Nevertheless, all this remains in the unconscious and Jung warns of

> the dangers of affinity, with its deceptive projections and its urge to assimilate the object in terms of the projection, to draw it into the family circle in order to actualise the hidden incest situation, which seems all the more attractive and fascinating the less it is understood.
>
> (1946, para. 452)

We know he was aware of what he was talking about. By the same token, he noted, 'doctor and patient thus find themselves in a relationship founded on mutual unconsciousness' (1946, para. 364). In other words this model of a double container which I am proposing could serve as a representation, or an attempt at a representation of something which remains permanently unconscious, something which eludes the one as much as the other.

The Setting

Then I said to myself: but if we are talking about analysis, we necessarily talk about a process in a setting. To my mind it is this setting then which ensures it can take place without being purely destructive, and probably, it is to be hoped, provide sufficient scope for differentiation. I conceive this setting as having two areas (Fig. 2), since I see it as an actual external setting, which, from the analyst's point of view allows him to survive, but which he experiences as outside himself, things like the number of sessions, the rules and conventions of practice, the interdict of enactment, and all that surrounds him beyond the consulting room, his colleagues with whom he has exchanges, wider society to which he must give an account of himself etc. The other area is the internal setting which for me stands for the analyst's internal position.

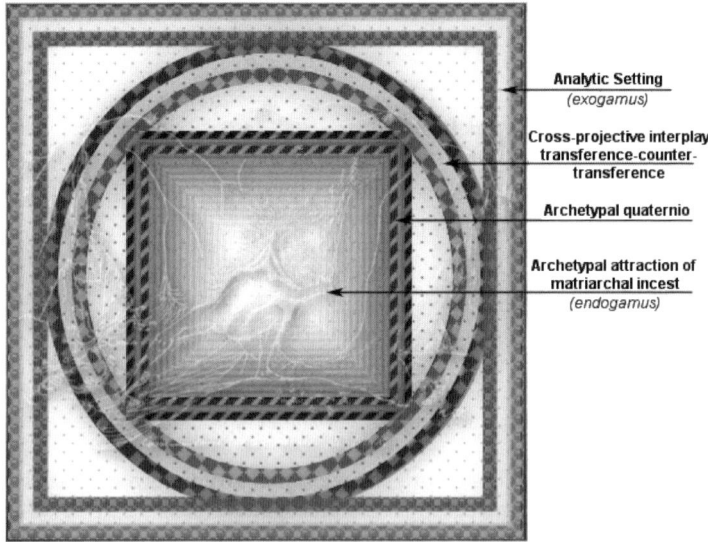

Figure 2

Going back to the original model, we note at its heart is maternal incest, a purely endogamous energy source, which tends wholly towards a return to unity, to identity, to undifferentiated identity, towards the identical. At the archetypal level, there exists a differentiation, since Jung tells us there is exogamy, an equilibrium between endo- and exogamy. Obviously at the projective level, we note exogamy since projections travel outwards, with a dynamic to and fro motion of endo- and exogamy; I project outwards partly because I want to rid myself of something that is inside, that is exogamous, but equally because I do not want the outside to remain outside of me, I want to gather it up, assimilate it within myself, that is endogamous.

All this leads me to the idea that for there to be a nucleus of a specifically analytic attitude at least some part of the analyst's commitment, conscious commitment that is, must remain purely exogamous, such that he remains in a relationship with his patient who in some measure will always be other, alien and unknown to him. The analyst needs to keep an awareness that the person he has been seeing for five years, once, twice, three, four or five times a week, well there is nothing he is able to say about him that is really true. All that he can say is at best tentative, but the other will definitely and radically always be unknown to him. I think this position is what permits containment, which maintains the distance which prevents total entrapment, even if it is desirable to be 98% trapped, at times, obviously.

Revisiting the Clinical Situations

It is time to revisit my clinical illustrations to try to convey how I imagined what was going on in those sessions, at the level of the chimera and the transferential space of the in-between.

In relation to Nymphéa, this is approximately how I understood it. I reckoned there was virtually no internal container (Fig. 3); I am not even sure there had ever been one for her, anyway I doubt there was one between us. She had begun suicide attempts from the age of eight, she managed to jump into a domestic well at fourteen, and when she got to me she was barely more together. I surmise that there had never been anything very solid in this woman's make-up,

Figure 3

nothing very differentiated, so that I felt utterly bombarded by her desire for maternal incest, battered and trapped from within. The way I conceived her migration to the couch, was an enactment on my part, but I was incapable of thinking anything else, I could do nothing other than what I did, it was my way of surviving, so I yielded to a non-destructive, minimal enactment, sufficient to ensure we both survived, one with the other. This is how I justify my reduction of the internal setting: my internal analytic attitude was severely at risk, I was 98% engulfed but fortunately in such situations, the outer setting persists, in that I was able to speak about it, have contact with colleagues who have had similar experiences, in order to stay upright, to contain myself. This is what allowed my enactment not only to avoid major destructiveness, but to be a source of genuine creativity in my representation of her, and of a resurgence of my capacity to think.

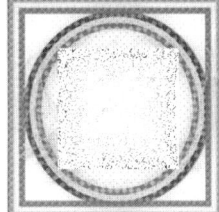

Figure 4

What transpired with Helen was quite different: it was pure and immediate projection from the very start, in an overwhelming way (Fig. 4). I immediately projected onto her the image of schizophrenic patients I had known in the psychiatric hospital, while she instantly projected onto me the image of a saviour, of an idealized father, the father she had not had in childhood. The whole thing eluded me completely at the time. Whereas I believed I had politely got rid of her, in fact I had proferred a helping hand. I executed exactly the opposite manoeuvre to that which I had intended. In fact, I think in this instance there was an element of the alchemical *quaternio* within, which was not at all in place, so that incestuous energy was immediately in contact with the projective level, hence the violence, the impulsiveness and the total unconsciousness which overcame us both – me probably much more than her.

The little session with Claire is I think a phenomenon which characterizes situations where there is a very powerful and fine interaction between the dynamic of the *quaternio* and that of those classic projections as described by Freud in relation to hysterical patients (Fig. 5). What appears to happen here is that elements of incestuous energy somehow cross the first projective level, tapping into the

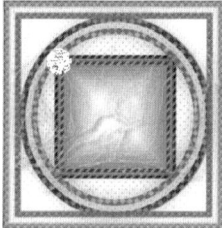

Figure 5

second projective level – I am unable to consider these things other than in terms of two layers or two thicknesses, like cell membranes – I say this because in Claire's case, there was a very important aspect upon which she insisted, and those were her refrains, 'as if'. Everything was as if, as if, as if, and then there was her 'it's not me and yet it is me'. I found there a kind of gap which, while it enabled her to be instantly in touch with archetypal energy, it also made her feel alien without being able to deny it was her. I recognized in her what I believe to be a very basic sense of otherness which it turned out to be for her, and about which I shall remain silent.

As to the story about Mother's Day (Fig. 6), it has remained for me one of those slightly miraculous sessions, which arrive from time to time, where everything works with textbook accuracy. There is not much to say about it. There is however much pleasure in experiencing it. I have nothing further to relate about it.

In conclusion, I just wanted to say that the foregoing is intended to disappear, to be

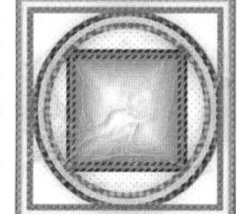

Figure 6

diluted, so that the patient can be allowed to continue on his way.

References

Agnel, A. (1999). 'Vide du mandala'. *Cahiers jungiens de psychanalyse*, 94, 81–92.

Coll. (2006). The Relativity of Scale, Encyclopédie Wikipedia, http://fr.wikipedia.org

Einstein, A. & Born, M. (2005). *The Born – Einstein Letters: Friendship, Politics and Physics in Uncertain Times 1916 to 1955*. London: Macmillan.

Freud, S. (1920). *Beyond the Pleasure Principle*. SE 18.

Freud, S. & Breuer, J. (1895). *Studies on Hysteria*. SE 2.

Gordon, R. (1980). *Dying and Creating*. London: Academic Press.

Jung, C.G. (1946). 'The psychology of the transference'. *CW* 16.

– (1953). *Two Essays on Analytical Psychology*. *CW* 7.

– (1956). *Symbols of Transformation*. *CW* 5.

– (1958). *Psychology and Religion*. *CW* 11.

– (1963). Aniela Jaffé: *Memories, Dreams, Reflections by C.G. Jung*. London: Flamingo / Fontana.

– (1967). *Alchemical Studies*. *CW* 13.

Martin-Vallas, F. (2002). Discussion at the Anglo-French-Belgian 'Consultation'. Windsor, UK.

– (2005). 'Towards a theory of the integration of the Other in representation'. *Journal of Analytical Psychology*, 50, 3, 285–93.

– (2006). 'The transferential chimera: a clinical approach'. *Journal of Analytical Psychology*, 51, 5, 627–41.

– (2008). 'The transferential chimera: some theoretical considerations'. *Journal of Analytical Psychology*, 53, 1, 37-59.

M'Uzan de, M. (1983). 'La chimère transférentielle'. In *De l'art à la mort*. Paris: Gallimard.

– (1994). *La bouche de l'inconscient*. Paris: Gallimard.

Sandor-Buthaud, M. (2004). 'Au-delà du bien et du mal: la réalité de l'ombre et de la destructivité'. *Cahiers jungiens de psychanalyse*, 112.

Solomon, H. (1999). 'The ethical self'. In *Jungian Thought in the Modern World*, eds. E. Christopher & H. Solomon. London: Free Association Books.

– (2005). 'Emergent theory in religion, spirituality and depth psychology'. In *The Self in Transformation*. London: Karnac Books, 2007.

Spielrein, S. (1912). 'Destruction as the cause of coming into being'. *Journal of Analytical Psychology*, 39, 2, 1994.

Winnicott, D. W. (1960). 'Ego distortion in terms of true and false self'. In *The Maturational Process and the Facilitating Environment: Studies in the Theory of Emotional Development*. New York: International Universities Press, 1965, 140–52.

Encounter with a Traditional Healer: Western and African Therapeutic Approaches in Dialogue

Suzanne Maiello
Italy (AIPA, ACP)

Abstract

The paper[1] explores the extent to which cultural aspects contribute to the modalities of human relations and consequently to the qualities of the internal objects and the sense of identity. Therapeutic relationships and techniques, as well as the theories on which they are based, are seen as being equally embedded in their cultural context.

An encounter with a traditional African healer offers the author, a western trained European analyst, an opportunity to think about similarities and differences in the therapeutic approach to mental distress, as well as in the training of therapists/healers in the two cultures.

Special attention is given to the role of ancestor reverence in African culture. The notion of the *ancestors* is related to what psychoanalysis describes as *internal objects*. Cultural differences in the role and importance of verbal language in the therapeutic relationship are described, and the importance and meaning of non-verbal forms of communication are explored.

Introduction

The cultural context contributes to shaping not only the basic patterns of our ways of living, but also, through the introjection of our interpersonal experiences from the very beginning of life, the development of our inner world. In particular, the impact of cultural factors on the ways in which human beings relate to each other and to themselves will be explored.

A few years ago, a three-months' stay in South Africa offered me the opportunity to meet a number of black South Africans.

---

1 Adapted extract from 'Encounter with an African Healer: Thinking about the Possibilities and Limits of Cross Cultural Psychotherapy' by Suzanne Maiello from the *Journal of Child Psychotherapy* (1999), vol. 25, no. 2, copyright © Association of Child Psychotherapists 1999, reprinted by permission of the Taylor & Francis Group. A version of the paper appeared in the *Journal of Analytical Psychology* (April 2008), vol. 53, no. 2, also with their permission. Permission has also been granted for the article to be included in the CD-rom version of the 17th IAAP Congress Proceedings.

At the time, very little cross-cultural research had been done in the country. One reason for this is likely to lie in the fact that for centuries the notion of cultural difference has been synonymous with white supremacy (Swartz 1996, 1998). After the apartheid regime, an excessively universalist view of social phenomena tended to develop, as a reaction to the previous policy of racial segregation. However, this tendency, undoubtedly connected with feelings of shame, fear and guilt in the white community, could have represented an attempt at both denial and manic reparation and contributed to a disregard of the reality of profound cultural differences existing between ethnic groups.

Psychoanalysis and Non-Western Cultures

Since the early days of the twentieth century, European psychoanalytic thinking has shown a keen interest in ethnology and anthropology. This interest derived primarily from the wish to explore the 'archaic layers of the unconscious', for which the authors searched for evidence in what they called 'primitive cultures' (Freud 1921; Jones 1924; Jung 1931/1950). Their objective was primarily the universal validation of the foundations of psychoanalytic theory. Later, authors like Roheim (1950), who had done anthropological research all over the world, tended to generalize the idea of the 'universality of the unconscious', which Jung had conceptualized with the notion of the collective unconscious (1936). Several authors (e.g., Devereux 1973) used western criteria for the definition of the 'healthy personality' and applied psychoanalytic and psychiatric categories to define 'cultural pathologies'.

From his cultural vertex, Kakar, an Indian psychoanalyst, states that so far psychoanalysis has been concerned with the individual's capacity to create culture more than with the individual being shaped by culture. He writes:

> The paramount concern of psychoanalysis seems to have been in protecting and gathering evidence in support of its key concepts rather than in entertaining the possibility that other cultures, with their different world-views, family structures and relationships, could contribute to its models and concepts.
>
> (Kakar 1985, p. 441)

In recent years however, psychoanalytic thinking has shown an increasing interest in the interactive reciprocity of intrapsychic, interpersonal and cultural processes. Berenstein and Puget (1997) introduced, alongside the intrapsychic and the intersubjective dimensions of subjectivity, the concept of the trans-subjective dimension, which consists of the culture-specific relations which the individual entertains in a shared social environment. Significantly, contributions in this area mostly come from psychoanalysts who live and work in multi-ethnic and multi-cultural countries.

The *trans-subjective* element becomes a central issue whenever individuals belonging to different cultures meet. This is all the more relevant in psychoanalytic or, more generally, in all forms of psycho-therapeutic practice which implies the use of conceptual tools and interpretative skills. There is often little awareness of the fact that cultural elements contribute to the patient's specific ways of com-municating and expressing distress. Furthermore, what we definitely tend to disregard is the fact that there is a cultural dimension to our own specifically western way of being as well, which in turn influences our professional approach.

During my stay in South Africa, the experience of cultural *otherness* made me more alert to the relativity of what I had previously relied on as obvious facts and certainties, and stimulated my interest in entering new ground. This was my state of mind when I had the opportunity to meet a traditional healer.

Encounter with a Sangoma

The encounter took place in a bush camp in the north eastern part of South Africa. Located in the wilderness, in the middle of wildlife, it consists of a few round reed huts hidden among the trees, and a larger central common hut.

A friend of mine who had been living there for several years drew my attention to a young man who was working around the place. He told me that Maboeta had been brought to the local *sangoma* from another village six months earlier in a confusional state, with hallucinatory symptoms, stereotyped movements and a total absence of contact with external reality. His symptoms were what we would describe as a schizophrenic breakdown. Now, he was integrated in the community, worked reliably and was being trained to become a tracker.

I got interested in hearing more about this undoubtedly successful therapy. The *sangoma* who had cured the patient was informed that a white healer had arrived and wanted to learn about traditional methods of treatment. She agreed to see me, and a meeting was arranged.

Like most black South Africans, the *sangoma* had an African name, but was generally known by her western name. When at a later date I started thinking and writing about our encounter, I read some literature by black authors born in the area, in order to choose an African name which existed in the *sangoma*'s culture. My research was motivated less by the preoccupation to protect confidentiality than by the wish to honour the healer's African identity. I found a name for her in Mamphela Ramphele's autobiography (1995). Only much later was I to learn that Makaba, the name I had chosen for her, *was* in fact the *sangoma*'s African name.

The encounter was to take place one morning in the round common hut at the camp. No precise time had been fixed. I had been around for maybe two or three hours in company of the friend who had arranged our meeting. An African proverb says, 'Western people have watches, we have time'. So, we waited. In the end, the old woman appeared in her full regalia, wearing her long embroidered skirts and white bead necklaces. In the centre of the hut, she unrolled her mat and sat down on the mud floor. Nyari, an old man who accompanied her, sat next to her, his long legs stretched across the floor. I was about to settle down on the ground in front of Makaba, but she shook her head and indicated the parapet at the open side of the hut. She insisted in having me sit up there and addressing me as 'madam', while my friend was allowed to sit on the floor. I felt uneasy because of the asymmetry of the set-up, not knowing whether it had to do with my belonging to the race of the white masters, or whether it was a sign of respect for a colleague who had come to visit from far away. There was also a language problem. Makaba belonged to the *Shangaan* tribe and spoke mostly *Tsonga*, and I spoke only English. In order to communicate verbally, we needed both Nyari and my friend for a double translation, from *Tsonga* into Afrikaans, and from Afrikaans into English.

Makaba's Report

The treatment took place in Makaba's hut. The patient lived with her day and night, for the whole duration of his illness. Now he was well, the healer said, and would not relapse.

During the initial period, the *sangoma* did nothing but observe the patient, until she understood what was 'not right' with him. In Maboeta's case, this period had been two and a half weeks. After this, Makaba knew what *muti*, what medical substance, she had to prepare for the patient to drink, so as to cleanse the inside of his body.

The next step consisted in rubbing Maboeta's legs with another *muti* whose specific function was to prevent the patient from running away. If he still tried to escape, his legs would bring him back to her hut even against his will.

At this point, the actual treatment could begin. Every night, Makaba introduced a *muti* into Maboeta's nose and ears during his sleep. The wind is believed to carry the healing substances into the inside of the head, where the illness is located. Makaba agitated her hands above her head to describe the patient's hallucinations. Both the nostrils and the ears are seen as ways of access for air and wind. The function of this *muti* is to stop the patient from hearing 'his own stuff' and bring him back to hearing and listening to his fellow human beings.

'One day', said Makaba, 'he gets up and recognizes you'. This marked the beginning of the last phase of treatment, which was given during daytime. From the moment the patient could hear and recognize another person again, he must go back to work. The therapy became verbal, but language remained closely related to concrete external reality. To my question what she actually did with Maboeta, Makaba explained that she would for instance tell him to bring her an object. Sometimes, he might go and fetch it, but not bring it to her, or bring another object, or keep it for himself, or he would pretend not to hear, like when he was ill. She worked with him, day by day, until he was 'right' again, i.e., until objects and names, words and actions matched, as they did before the illness.

When Makaba had finished her report and replied to all the questions I had asked during her account, she said that now it was my turn to tell her how I would treat a patient like Maboeta.

I found myself in great difficulty, with a feeling that I could say nothing that would in any way be meaningful to an African healer. I first tried to explain the difference between psychiatry and psychoanalysis by saying that I did not use any plants or other substances to cure patients, and that the only *muti* I used were my words. From what the patient did or said, I tried to understand what his illness was about. Then, I transformed into words what I thought was hidden in his behaviour or speech that made him sick. And if I found the right words for him, they would enter into his ears and go into his head. Gradually, he would hear me, and the words would have the effect of a *muti*.

Makaba seemed satisfied with my attempt to describe a psychoanalytic session and said that after all our treatments were similar. As a token of her appreciation, she offered to give me a recipe of a *muti*, if I was prepared to give her one of my *muti* words in return. This was one of the moments when I painfully perceived the depth of the gap between our cultures. None of my English words would have been of any use to her. I expressed my gratitude and my appreciation for the effectiveness of Maboeta's treatment, but we parted without exchanging any of our therapeutic tools.

Comment

In thinking about this indigenous healer's therapy, I tried to 'translate' its various stages into psychoanalytical terms, so as to make them meaningful to me. In a way, I felt that Makaba was right when she noted similarities.

As to the phases of Maboeta's treatment, we could say that the initial observation and assessment period ended when the *sangoma* had made a diagnosis of the patient's disorder. The following 'cleansing' phase could be seen as the creation of a therapeutic space and setting inside the patient, or, in other terms, as the beginning of the process of establishing the therapeutic alliance and fostering the positive transference.

The subsequent treatment of the patient's legs with the *muti* which would have brought him back into therapy if he was tempted to escape, showed the special attention given to the part of the body that regulates distance. Makaba knew about the danger of the patient not tolerating the closeness of the therapeutic relationship at moments when his anxieties would increase. In psychoanalytic terms, we would say that she expected the emergence of the negative transference, which could lead to the patient's attempt to interrupt the treatment under the pressure of unbearable emotional states.

What particularly struck me was the fact that the central part of the therapy occurred during the patient's sleep. When the *muti* was introduced into Maboeta's ears and nose to be carried into his head by the wind, the *sangoma*'s function seemed to be to re-establish channels of communication between the internal and the external world at deep unconscious levels while the patient was asleep.

When thinking about her account, I could not help associating Maboeta's night treatment with what I learnt during my infant observation in the township. The baby used to be fed at least twice during every observation. The feeds were brief and unspectacular. All through the first weeks of the infant's life, he almost invariably slept at the breast. He did suck and take in milk, just as the *muti* was carried by the wind up the patient's nostrils and ears, but the baby's mouth movements did not appear to be linked to any wish or need deriving from the perception of hunger. In thinking about Maboeta living in the *sangoma*'s hut day and night, I was also reminded of the surprise of the baby's mother on hearing that European babies do not usually share their mother's bed, but sleep in a cot on their own. Maboeta's night treatment also made me think of African weaning practices, according to which, in contrast to western habits, night feeds are the last to be abandoned (Ainsworth 1967).

During the nights, Makaba may have restored in her sleeping patient a deep unconscious experience of containment and relatedness, which had a therapeutic effect on his state of alienation and fragmentation. I would suggest that the healing force of the night *muti* might be connected not only with the intrinsic qualities of the drug, but with the mental containment offered by Makaba's constant presence throughout the night and to her care and dedicated attention over her sleeping patient. I did not know at the time of the encounter with Makaba that the restoration of links has, as we shall see, wider implications in African culture than in the western world.

The morning on which the patient woke up and recognized the *sangoma*, the night treatment ended, and the day treatment began. The healer's remaining task seemed to consist mainly of what we would describe as rehabilitation exercises. It was only at this point, in the phase of re-establishing the connections with external reality, that the verbal component became part of the treatment at all. Maboeta had to learn to listen and understand Makaba's requests, to differentiate between persons and objects and to perform the movements and activities which would have connected him with his social environment again. In terms of verbal communication, Makaba did use language during this last phase of treatment, which coincided with the patient resuming work and with his concomitant reintegration in the community, but her words never had more than a purely practical descriptive or pointing function. By naming concrete reality rather than mental and emotional states, these words were not invested with any deeply shared symbolic meaning. In the conclusive part of this paper, further thought will be given to the crucial difference between African and western culture in the area of the use, value and position of verbal language in human communication in general, and in healing practices in particular.

Illness and Healing in African Traditions

For a better understanding of Maboeta's treatment, it may be necessary to underline a few culture-specific aspects of African traditions in connection with health and ill-health.

The authors whom I shall quote in this part of the paper are black South African healers or thinkers, whose writings are rooted in the cultural soil of Africa. In order to avoid generalizations, I do not refer to 'African tradition'. Some regional differences exist even within South Africa between *Xhosa*, *Zulu* and *Shangaan* traditions. But I shall attempt to convey some perception of the essence of traditional healing practices. I shall refer in particular to the writings of Vusamazulu Credo Mutwa, a Zulu healer, *sanusi* (an uppermost *sangoma* of all *sangomas* in Southern Africa), storyteller and author of many books. Incidentally, Credo Mutwa and Makaba had met, and he is said to have had high respect for her. Another important source of information comes from the writings of an influential Xhosa healer, Nokuzola Mndende.

The only white South African among the quoted authors is Vera Bührmann. She had spent her childhood in close contact with black South African people and spoke Xhosa. She was the first Jungian analyst who returned to South Africa after her training in London. My references to her courageous work, done in the middle of the apartheid years, are a tribute to the invaluable intercultural 'bridging' quality of her research and writing.

About illness and healing, Credo Mutwa writes: 'Where illness or madness have come, the *sangoma* knows that some power of the universe is disrupted and must be balanced or restored to harmony again' (1996, p. 27).

This basic truth must be kept in mind, as it is the foundation on which traditional healing practices have grown.

Body and Mind

In the view of African traditions, disease is generated by a global problem, and healing practices have an equally global dimension and meaning. Illness is not split into either physical or mental suffering. Body and mind are a unit, and the mind is never experienced as separate from the body. This is the first important cultural difference. Vera Bührmann, who did an extensive study of traditional healing practices amongst the Xhosa population in the south eastern rural areas, quotes an African patient who said: 'When part of me is ill, the whole of me is ill' (1984, p. 36). Physical symptoms belong to every illness, including mental disorder. Consequently, the approach of traditional healers to illness is holistic and includes the biological, psychological, social and spiritual dimensions. A *sangoma* can be said to be a general practitioner, a psychiatrist and a psychotherapist in one, but also in many respects a 'minister' or 'priest'. Healing can involve ritualistic elements. 'Rituals are holistic in the sense that they address social, moral and spiritual aspects of individuals' (Mndende 2006, p. 1).

The primary and indivisible *unity* of body and mind represents the core of the African view of the human being, rather than the Western body/mind split, which leads, in the most favourable circumstances, to *reciprocity* between mind and matter (Gumede 1990). This has obvious consequences for the basic metaphors of mental functioning and human life.

When Makaba agitated her hands over her head to describe her patient's symptoms, I interpreted them as hallucinations, i.e., as pathological productions of his *mind*, whereas the *sangoma* seemed to understand them as a mix-up that occurred concretely inside his *head*. And the *muti*, which was introduced into the orifices of the ears and nose, was supposed to display its healing forces by reaching the patient's illness directly inside his head.

In thinking about the special *muti*, which was rubbed onto the patient's legs to prevent him from running away, a western mind would imagine that Makaba saw the legs not only as the vehicle for escaping from the treatment, but attributed to them some form of intelligence.

But I am aware that this very hypothesis already presupposes a split between body and mind.

Abstract western categories of physio- or psycho-pathology have no meaning in traditional African culture. Bührmann reports that a term like *depression* is unknown. A depressed patient might describe his symptoms by saying that 'his body is broken', or 'his body is down'. 'The general use of body terms for what Westerners would call emotions is very common' (1987, p. 276). An episode in my personal experience confirms this.

One year, on the drive to the bush, the young driver asked me what my 'business' was. I said that I was a psychologist. He looked blank. I explained: 'I am a doctor who works with people who have problems and try to help them to get better'. He still looked puzzled. So, I added 'I am a white healer'. This made sense to him. He immediately started complaining about his ailments in great detail. I understood that the idea of one doctor for psychic problems and another doctor for physical illness did not make sense to him. If I was a healer, I was a healer of the whole person.

Individual and Community

The second point which needs to be explored is that in African culture individuals remain in a life-long close connection with the family of origin, the clan and the wider community. This has far-reaching implications both in terms of social and cultural values, and the definition of psychic development. Where western culture encourages the individual to strive towards personal achievement and face the loss and relinquishment of primary dependency and relationships, the individual's wellbeing largely coincides, in African culture, with being integrated in the community of origin and contributing to its development (Bührmann 1984).

If the normal life not only of children, but also of adults, is so closely intertwined with primary group relations, it is understandable that illness is an equally shared event. 'The African gets sick within his community and will also recover within his community' (Gumede 1990). It is particularly important for western psychotherapists to keep this aspect in mind when they see immigrants who belong to a culture in which integration in the primary family group remains a pillar throughout life. These patients have suffered a loss in terms of containment. This loss seems to touch more and deeper levels than in a western patient.

As far as the healing process is concerned, Bührmann writes that 'Treatment, especially for any mental dysfunction, is not individual, but requires the cooperation of the family and at times the active treatment of others in the family' (1984, p. 25). I remember a communication of a western-trained black South African psychotherapist who presented clinical material in a supervision group in Johannesburg. She complained about the unreliability of the patients she saw in a mental health unit in Soweto. It happened frequently that a patient did not turn up at the time of his appointment. He might drop in at any other time of the day or of any other day, or else some other members of the family might turn up without the patient. What to western psychoanalytically trained professionals would appear as resistance and acting out could be seen under a different light in the framework of traditional African social structures.

A crucial general issue arises from this episode. It concerns the complex meaning of undertaking training in a healing profession according to a method whose social references are rooted in a cultural model which is different from the therapist's and the patient's. Yet another facet of the problem, which is highly relevant in our times of globalization and migration, concerns the possibilities and limits of cross-cultural psychotherapy (Maiello 1999).

Ancestor Reverence

The third cultural aspect, which is crucial for the understanding of the meaning of both illness and healing in African cultures, concerns the role of the ancestors. A deep feeling of belonging to the clan and family of origin accompanies the individual throughout life. These relationships concern not only the living relatives, but also the forefathers, the 'living dead', who are revered through rituals and ceremonies.

Bührmann writes:

> The clan ancestors have retained many of their human qualities. They can feel the cold, and hunger and thirst; they can feel neglected or happy and well cared for; they can get annoyed, angry and even *vengeful*. On the whole however, they are kindly mentors, guides and protectors, especially when the customs are kept and regularly performed.
>
> (1984, p. 28; italics added by the author)

In connection with this quotation, the Xhosa healer Nokuzola Mndende stated that 'ancestors may *punish* people, but they are never *vengeful*' (2007, personal communication). In other terms, ancestors will never retaliate: they have unquestioned authority. This short hypothetical 'dialogue' across time between a western and an African healer is but a minute example of how much caution and careful attention is required when we approach and try to interpret another culture. The choice of one word instead of another can be the result of a different view of the world.

The ancestors have a concrete space in the hut or in the cattle area of every homestead. Special African beer is brewed before performing ceremonies, and some is spilled on the ground for them to drink. They are consulted whenever an important decision has to be made or when a serious problem has arisen. Their presence is constant, and a good relation with them is vital for the wellbeing of the individual and his family. There is an aspect of reciprocity in the relationship, in so far as the living and the ancestors must keep each other happy.

The ancestors communicate with the living mostly through dreams, which play an important role in the lives of African people. However, these tend to be interpreted, according to Bührmann (1984), not at what western culture conceives as the symbolic level, but more like pieces of concrete reality. Advice received by an ancestor in a dream tends, according to the author, to be taken at face value and acted on concretely in waking life. The *Xhosa* healer Nokuzola Mndende commented on this statement by affirming that this is both true and untrue, as dreams *are* interpreted at a level, which, within the African cultural framework, is symbolic (2007, personal communication). This second example shows again, how cautious we must be in interpreting notions which western culture tends to consider as universally shared, but which may need to be reconsidered in the light of another cultural system.

If good health is related to the ancestors, the same is true for some forms of ill health, which are connected with a disturbance in the relationship with the ancestors. Breaking the links with the ancestors and their consequent withdrawal can bring about illness directly, but also, and this is far more dangerous, make the individual and his family vulnerable to the deadly spells of witchcraft. If the benevolence of the ancestors is the source of health and their withdrawal the cause of some illnesses, recovery from these necessarily involves reconciliation with them.

This means that in Maboeta's night therapy, the wind, which had to carry the *muti* through his nose and ears into his head, had less to do with the patient's actual breath than with the spirits of the ancestors who had been called upon by the *sangoma*. Their willingness to enter the patient's head again was the prerequisite for his recovery, and Makaba's ability to reconnect and reconcile the patient with his ancestors was at the core of her healing power.

Training as a Sangoma

If health and some illnesses are connected with the ancestors, the same is true for the decision to become a healer. This is not the result of an individual's personal choice, but quite literally a vocation. In fact, a call from the ancestors is at the origin of every *sangoma*'s training (Bührmann 1984; Mutwa 1996). The call can occur in dreams and is often accompanied by serious, often long-lasting and seemingly incurable illness, including symptoms which a western psychiatrist might diagnose as a psychotic breakdown. Bührmann writes 'The clinical picture ... resembles an emotional disturbance of greater or lesser degree, which is, however, always accompanied by physical symptoms ...' (1984, p. 36). Credo Mutwa comments on his own illness before he went into training: 'my sickness was really not a sickness at all, but rather I was undergoing the great illness which all *sangomas*-to-be had first to undergo' (1996, p. 11). Mndende specifies:

> For the most part, physical sickness occurs due to a *rejection* of the call, sometimes as a result of a deliberate delay because one is reluctant to accept the call, sometimes because an individual is unaware of the significance of his/her dreams. This is why the involvement of the clan is crucial, the elderly of the clan being the experts in the analysis of such symptoms.
>
> (2006, p. 51)

A general cultural statement must precede the exploration of some contents of the process of training of a *sangoma*. Nokuzola Mndende writes:

> African healing methods should be studied in their own context first. For one to be healed of *intwaso* (call to divination), for instance, no Western medical approach could help. The only cure is for the 'sick' person to obey the ancestors who convey their wishes through dreams or visions. There are several case studies where people are cured only by accepting the ancestral call to heal. Most scholars have identified sickness as the most common symptom occurring in the call to become a diviner....However, it should be argued that it is actually dreams and the experience of visions which signify the call of ancestors.
>
> (Mndende 2006, p. 51)

In some cases, a healer may be consulted and will decide whether the patient's illness is the result of a call of the spirits to become a *sangoma*. If so, he/she undergoes training, which implies moving to the home of the *sangoma* of his/her choice. The student will live with his master for the whole training period, which can run over many years. 'It is long, demanding and expensive and can interfere with other duties and relationships' (Bührmann 1984, p. 37). It includes getting to know the therapeutic powers of plants, the preparation of *muti*, purification rituals necessary for opening the person to receive the messages of the ancestors, ritual dancing, performing of ceremonies, discussion of dreams, divination and diagnosis of illness. All disciplines are interrelated and convergent in the endeavour to enhance the harmonious relationship with the ancestors.

As for divination, Mutwa affirms that there is nothing supernatural in this capacity, which is skilfully developed during the healer's training. What to western eyes might look like magic and be described as 'para-psychological' or 'para-normal' phenomena, is related to the idea that the human being is believed to have twelve senses in African culture, and not only the five known in the western world (1996). When Bion says that 'there are no sense-data directly related to psychic quality, as there are sense-data (directly) related to concrete objects' (1962, p. 53), his statement is based on the western conception of the existence of five senses. But Bion felt that an element was missing in our approach, when he added 'I have no doubt whatever of the need for *something* in the personality to make contact with psychic quality' (1962, p. 54). If Bion and Credo Mutwa had had an encounter, the *sangoma* might have replied to the psychoanalyst that this *something* capable of making contact with psychic reality might be found among the other senses known in African tradition.

The *sangoma* seems to be constantly and deeply committed to his or her activity as a healer. One day, I saw Makaba coming back from the bush across the sandy ground of the dry river bed. She carried a couple of twisted sticks. I greeted her from the distance and asked whether she had gone to collect wood. She shook her head, only said '*muti*' and walked on. She looked absorbed. Collecting medical substances seemed to be an intrinsic part of her healing activity, which needed her full attention at any moment. I remember also being worried about her walking out into the bush unprotected and exposed to potentially dangerous animals. I was told that before she set out into the bush, Makaba rubbed a special *muti* onto her eyebrows. This keeps wild animals away.

The call from the ancestors to undergo training as a *sangoma* can occur at any time in life and is not always welcome to the individual and to his or her family. In this case, a special ceremony can be performed in the attempt to 'block' the call. However, these efforts seem to be of doubtful effectiveness (Bührmann 1984).

A clinical example may illustrate this[1]. On the initiative of the child psychiatrist and analyst Dr. Astrid Berg, a parent-infant mental health service was established in Khayelitsha, a township near Cape Town. Consultations take place in the presence and with the participation of one or two *Xhosa* consultants who also act as interpreters.

Berg's report is about the failure to thrive of the nine months' old child of a young *Xhosa* mother. The baby had developed normally up to the age of four months. At this point, the little boy stopped growing and his weight even began to drop. It seemed difficult to find a cause for his condition. The psychiatrist noted a band of animal hair around the mother's neck. At first, the mother was reluctant to talk about this

---

1   I thank Astrid Berg for the permission to quote her clinical material.

and to see any connection with the child's failure to thrive. But then, she said that, five months ago, she had a dream in which the ancestors put around her neck the band that is the distinctive sign of being in the process to qualify as a *sangoma*. In external reality, her mother as well as her sister were healers. Her husband's family however opposed the call of her ancestors, and she was sent to the husband's village, where a 'blocking' ceremony was performed. The band around her neck was made of the twisted tail hair of the cow, which had been slaughtered on that occasion. Since then, she said, her dreams had stopped, and she thought things were much better.

The psychiatrist's further inquiry however brought forth that the mother still wanted to become a healer, and it was clear that her underlying depression was linked with the repression of her ancestors' call, and the baby boy's failure to thrive was his response to her emotional withdrawal. His symptoms had in fact started shortly after her dream about being in training as a *sangoma* and the ensuing blocking ceremony (Berg 1998).

This clinical example gives an idea of the complexity of a western health worker's task in another culture and shows how indispensable accurate translation and cultural mediation is in a transcultural therapeutic setting. The presence and interpreting function of local participants, both in my conversation with the *sangoma* and in Dr. Berg's consultation with her *Xhosa* patients, means much more than the mere bridging of different languages. Local cultural mediators hold a key position for the understanding of social and cultural aspects of a patient's symptoms.

Ancestors and Internal Objects

Two basic concepts will be discussed in comparative terms, namely the African notion of the *ancestors* and the western psychoanalytic concept of *internal objects*. The notion of internal objects is used in a wider and deeper sense, in so far as they are not confined to the internalized image of the biographical parents. This restricted view would not do justice to the meaning and power of the African ancestors. There are both differences and similarities between the notion of *internal objects* and *ancestors*.

One difference lies undoubtedly in the fact that for African people the ancestors reliably exist in external/internal reality, whereas in western culture, the notion of the internal objects is a metaphor construed to describe mental processes related to projective and introjective identification, as well as to transgenerational transmission. Black South Africans receive support and advice from their ancestors, where westerners rely on their good internalized parental objects, both in their personal and their transpersonal dimension.

An important difference however lies in the degree of their power. Bührmann claims that 'the unquestioning belief in the presence and role of the ancestral shades acts as a powerful therapeutic agent which the rational science-oriented Westerner has difficulty in understanding'. 'In contrast', she adds, 'Western therapy is undermined by doubts and uncertainties, inner strife and a bewildering variety of techniques – such a state can be anti-therapeutic' (1979, p. 23).

The ancestors are both in the external world and inside the person. Berglund quotes a Zulu person who said about his ancestors; 'They are in me. When they are in me I know that they are there. I feel them. They are happy with me and I am happy with them. I think of them always. They know that I am thinking of them' (Berglund 1976). In this instance, the ancestors seem to be halfway between concretely existing external entities and internal mental objects.

There is another element which the therapeutic approaches of both cultures have in common, namely the central importance of the restoration of a feeling of relatedness. This basic requirement for the maintenance of good health is expressed through the connection with and reverence for the ancestors in African tradition, and through the link with and between internal objects in western psychoanalysis.

Breaking the relation with the ancestors brings about illness, just as massive splitting, projective identification and 'attacks on linking' lead to severe psychopathological symptoms. In African traditions, recovery is possible only if the voices of the ancestors are heard and listened to again, which means that the patient's relationship with them is restored. The western patient's psychic recovery occurs thanks to his increasing ability to bear the pain of the contact with formerly split off parts of the personality, and their reintegration in the world of his internal objects.

A Xhosa proverb says *umntu ngumuntu ngabantu*, which means 'a person is a person because of persons'. In other terms, 'I am because we are, and since we are, therefore I am'. *Umntu ngumuntu ngabantu,* three words which could have inspired object relations theory. Inversely, if something has gone wrong in the growth of relationships, there seems to be a shared conviction that another relationship is needed to repair the damage.

The essential prerequisite in approaching people from and in another culture is to be open to *see* and *acknowledge* existing differences before making attempts to *bridge* them.

Verbal and Non-Verbal Language

Western culture attributes high priority to verbal language as a means of interpersonal communication. In African traditions, words do not have the same value and do not occupy such a high-ranking position.

My observation of an African mother-infant couple gave me a first-hand experience of this basic cultural difference. This is confirmed by the descriptions of childhood experiences in autobiographies of black South African authors (Mandela 1994; Ramphele 1995). They give evidence of how unimportant verbal interaction is for the development of interpersonal relations in African tradition. Nelson Mandela writes:

> Like all Xhosa children, I acquired knowledge mainly through observation. We were meant to learn through imitation and emulation, not through questions. When I first visited the homes of whites, I was often dumbfounded by the number and nature of questions that children asked their parents – and their parents' unfailing willingness to answer them.
>
> (1994, p. 11)

If this is true both of parent-infant interaction and adult communication, it is true also, as we saw in Makaba's description of Maboeta's treatment, for the relationship between the healer and the patient. In comparison with the western psychoanalytical 'talking cure', verbal language seems to have a marginal function in traditional healing practices. Bührmann states that what western people think and talk about in psychotherapy, African people tend to act and represent in dancing, singing, rituals and ceremonies. Quoting a Xhosa healer, she writes 'There are things you can never put into words; you can only feel them in your body' (1984, p. 22). It is known that the rhythmical stamping of the feet in prolonged ritual dancing brings about chemical and neuro-physiological changes and an alteration of mental states.

Even dream interpretation is not a matter of verbalization in the western sense. It is usually dealt with in a group situation. Bührmann describes how the dream is told bit by bit and accompanied by singing and dancing to the beat of a special drum to invoke the help of the ancestors (1977). The author also states that insight in the western sense of 'conscious understanding' does not play a significant role. It is as if the dialectic process of western psychotherapy between the analyst's and the patient's consciousness and unconscious was circumvented by direct unconscious communication between the healer and the patient (Bührmann 1979).

At another level, words *are* attributed great power in African healing practices, but their therapeutic effectiveness does not seem to stem from the same source as in western culture. In traditional

African ritual and medicine, the power of verbal language unfolds at other levels, for instance in incantations, which form a vital part of the healers' therapeutic tools (Gumede 1990; Koumare 1983). These words seem to draw their power from a transpersonal dimension and to have a healing effect not only through their meaning, but also through their sound.

This brings me back to my conversation with Makaba. If I think about the *sangoma*'s verbal report of her patient's treatment, which reached me through a double translation, I have legitimate doubts about the literal accuracy of the narrative on which I have based my considerations. After our meeting, I asked my friend who himself knew a few words of *Tsonga* and who had translated Nyari's Afrikaans translation into English, whether he thought that Nyari had left out part of Makaba's communications, as she spoke at length, and the translations were much shorter. He replied that Nyari's translations had been quite accurate, but that Makaba had repeated the same things over and over again in similar versions. This corresponded to what I had felt myself while watching her and listening to her voice. As she talked, she made circular movements in the air with her hands and arms, in front of herself or above her head. Her voice was rather monotonous, as if she had been speaking more to herself than to another person. The same sequences of intonations were repeated in accordance with her movements. I now feel that she may have used verbal language in her own way. Her voice and gestures may have helped her to get into a mental state which made it possible for her to say things in words at all, with the support of repetitive, rhythmical and ritualized vocal and kinesthetic elements. In her mind, she may have been immersed in a ritual dance, which created the necessary frame for insight and communication to emerge at a verbal level. It occurred to me that ritual dancing and singing is always performed in concentric circles, that Makaba had settled on the floor in the centre of the circular hut and drawn circular shapes in the air with her hands. May this have been the deeper and probably unconscious reason, why Makaba insisted that I sat on the parapet of the hut, at the outmost rim of the circle, well knowing that I was not familiar with African ritual?

Incidentally, Gumede mentions the tremendous cultural transformation brought about in African culture by western building practices, which introduced square houses, where formerly roundavels had been the only traditional form of housing (1990).

Listening to Makaba's account, I felt that in a way the process of understanding occurred not only at a conscious semantic verbal level, for which I depended entirely on the two interpreters' help. The repetitive circularity of the *sangoma*'s non-verbal expressions, through her gestures and her voice, were part of the meta-code of her message. When I tried to describe to her verbally the basic principles of western psychotherapy, and Makaba felt that there were similarities in our methods of treatment, she referred to a deeper shared understanding of our basic common therapeutic commitment.

One of the *differences* of our respective cultures manifested itself precisely at the level of our diverging conceptions of the use and function of verbal language. I was unable to bridge the gap, whereas within the *sangoma*'s cultural frame, her request to receive a *muti* word from me in exchange for one of her *muti* recipes made perfect sense. In her terms, they were two equivalent and interchangeable therapeutic elements.

In Conclusion

I shall never know what exactly our encounter and exchange had meant to Makaba, but when she thought that our treatments were similar, this was a precious gift to me and showed that there had been a deep human encounter between us. As to my own experience, I shall try to espress it in terms of Bion's concept of the K-link. Referring to the psychoanalytic relationship, Bion states that 'x is concerning himself to know the truth about y …'. However, this does not mean that 'x is in possession of a piece of knowledge called y but rather that x is in the state of getting to know y and y is in a state of getting to be known by x' (1962, p. 47). The *sangoma* and myself were not an analytic couple. Ours was a relationship of peer reciprocity, and there was a mutual human and professional interest in the other therapist's approach. By this I mean that both of us were subjects (x), and both of us were objects (y) and our common endeavour consisted both in getting to know the other and to be known by the other.

At a deep level, Makaba's experience seemed to correspond to mine. When I expressed my hope to come back and learn more from her, she replied 'I also want to learn from you. We can learn from one another'.

> After the end of the apartheid years, Credo Mutwa wrote: 'Under western civilization, we live in a strange world of separatism, a world in which things that really belong together and which ought to be seen as part of a greater whole are cruelly separated. The result of this separatist attitude is that humanity is denied a great deal of valuable knowledge.'
>
> (Mutwa 1996)

The acknowledgement of the responsibilities of western civilization for this breach of potential communication between cultures may contribute to bring together 'things that have been torn apart' and create the conditions for the development of new forms of mutually respectful inter-cultural dialogue.

References

Ainsworth, M.D. (1967). *Infancy in Uganda – Infant Care and the Growth of Love.* Baltimore: The John Hopkins Press.

Berenstein, I. & Puget, J. (1997). *Lo vincular.* Buenos Aires: Paidos.

Berg, A. (1998), 'Coming-together – Reflections on mother-infant work in Khayelitsha'. Paper presented at the International Conference, 'Change: A Psychoanalytic Perspective'. Cape Town, 3-5 April 1998.

Berglund, A.-I. (1976). *Zulu Thought Patterns and Symbolism.* London: Hurst.

Bion, W.R. (1962). *Learning from experience.* London: Heinemann.

Bührmann, M.V. (1977). 'Dream therapy through the ages'. *Psychotherapeia,* 3,1, 16-18.

– (1979). 'Why are certain procedures of the indigenous healers effective?' *Psychotherapeia,* 5, 3, 20-25.

– (1984). *Living in Two Worlds.* Cape Town & Pretoria: Human & Rousseau.

– (1987). 'The feminine in witchcraft (II)'. *Journal of Analytical Psychology,*32, 2, 257-77.

Devereux, G. (1973). *Essais d'éthnopsychiatrie générale.* Paris: Gallimard.

Freud, S. (1921). *Group Psychology and the Analysis of the Ego. SE* 18, 67-143.

Gumede, M.V. (1990). *Traditional Healers – A Medical Doctor's Perspective.* Braamfontein: Skotaville Publishers.

Jones, E. (1924). *Essays in Applied Psycho-Analysis.* London: Hogarth Press.

Jung, C.G. (1931/1950). 'Archaic Man'. *CW* 10.

– (1936). *The Archetype and the Collective Unconscious. CW* 9i.

Kakar, S. (1985). 'Psychoanalysis and Non-Western Cultures'. *International Review of Psychoanalysis,* 2, 441-8.

Koumare, M. (1983). 'Traditional medicine and psychiatry in Africa'. WHO Report.

Maiello, S. (1999). 'Encounter with an African healer: thinking about the possibilities and limits of cross-cultural psychotherapy'. *Journal of Child Psychotherapy,* 25, 2.

Mandela, N. (1994). *Long Walk to Freedom.* London: Little, Brown and Company.

Mndende, N. (2006). *African Spiritual Journey – Rites of Passage among the Xhosa Speaking of South Africa.* Cape Town: Icamagu Institute.

– (2007). Personal communication.

Mutwa, V.C. (1996). *Song of the Stars – The Lore of a Zulu Shaman.* Barrytown: Station Hills Openings.

Ramphele, M. (1995). *A Life.* Cape Town & Johannesburg: David Philip.

Roheim, G. (1950). *Psychoanalysis and Anthropology – Culture, Personality and the Unconscious.* New York:

Swartz, L. (1996). 'Culture and mental health in the Rainbow Nation: transcultural psychiatry in a changing South Africa. *Transcultural Psychiatric Research Review,* 33.

– (1998). *Culture and Mental Health – A Southern African View.* Cape Town: Oxford University Press.

Brain Mechanisms of Dreaming

Mark Solms
South Africa

Abstract

In his presentation, Professor Mark Solms, known for his attempts to integrate psychoanalytic theories and methods with those of modern neuroscience, shares with us his research interests into the neuropsychology of dreaming. His focus is on how the brain generates dreams and their meaning and function.

* * *

I am unfortunately not very knowledgeable about the sorts of things that interest you most, but I do hope that I'll be able to convey to you something about my own field and the interest that attaches to it because I think it is very interesting and very relevant to the broader topics that you're discussing.

I come from a very particular culture, a natural-scientific one, in which we hold the view that there are facts and there are falsehoods, and if different people hold different views they can't all be right. And we have a method by which we seek to choose between the different views to determine which view tallies more closely with the facts. The approach of my natural-scientific culture has great merits, but it also has some interesting flaws, and my presentation will have that as a sort of subplot. The primary plot of my presentation is to tell you something about how the brain generates dreams. I'm going to divide what I have to say into roughly four sections. Firstly I'm going to tell you what we used to think, what we thought we knew about how the brain generates dreams, then I'll go on secondly to tell you what was wrong with that view, how we found that it was grossly mistaken about how the brain generates dreams. Thirdly I will tell you what we more recently have begun to think we know about how the brain generates dreams, something which we hope tallies more closely with the facts. Lastly, I'll say something about the implications of this new view of how the brain generates dreams for dream psychology, for questions relating to the meaning and function of dreams, and I'll try to be brief in doing all of that.

So, no matter what your psychological affiliation, the school of wisdom that you attach yourself to in psychology or in psychoanalysis, the discoveries that were made in the 1950s about how the brain generates dreams must have come as something of a blow to all of us; in fact, they were trumpeted as a blow to all of us who think that dreams might have meaning, and might be worthy of the attentions of psychotherapists. I'm referring to the discovery in the early 1950s of the phenomenon now known as REM sleep (rapid eye movement sleep). This was discovered by two eminent University of Chicago researchers, who observed that roughly every ninety minutes or so, all of us human beings fall into a curious physiological state in which although we're asleep, unconscious and asleep, our brains become very active. It's for this reason that they initially described this state as 'paradoxical' sleep. The paradox being that you're asleep in a restful state and yet your nervous system is highly excited. The primary feature of the REM state is the one I've just referred to; when measured by EEG it shows that the brain is very active, more or less as active as during waking. The other principle features are that whilst the brain is thus activated, the eyes move around in a saccadic fashion. These are the 'rapid eye movements' which eventually became the name of this physiological state. Its third major feature is that you basically are paralysed. You lose all muscle tone below the neck during this state. There are other things about it too, changes in body temperature, breathing, heart rate and what not, but those three are the cardinal features, the ones by which we identify whether one is or is not in REM sleep.

I said this happens every ninety minutes or so during sleep; it takes up (in total) roughly twenty percent of your sleeping hours. The paradox that I referred to, contrasting the fact that physically one is resting and yet one's brain is in a highly active state, is matched of course by a psychological paradox: that when we go to sleep, we close down our minds and yet, as we all know, this unconscious state of sleep is punctuated by moments of great mental activity, great mental excitement, this being what we know as dreams. So it's not surprising that Azerinsky and Kleitman, the researchers in Chicago that I referred to earlier, on discovering paradoxical sleep, had the idea that perhaps this physiological state coincided with the psychological state of dreaming; and they then sought, being of the same cultural background as me (natural scientists), to test this hypothesis. And the way that they tested it was to wake people up during REM sleep and during non-REM sleep, during the other eighty percent of sleep when the brain is quiet. And what they found they took to be confirmation of their hypothesis: they found that roughly ninety percent of the time, when you awaken a human being from REM sleep, they will report a dream to you. By contrast, roughly ten percent of the time, when you awaken a human being from non-REM sleep, they will report a dream. This is a vast difference, ninety percent versus ten percent. It's about as close as you could hope to get to a perfect correlation between

REM sleep and dreaming, bearing in mind that your research subject is asleep and we all know how difficult it is to remember dreams, so you can't expect a hundred percent of REM awakenings to produce dream reports and nought percent of the non-REM awakenings to do so. And so it came to be generally accepted wisdom that dreaming is the psychological equivalent of REM sleep, REM sleep is the physiological equivalent of dreaming; they are, or were, considered to be literally the same thing.

It's not only, as it turns out, us human beings who have this physiological state; all mammals (bar one, a strange Australian creature) have REM sleep. This presented a great opportunity to neuroscience because the theoretical importance of dreaming, due largely to people in the psychologies and in psychoanalysis in particular, dreaming had come to occupy quite an important place theoretically, also in psychiatry and cognate disciplines. So the discovery of a physiological marker, a physiological equivalent of the dreaming state, was really grasped with great enthusiasm, and the intention immediately was to identify what the brain mechanisms were that generated this physical state. Now that we had an objective physiological state defined by those three criteria all we had to do was find what in the brain makes us have this state, and then we would have understood something terribly important about how dreams are generated, which would presumably have significant implications for our theories about dreaming and their meaning (or lack of it) and their function.

The fact that animals other than humans had the same state, especially in the 1950s when ethical concerns were not quite what they are aiming towards today, presented the opportunity of being able to chop the brain up and see what happens if you remove this bit or you remove that bit from some non-human creature; does it prevent them from dreaming? The race was on to find which part of the brain makes this REM state. It started with the work of a man named Jouvet on cats (he chose cats as his particular victims). He sliced the brain going further and further down the neuraxis, one slice at a time, wanting to see at what point the slice would remove the critical bit, and make the cat no longer able to dream. He sliced right down to the diencephalon, separating the entire forebrain from the brainstem, and found (I don't know if it was to his surprise or not), that the cat continued to have normal REM sleep. Therefore whatever it is that generates dreams must be in the brainstem. He continued to slice and it was only once he got right down into the pons that the REM state started to falter and ultimately to stop. Jouvet's conclusion was that dreams are generated from here, from a very primitive, lowly part of the brain, in fact a part of the brain that we share with all reptiles. This part of the brain has no known, no recognizable mental function. It is at the level of brain mechanism that regulates heartbeat and the like: a very, very basic part of the brain. It doesn't have anything to do with motivations, with wishes, with memories, with embarrassments at all. Combining this with the fact that it switches dreams on regularly, automatically, every ninety minutes, you can see why I said at the outset that all psychologists and psychiatrists with an interest in dreams were put on the back foot by these findings. It was left to a student of Jouvet's by the name of Hobson to finish the job. He identified precisely which nuclei within the pons switch REM sleep on and precisely which ones switch REM off. I'm going to have to quickly tell you what these nuclei are because they become major characters in the story that I'm going to proceed to tell you. There's an area called the mesopontine tegmentum, which when you go into REM sleep switches on dramatically: the neurons fire at an extremely rapid rate, and they release, upwards, via the long axons into the forebrain, a chemical called acetylcholine. You have to remember that one, acetylcholine. While this area is switched on, there are two other areas called the dorsal raphe and the nucleus locus coeruleus, which switch off. Their firing rates dramatically plummet. And as a result of this, the level of two other chemicals which would normally be released in the forebrain, goes right down. Those chemicals are noradrenalin (if you're American it's norepinephrine), and serotonin. So the level of these chemicals goes down due to the dropping firing rate of those nuclei, and the other chemical, acetylcholine, goes up due to the increased firing rate of that nucleus; and it is as simple as that. It's a very simple switch. And that, according to Hobson's very elegant, thorough scientific work is what generates dreams. Really, I mean it, not sarcastically, when I say very elegant, very thorough research. It was proven by Hobson, beyond a shadow of doubt, that REM is switched on by acetylcholine and switched off by serotonin and noradrenalin, due to this reciprocal interaction between these two very primitive nuclei in the brainstem. He went on to draw conclusions for people like yourselves, he said, 'Cholinergic brainstem mechanisms cause REM sleep and dreaming, therefore they have no primary ideational, volitional or emotional content', because that part of the brain as I said to you doesn't generate things like ideas, wishes or feelings. 'Automatic, mindless, intrinsically meaningless' was the conclusion that Hobson's research led us to. That was 1977, and since then the neuroscientific world could not possibly take seriously any psychological account of what causes dreams; any psychological view of the mechanism of the meaning of dreaming was severely question-able in the neurosciences from that date onwards. And, I might add, this gave Hobson great pleasure.

Now twenty years later, your speaker did a piece of research in which he did a strange thing. He decided that he would speak to his patients and ask them about their experiences after different parts of their brains had been damaged, not by him but by natural forces outside of his control. I thought: maybe we'll learn something by asking these patients about how their dreams are changed by damage to different parts of the brain. I did this with three hundred and sixty-five patients. Definite patterns emerged which I don't have time to go through with you in detail; I will just focus on three particular findings, but before I do that, I want to tell you that damage to various parts of the brain caused distinctive changes in the quality of their dreaming. I don't have time to describe all of them to you, but the thing that's important is that some parts of the brain do specific things in dreaming and other parts of the brain do nothing in dreaming, and the parts that do things in dreaming do different things from each other.

The important thing, before I go into telling you the three main findings that arose out of my study, that I should've said to you a few minutes ago and will quickly catch up on, is this: Hobson's view of how dreams are generated by the mechanism that I outlined for you, was called the 'activation synthesis model'. According to the activation synthesis model, the forebrain (the thinking, feeling, wishing part of the brain, the mental part of the brain), is activated by this cholinergic switch that I mentioned earlier. Because it's been activated broadly (not by anything meaningful, not by any actual event in the outside world, but because it represents the outside world) it generates thoughts, memories, ideas and the like; it starts to have them randomly and meaninglessly. It then connects them up with each other because what else can it do? And this is the dream. That was Hobson's activation synthesis theory. The forebrain has been activated in an inherently meaningless, random fashion, thereby generating inherently meaning-less, random sensations, perceptions, memories, feelings and the like, and all that it can do, poor thing, is join them together, and there you have the dream, and no surprise under the circumstances that dreams should be so disjointed, so irrational and so senseless. Already the pattern that I'm describing to you begins to not quite fit with that view because as I have just said to you, different parts of the brain tend to do very definite things and other parts do nothing much at all during dreaming. This doesn't fit with a random activation of the forebrain, but I must not digress too much.

The three things that I found, that I'm going to focus on, are the following. The pons, which I introduced to you just now, is the part of the brain that generates REM sleep. I had eighteen patients with lesions there, and I had six of them who were sufficiently lucid to be able to reliably tell me about their mental experience. These six patients all reported, as if it was the most obvious thing in the world that, of course, they do still dream. This came as a great shock to me because the ABC's of behavioural neurology, the ABC's of cognitive neuroscience, stipulate that if a particular part of the brain performs a particular function, then when you damage that part of the brain, that function should falter, if not disappear. I've already said with regard to REM sleep that that has been demonstrated. It's been shown with all manner of mammals, rats, cats, and human beings, that damage to that part of the brain indeed leads to a loss of REM sleep. What nobody had thought of doing before this study though, bizarre as it may seem (and it was only in the doing of it that I realized that nobody had done this before), was to actually ask these patients whether they dreamt or not. There's a particular bias in my field which I think might be becoming apparent to you. So, upon finding that my patients, whom I did think of speaking to, were dreaming (and indeed even dreaming when woken up in the sleep laboratory; every possibility was given to get them to not dream and tell us so), I went back to the literature. There is a gigantic literature on REM sleep, it is really fair to call it an industry, and it has never been demonstrated, ever, that loss of REM sleep or damage to that part of the brain leads to a cessation of dreaming. It's an absolutely astonishing omission. That's my first finding.

The second finding pertains to the white matter at the bottom part of the frontal lobes of your brain; it's sort of behind your eyes near the middle. Nine patients of mine had damage to this part of the brain and stopped dreaming completely. Nine is not a large number, but there you have it. These patients were quite clear that they no longer dream; they used to dream, they don't dream any more. I put them in a sleep laboratory. They continue to have REM sleep, but when you wake them up from REM sleep, they report no dreams. This is called a double dissociation: if you take these two findings together, the first one and the second one, what it means is there's a part of the brain which, when damaged, leads to a loss of REM sleep with preservation of dreaming and there's another part of the brain which, when damaged, leads to loss of dreaming with preservation of REM sleep. That means these are two different things; they are doubly dissociable from each other. This is a paradigmatic method in the neurosciences for establishing whether two functions are separate or not identical. This proves beyond a shadow of doubt that REM sleep and dreaming are two separate things.

The third finding that I want to point to relates to patients with damage to what is called dorsolateral prefrontal cortex. These patients, despite having substantial and significant brain lesions which greatly affected their ability to think and behave normally, had absolutely no change in their dreams. If you take the dream reports of these patients and give them to blind raters together with dream reports of people like you and me with more or less intact brains, they are unable to distinguish the two groups from each other. So this part of the brain has no role to play in dreams, it is involved only in the negative sense that we were able to show for this particular part of the brain, absolutely no effect on dreaming.

OK, so what I've just done is give you the second section of my talk, the proof that we were wrong. The identification of dreaming with REM sleep was a mistake. Therefore everything that we learnt about the physiology and anatomy of REM sleep is all well and good, but it doesn't tell us anything about dreaming, because dreaming has a different mechanism. This mechanism co-activates with REM sleep, but is in fact separate from it, and in the interests of time I will resist the urge to underline that in various verbal ways and just take it that you've got that point.

I now move onto the third section of my presentation which is: well, what does cause dreams? If it's not REM sleep, then what is it? Before I go onto that, I'll just make a sort of bridging comment. Once we look again at the findings of Jouvet and Hobson and the whole industry that grew around the phenomenon of REM sleep, certain things spring out now as having great significance which at the time were sort of overlooked if not actually brushed under the carpet. And I am drawing your attention to these because I think it really does say something about our hallowed cannons of natural science, in terms of how it really works. When we looked back again at this gross mistake that we made in thinking that REM sleep was the same thing as dreaming, and therefore that the parts of the brain that generate REM sleep must be the parts of the brain that generate dreams; once we had decided this (on the basis of that correlation study from the 1950s), we then moved on to studying only animals who can't speak and who could therefore never give any evidence of any kind to the topic of dreaming. We wanted to look only at the objective facts, at the material facts, and you know, you do that at a certain risk, it carries a certain price. It was only when I did the same sort of study on human beings who can speak that the error emerged.

Looking back then at the previous assumption that dreaming was identical with REM sleep because of this ninety-ten distinction, this near perfect correlation between REM and dream reports: When I look back at the old data, striking things emerge and I want to tell you about one of them. I said that about twenty percent of your sleeping time is REM sleep, which means eighty percent of your sleeping time is non-REM sleep. If you wake somebody up during REM sleep and you get ninety percent dream reports and you wake them up during non-REM sleep and you get ten percent dream reports, it sounds almost, as I said, like a hundred to nought; but it doesn't take account of the fact that you spend four times more hours in non-REM sleep than in REM sleep. If you do exactly the same sum with a different spin (and I grant you that both ways of doing it turns out to be spin), and you say: OK, let's take all the dreams and see how many of them occur during REM sleep and how many of them occur during non-REM sleep, you're being a little bit more fair to the non-REM sleep because it takes up four times more of the hours, and what you find is that just over twenty percent of all dreams occur in non-REM sleep. It starts to sound a little bit less perfect, that correlation. If you take all dreams that occur during a night, twenty percent of them occur during non-REM sleep. Maybe REM and dreaming are not so identical after all. Then you look at those non-REM dreams and see where they occur during sleep; they don't occur randomly throughout the night, most of them occur just after you've fallen asleep, ninety minutes before you go into your first REM phase, or at the end of sleep, in the late morning, so the longer you sleep, the more dreams you have in non-REM sleep. So the picture that emerges is one, not of dreaming equals REM sleep, but rather that one dreams straight after one falls asleep, then one dreams during one's REM phases, and then one dreams before one wakes up in the morning. So it's not the unique physiological signature of REM sleep that gives us dreams, perhaps, but rather anything that might be described as a relative state of arousal (just fallen asleep, about to wake up and REM are all states of arousal). So when you have something disturbing your sleep, during this time you dream. That seems like a more fair description of the facts that were in fact available to us even before I did this study that made me realize there was something fundamentally wrong with the old view. Those facts were available but just looked at in a particular way, or in many cases just not looked at at all.

So now we come to the question, this third part of my presentation: what then is generating dreams? I said to you that I had nine patients with damage in the ventromesial frontal white matter. Nine patients I regret to tell you is not enough. It's not enough to overturn a theory that's dominated a field for twenty years, if not forty years. So, what could I do?

Unfortunately, the brain doesn't frequently damage itself in that area on both sides simultaneously, which is what was necessary to produce this loss of dreaming. I, unlike Jouvet and Hobson, didn't feel inclined to damage more patients brains so that I could see whether the finding was reliable, but on looking at those nine brain scans, something popped out of my memory, which is that once upon a time in psychiatry we did use to inflict lesions on people's brains and it was as a matter of fact in this exact area, the old prefrontal leucotomy. This procedure was performed with gay abandon on many thousands of people in the 50s and 60s, and a sort of smattering in the 40s and 70s too. These were patients who were seriously mentally ill. The operation was done predominantly on patients who had positive psychotic symptoms, that is to say hallucinations and delusions, because it was found that if you produce a lesion in this part of the brain deliberately, you have a very good chance of reducing if not absolutely stopping the patients' hallucinations and delusions. That's why this operation was done. It also had other effects, one of which struck me because I noticed this other effect in my nine patients too. The other effect was that the patients became sort of apathetic, indifferent, inert, aspontaneous, avolitional, they kind of lost their spark. This is well known from 'One Flew over the Cuckoo's Nest' for example, the Indian chap when he came back had lost his zest for life. I went back to the literature on this psycho-surgical procedure which was performed literally on thousands of people with my heart in my mouth, if that's the right expression, wanting to see what was said about these patients' dreams, because these studies were done in the 50s when people still talked to their patients about dreams, if they were psychiatrists. I was sure that if what I'd found in my nine patients was valid, that somebody would have noticed it before. I was not disappointed. In the very large studies of Schindler in Germany, of Partridge in England and of Frank in America, they all reported the same thing. That this operation leads to reduction in hallucinations and delusions, it leads to a reduction in general motivation, and it leads to a cessation of dreaming. So another fact was out there for decades and yet somehow excluded from the official picture that dominated my science. In fact Schindler and another colleague named Müller both observed that when the operation has been done, if the patient carries on dreaming, it's a bad prognostic sign, it means the operation is probably not going to work. And then if you think about that for a moment, you begin to see something that I think is rather important. You realize dreams are a form of hallucination and delusion, and it's not so surprising that an operation that prevents people from being able to hallucinate and delude themselves anymore, also deprives them of the ability to dream.

So I took this as my point of entry into trying to understand what it was about this part of the brain that was so important for dreaming. This part of the brain has many different fibre pathways coursing through it, it was far from clear what was the essential mechanism that I'd identified in finding that this part of the brain was crucial for the ability to dream. Needless to say there were different opinions about which one of these many fibre pathways was the critical one, and needless to say Hobson had a very definite opinion. He didn't dispute the finding, but he gave it a different spin. His interpretation was: well we all know that there are cholinergic pathways that course through this part of the brain, we also know that there are some nuclei down here which are cholinergic called the basal forebrain nuclei. It was surely the cholinergic pathways, according to Hobson, which had been lesioned which led to the cessation of dreaming. This was a rather desperate attempt to save the old theory. I'll just quickly tell you; I studied a group of patients who had damage to precisely those cholinergic nuclei, and what happened to them was they dreamed a hell of a lot more than normal. In fact many of them dreamed constantly throughout sleep, in fact many of them I'm afraid to say dreamed even when they were awake. It was the exact opposite of the prediction one would make from Hobson's interpretation, and that's the value of this way of approaching the mind. You can make predictions and you can test them. So we tested Hobson's prediction, first of all by drawing to his attention this group of patients who were cholinergically deprived and in fact had more dreams. We then gave anti-cholinergics to normal subjects to see what would happen to their dreams, in other words we reduced their acetylcholine and what we found was the same as the lesioned patients, they dreamed a hell of a lot more and had the entertaining phenomenon of dreaming while awake too. So clearly it's not the cholinergic pathway that's the critical one. I'm not going to go systematically through all of the possibilities, that's the one I want to highlight because that was Hobson's view, and now I'll tell you what my view was and what it led me to.

There is another pathway coursing through this part of the brain, it's a dopaminergic pathway; the chemical released by these neurons is dopamine. I thought it might be dopamine that's the important one because, as I said to you, there seemed to be an important link between positive psychotic symptoms and dreaming, and we knew that positive psychotic symptoms could be reduced with dopamine blockers. Dopamine blockade is the essence of what antipsychotic drugs do, all antipsychotic drugs more or less, first and foremost block dopamine in this system. This is where the damage is in patients who can't dream. So I tested my hypothesis that this is the system that's generating dreams by giving patients dopamine agonists, increasing the activity of that system, and giving them dopamine antagonists, decreasing activity in that system. And what I found was dopamine blockers lead to a gross reduction in dreaming and dopamine boosters lead to a great increase in dreaming. Dopamine seems to be causally manipulable of dreaming. In fact if you give normal subjects dopamine, they not only have more dreams, they also have more emotional dreams, they also have more bizarre dreams, they also have more nightmares. Everything about 'dreamness' increases with dopamine. It has no simultaneous effect on REM sleep, again underscoring the dissociation between these two things. Colleagues of mine measured the activity of these dopominergic neurons during dreaming versus non-dreaming sleep, and found that they are massively active during dreaming sleep. In fact these neurons stay active throughout the night, unlike all the other amminergic systems which vary greatly according to whether you're asleep or awake, and which phase of sleep you're in, these dopaminergic ones don't care, they just keep going. They keep going at the same rate when you're asleep as when you're awake. That's important and I'll come back to it. Other colleagues also did microdialysis studies, looking at dopamine release at the terminal ends of this system, and we found it was maximal during dreaming sleep. There is more dopamine released during dreaming sleep than at any other time of the day, including active wakefulness. So the evidence points strongly to the view that it's this system, this dopamine system that generates dreams.

By the way, in PET imaging, a positron emission tomography images of the human brain during dreaming, that same pattern that emerged in my lesion studies, emerges also in the functional imaging studies. The same structures that were important when they were damaged, that caused changes in dreams, those are the ones that are activated during dreaming sleep, and the dorsolateral prefrontal convexity, the part that I said when damaged has no effect on dreams, it's not switched on during PET imaging of dreams. So there was a wonderful coming together of the lesion findings and the functional imaging findings. I am now going to focus on this system in order to move onto the last bit of my talk, or heading towards the last by asking: well, what is it about this part of the brain that is so critical for dreaming?

I've summarized for you the evidence that this is the critical part of the brain, this is the system that is at issue, now the question is: what does this system do? Because clearly whatever this part of the brain does is very important for what dreams are, and all the interesting psychological questions that concern us relate to this. Well, we know this system very well, anatomists call it the mesocortical-mesolimbic dopamine system, and functional neurobiologists call it by different names; it's very well known to animal neurobiologists because this system exists in all mammals, not only in us, all mammals right down to mice have exactly this same structure as we do. And it works in the same way, releases dopamine in the same parts of the brain, starts in the same part of the brain, has fibre pathways connecting the same parts of the brain. My favourite term for this area, this structure, this system, is the 'seeking' system. This is what Jaak Panksepp calls it, the 'seeking' system. Kent Berridge calls it the 'wanting' system, Edmund Rolls calls it the 'reward' system, others call it the 'expectancy' system, or the 'curiosity' system. You get a common denominator of all these terms: seeking, wanting, rewarding, expecting, interest, curiosity; this tells you what this system does. We know what this system does so well because, as I said, all our mammalian cousins have it, and a great many experiments have been done to see what happens if this system is damaged, or if it is stimulated.

It is, in a word, a motivational system. What I'm summarizing for you now is the generally accepted view. This system is bequeathed to us by our ancestors in a deep sense of the word. This system

evolved in early mammalian evolution, and was preserved through the
millennia because it does a very important job, which greatly enhances
our chances of surviving to reproduce. Which is why those of our
ancestors who had this system passed it on to us, those of our ancestors who didn't have this system didn't pass on their genes and fell by
the wayside. What it does is this: whenever you have a need detected
by the hypothalamus need detectors, but also when you have a need
coming from above, a want, a desire, a hunger, an appetite, an urge of
any kind, it switches this system on. This system makes you go forth
and look in the world for what it is that you want. That's what it does.
It's a seeking system, a wanting system, a foraging system, a looking
about for a good time system, it's a sort of 'cruising' system, it makes
the animal perk up and think: I'm going to get what I want and it's out
there. It's not in me, I can't satisfy this want, it's out there, so go forth
and seek, that's what that system does. And so the mouse twitches
its whiskers, wags its tail, most important of all peddles along with
its feet, looking for something good, looking for a good time. Human
beings who have been naughty enough to snort cocaine will know
this state of mind very well. Cocaine activates this system beautifully.
There's a party tonight, I'm gonna be there, if anything good happens,
I'm gonna be there, and I'm going to be interacting with everybody,
I've got a sort of slight positive expectation, I'm there, I'm there, hi, hi,
interact with me, talk with me, I'm sort of randy. That sort of feeling
is what's generated by activation of this system. Now, you see why
damage to this system makes people lose all interest in the world? I
won't, due to lack of time, go into why it should be that over-activity
of this system pushes us into psychotic states, and indeed it does; this
is unequivocally the case. What I will just say is this: is it not a curious
fact that this system stays active throughout sleep? Bear in mind what
it does. It motivates us, makes us have positive expectations, and
most important of all makes us go out into the world and do things,
interact with other objects, in the hope that they'll meet our needs,
in the belief and expectation that they'll meet our needs. This system
which makes you do that is fully active throughout sleep, and it is even
most active during dreaming sleep, and when it's damaged you can't
dream anymore.

Here we have a new paradox, and I think this begins to point to one
of the possible functions of dreaming. Instead of waking up and going
out into the world and going to a party, you have a dream. The dream
occurs instead of this foraging or cruising in the outside world. This is
a speculation, but it coincides with far more facts than the old speculation, which is that dreams are meaningless, random noise. If the brain
is activated, it doesn't generate dreams, by itself: that sleep onset
effect and that late morning effect and those REM effects that I mentioned, these times during sleep when we have most of our dreams by

themselves, this relative activation of the brain is not enough to cause us to dream, because if this one system is damaged, despite all those things remaining intact, we don't dream. So you have to have activation plus appetitive interest, activation plus motivation; the activation has to attract motivational interest, then you can have a dream. So the view that I am led to, is that, dreaming is a kind of imaginary acting, it's a kind of imaginary motivated behaviour, it's a kind of doing something in your internal world rather than having to do it in the outside world. It's having an imaginary kind of seeking, wanting, cruising and whatnot. Dreams are a kind of motivated behaviour occurring in virtual reality, rather than in actual reality. Certainly, at the very best, it would have to be concluded that dreams are a motivated mental state, and that there's every reason to believe that they tell you something about the wants and desires and interests of the dreamer.

I realize there are many possible interpretations that can be put on my findings, and I don't want to make the mistakes of the past. What we have to do is test the different alternatives, compare them with each other and see which one is right. I'll just give you one example of an alternative hypothesis, it might be that what we humans do, or what we mammals do during dreaming is search our minds, search our memories, seek things in our minds. It might be some kind of motivated doing things with your memories, doing things with your thoughts, not necessarily an 'instead of' in the outside world. All of these things are possible, but as I said, for natural science, we have to formulate a prediction which we can test in order to start sifting through these different possibilities, and the prediction that arises or one prediction that arises from my hypothesis is that if you cannot dream, then you cannot stay asleep. So anything that disturbs your sleep significantly when you cannot dream will lead you to wake up, rather than what the dream normally does, which is allow you to stay asleep and do the thing in the privacy of your mind. In a word, patients who can't dream should suffer sleep maintenance insomnia, and we're now doing a study to test that hypothesis, and so far we've had three patients whom we've tested in this way. Three patients who cannot dream due to brain lesions, and we find that these three patients have dramatic sleep maintenance insomnia. They have great difficulty staying asleep. Usually they spend between thirty to forty percent of the night awake, and usually the awakenings come during the REM phases. So I'm hopeful that we're going to finally button down an answer to this question as to why we dream, what the function of dreaming is.

But whatever the function of dreaming turns out to be, the important thing is we now have a paradigm for testing any hypothesis. Anything that you say dreams contribute, what they're there for, what they do, we can look in the patients who are no longer able to dream and see whether they are deficient in regard to this thing. So that, my dear colleagues, is what we thought we knew about dreams, how we realized we were wrong, what we then started to think about dreams and where I think it's leading us to and some of the implications for our broader field. Thank you very much indeed.

Response to Mark Solms' Presentation on 'Brain Mechanisms of Dreaming'

Margaret Wilkinson
UK (SAP)

Abstract

In this response to Mark Solms' paper I will discuss the nature and role of dream and the dreaming process and the long-running debate between dream researchers such as Hobson, whose large-scale studies have focused on dreaming that occurs in REM sleep, and Dr Solms' research into dreaming. I assert that insights from contemporary neuroscience support rather than contest Jung's view that emotional truth, not censorship or disguise, underpins the dreaming process.

I discuss the large scale evidence-based research that reveals that dreaming is caused by brain activity during sleep that is both biochemically and regionally different from that of waking states and asserts that dreams are the mind's vehicle for the processing of emotional states of being. Dream sleep is also understood as being the guardian of memory, playing a part in forgetting and encoding memory.

* * *

Introduction

I thank Dr Solms for his enlightening and creative presentation. Driver reminds us that neuroscientists are, in many ways, asking the same questions that we do as therapists: 'what is going on inside, what are the inner connections, what are the inner conflicts, what are the inner conversations?' (Driver 2006). It is these issues that I wish to address as I focus on the mechanisms of dreaming and Dr Solms' presentation. Dr Solms wanted to speak 'out of the moment' at the Congress. Having heard his paper I am now able to respond with some thoughts concerning its content. Underpinning Dr Solms' presentation is the long-running debate between dream researchers such as Hobson, whose large-scale studies have focused on dreaming that occurs in REM sleep, and Dr Solms' research on the dreaming process in patients with varying types of brain damage.

The Dreaming Process

Dr Solms focused our attention on the significance of non-REM dream sleep. ['90-95% of awakenings from REM sleep produce dream reports, whereas only 5-10% of awakenings from NREM produce equivalent reports' (Solms & Turnbull 2002, p. 183)]. Solms' argument is supported by evidence from sleep laboratory awakenings demonstrating that at least 10% of NREM reports are similar in their form and contents to reports from REM awakenings, which is enough to reject the tight relationship between REM and dreaming originally emphasized by Hobson (Domhoff 2005). Dr Solms suggested that dreaming is generated by a different mechanism from the one that generates REM sleep. He understands the activation of the dopaminergic mechanism to be crucial to the generation of the dream state in all sleep states. This is the hormone that activates the seeking system of the mind-brain being (Panksepp 1998). Solms surmises that REM only causes dreaming via the intermediary of this motivational mechanism. Thus he significantly posits that a continuous thought process during sleep is converted into dreaming by an arousal stimulus. He concludes that such a stimulus has much in common with the Freudian view of dreaming. As early as 1968 Kirsch drew attention to the significance of dream research for the Jungian analytic community, urging 'the need for a reassessment of our psychological understanding of dreams based on the recent research' (Kirsch 1968, p. 1462). As we heed his words and look at the broader spectrum of research it becomes clear that we need not automatically reach the rather Freudian conclusions that Dr Solms offered us at the Congress.

Key chemicals in the brain are thought to influence the dreaming process and the debate concerning clarity or censorship as the purpose of the dream rages around their relative roles. The exact nature of these preoccupies both Hobson and Solms, two of the main protagonists in the field; however they reach very different conclusions. Hobson emphasizes that in waking states the noradrenergic and serotinergic systems are on and the cholinergic system is damped, and that in REM sleep just the opposite pertains, that is the noradrenergic and serotinergic systems are damped and the cholinergic system is dominant. Hobson and Pace-Schott, as a result of large scale studies focused on REM sleep, conclude that REM dreaming consciousness contrasts with waking consciousness in that the brain is activated in a 'bottom-up' manner rather than the 'top-down' mode of waking thought. They argue that in dreaming ascending activity begins in the brain stem, progresses through the limbic system, reaching the medial frontal cortex (that deals with arousal and attention). They note that the executive portions of the frontal cortex (i.e. the dorso-lateral cortex and the orbito prefrontal cortex) are deactivated. They conclude: 'dreaming cognition is bizarre because of the loss of the organizing capacity of the brain, not because of an elaborate disguise mechanism that rids an internal stimulus of an unacceptable meaning' (Hobson & Pace-Schott 1999, p. 211). Hobson's early understanding of brain stem activity as having an intrinsically chaotic influence on the cortex has been rejected by several prominent critics, including Solms, who argue that he underestimates the degree of cortical control over the dreaming process (Jones 2000; Domhoff 2005).

Solms, a long-time critic of Hobson, as we have seen, marshalled a strong defence for the classical Freudian view of the dream. He stressed the importance of the activation of the dopamine circuit in the brain at the time of dreaming and argued that it is this, rather than the dominance of the cholinergic system, that gives rise to all peculiar states of dream-like experience including actual dreaming. He suggested that this activates the seeking circuit that is characterized by curiosity and eagerness causing the sleeping ego to protest against the seeming wish fulfilment of the dream state.

Meaning not Madness

Both Hobson and Solms have likened dream-states to psychotic states: Solms draws attention to the functional anatomy of dreaming as 'almost identical to that of schizophrenic psychosis' (Solms & Turnbull 2002, p. 213). Hobson, in his early work, emphasized the bizarre characteristics of dream sleep, similar to states of delirium, but as a result of more recent research he now urges the therapist to ignore the bizarreness and instead to attend to the 'emotionally salient concerns' of the dreamer's mind that are revealed through the dreaming process. As Jung commented, 'Dreams do not deceive, they do not lie, they do not distort or disguise, but naïvely announce what they are and what they mean … they are invariably seeking to express something that the ego does not know and does not understand' (Jung 1946, para. 189).

Domhoff, a rigorous critic of both Hobson and Solms, argues that the best starting point for gaining an insight into the nature of actual everyday dreaming is in the sleep laboratory, where immediate awakenings from REM and NREM provide the maximum possibility of accurate recall (Domhoff 2005). He examines several large-scale studies for bizarreness and intensity of emotion, all of which failed to find significant evidence of these. He concludes that dreams have more in common with stories than with psychosis. Domhoff argues that some of both men's 'speculations concerning the neurophysiology of dreaming are as questionable as their beliefs about dream content' (2005, p. 4). His strongest criticism is reserved for the way in which both depend solely on neurophysiological arguments and ignore the information that is available from the large-scale studies of dream content (Wilkinson, in press).

Braun, in reviewing the wider debate in the light of his own and other research findings, also argues that neither the cholinergic nor the dopaminergic hypothesis will prove conclusively to be an adequate explanation of the dreaming process (Braun 1999, pp. 196-200). He warns against an 'either' 'or' approach to understanding the chemical aspects of the dreaming process and emphasizes the common ground amongst the protagonists, stressing that 'the activation of the limbic system, in the absence of top-down control by the frontal cortex, provides a context in which salient memories and emotions are manifest' (Braun 1999, p. 198).

Siegel also argues that:

> one must not view the rest of the brain as merely a passive responder to a REM sleep-state generated in the pons and caudal midbrain; instead, present evidence suggests a dynamic interaction between the forebrain and pons in molding the structure and timing of PGO spikes and the other "phasic" events of REM sleep and, in all likelihood, the dream imagery of REM sleep.
>
> (Siegel 2000, p. 121, cited in Domhoff 2005)

Sleep as the Servant of Predictive Patterns in the Mind

Bar-Yam (1993) suggests that the temporary subdivision of the brain during sleep enables a selective re-learning process to take place that in turn permits the development of predictive patterns in the mind. The fundamental motivation for subdivision of the brain is the need to generalize experiences by isolating aspects that may recur in other contexts. Here we have the grounding for the rich experience that occurs in the transference and the countertransference. Such selective re-learning also results in a selective forgetting of information that prevents the mind-brain being stretched beyond its limits (Wilkinson, in press).

Conclusion: Meaning, Metaphor and Patterning

One might ask whether there is any common ground amongst the researchers? What has become increasingly clear is that dreams have meaning, and that as Dr Solms has explained non-REM sleep has as significant a part to play in our understanding of the dreaming-process as REM sleep. I would like to emphasize that, with Braun, we should assume that the meaning of the dream is mapped on its surface, not disguised and in need of decoding; indeed Braun himself comments that he is rather inclined to agree with Jung, who said, 'I am doubtful whether we can assume a dream is something other than it appears to be' (Jung 1938, para. 41). I conclude that, as clinicians, we should take note of Jung's recommendation, we should appreciate that

> The 'manifest' dream picture is the dream itself and contains the whole meaning of the dream … What Freud calls the 'dream-façade' is the dream's obscurity, and this is really only a projection of our own lack of understanding … We say that the dream has a false front only because we fail to see into it.
>
> (Jung 1954, para. 319)

Braun and his associates note that REM sleep constitutes in the cortex a unique condition of information processing, functionally isolated from input from the external world or output to it. The dream is therefore in a unique way the expression of the internal, the intra-psychic world of the dreamer (Braun 1999). Hartmann stresses that 'as we move along our continuum from focused waking thought to dreaming, our mental processes become increasingly metaphoric' (Hartmann 2000, pp. 69-70). He argues that a dream provides 'the explanatory metaphor for the dominant emotion or concern of the dreamer' (ibid.). The dreaming mind-brain's use of emergent metaphor allows the possibility of an encounter between conscious and unconscious, such as Jung envisaged; such an encounter with the symbolic facilitates the individuation process. Jung likened the dream to a theatre in which 'the dreamer is himself the scene, the player, the prompter, the producer, the author, the public and the critic (Jung 1960, para. 509). The dreaming mind-brain uses imagery to process emotional states of mind that are implicit, not yet available to consciousness, and which seek to emerge, through the dream, into consciousness where they may be thought about. Despite the amnesia associated with dreaming, it has become clear that dreaming has a vital role to play in the affective organization of memory. Reiser draws our attention to 'the principle of affective organization of memory' (Reiser 1999, p. 203). He explains

> Each of us carries within the mind-brain an enduring network of stored memories encoded by images … perceived during significant emotional life experiences. Such images and the memories they encode are associationally linked by a shared potential to evoke identical or highly similar complexes of emotion. Such networks are organized around a core of perceptual images or part images that encode memories of early events.
>
> (Reiser 1999, p. 203)

The work of Rossi (2004) and Ribeiro (2004) stresses the value of dreams and the dreaming process in respect of memory. Both emphasize the importance of the zif-268 gene, a learning-related gene devoted to experience-dependent strengthening of synaptic connections that is released in the dreaming state (Ribeiro 2004, p. 7). I suggest that the plasticity of the brain in response to the experiences of the day is central to an understanding of the value of dreams and their contribution towards the restructuring of the internal world.

I give the last word to Panksepp. He argues that REM sleep permits information-processing whereby transient memory stores become integrated into subconscious behavioural habits, adding 'Perhaps the dream theories of Freud and Jung, which suggested dreams reflect unconscious and symbolic emotional forces affecting an individual, may still hold some basic truths' (Panksepp 1998, p. 129). He concludes REM sleep may help

> to solidify the many unconscious habits that are the very foundation of our personality. In the final accounting dreams may construct the powerful subconscious or preconscious affective psychological patterns that make us ... the people that we are. They may help construct the many emotional myths and beliefs around which our lives revolve.
>
> (Panksepp 1998, p. 142)

References

Bar-Yam, Y. (1993) 'Sleep as temporary brain dissociation'. NECSI Research Report YB-0005, http://necsi.org

Braun, A. (1999) 'Commentary on the new neuropsychology of sleep', *Neuro-psychoanalysis*, 1, 2.

Domhoff, G.W. (2005) 'Refocusing the Neurocognitive Approach to Dreams: A critique of the Hobson versus Solms Debate'. *Dreaming*, 15, 3-20.

Driver, C. (2006). 'Response to Margaret Wilkinson's paper 'Windows to the Mind: Contemporary Neuroscience: A Jungian Clinical Perspective'. Given at the Royal Society of Medicine, 7 October, 2006.

Hartmann, E, (2000). 'The psychology and physiology of dreaming. A new synthesis'. In Binghampton University Art Museum, *Dreams 1900-2000. Science, Art and the Unconscious Mind,* ed. E. Gamwell. New York: Cornell University Press.

Hobson, J.A. & Pace-Schott, E.F. (1999). 'Response to commentaries on the new neuropsychology of sleep: implications for neuropsychoanalysis'. *Neuropsychoanalysis*, 1, 2, 206-24.

Jones, B.E. (2000). 'The interpretation of physiology'. *Behavioural and Brain Sciences,* 23, 955-56

Jung, C.G. (1938/1958). *Terry Lectures. CW* 11.

–(1946). 'Analytical psychology and education'. *CW* 17.

–(1954). 'The practical use of dream-analysis'. *CW* 16.

–(1960). 'General aspects of dream psychology'. *CW* 8.

Kaplan-Solms, K. & Solms, M. (2000). *Clinical Studies in Neuro-Psychoanalysis. Introduction to a Depth Neuropsychology.* Connecticut: International Universities Press.

Kirsch, T.B. (1968). 'The relationship of the REM State to analytical psychology', *American Journal of Psychiatry*, 124, 1459-63.

Panksepp, J. (1998). *Affective Neuroscience. The Foundations of Human and Animal Emotions.* New York & Oxford: Oxford University Press.

Reiser, M.F. (1999). 'Commentary on the new neuropsychology of sleep', *Neuropsychoanalysis,* 1, 2, 196-206.

Ribeiro, S. (2004). 'Towards an evolutionary theory of sleep and dreams', *MultiCiência,* 3.

Rossi, E.L. (2004). 'Sacred spaces and places in healing dreams: gene expression and brain growth in rehabilitation'. *Psychological Perspectives,* 47, 1, 48-63.

Siegel, J. (2000). 'Brainstem mechanisms generating REM sleep'. *Principles and Practices of Sleep Medicine*, eds. M. Kryger, T. Roth & W. Dement. Philadelphia: Saunders, 3rd ed., 112-33.

Solms, M. & Turnbull, O. (2002). *The Brain and the Inner World. An Introduction to the Neuroscience of Subjective Relationship.* New York: Other Press.

Wilkinson, M.A. (2006). *Coming into Mind. The Mind-Brain Relationship: A Jungian Clinical Perspective.* Hove & New York: Brunner-Routledge.

– (in press). *Changing Minds. Neuroscience, Attachment and Trauma: A Clinical Perspective.* New York & London: Norton.

Friday, 17 August 2007

New Direction Home:
African Oracles and Analytic Attitudes

Sherry Salman
USA (JPA)

Abstract

The prophetic and oracular dimension of psychological process is integral to Jungian theory and our on-going vision of therapeutic action. Working constructs such as teleology, synchronicity, Self-processes, and the mythopoetic construction of narrative, support the ultimate concern with analysis as a meaning-making endeavour. At this juncture, we understand analysis within a model of unfolding field interactions between essentials, events, process, and imagination. This paper draws forth the clinical implications of the oracular tradition in Africa, as it pertains to this mosaic – to the transference field, the dynamics of interpretation and amplification, and the relationship of clinical process to culture and context.

As Jungians we explore both childhood fantasies, and psychoanalytic fantasies of childhood, not to recover memories or inner children, but rather to commune with the source, with origins and originators, creators, spirits, the entire trajectory of archetypal ancestry, or, as referenced in Africa, with the 'village of truth'. We listen to clinical narrative with an imaginal ear tuned to the essentials and potentials prevailing at the time of origin, in the present moment, and in the possible futures.

There has always been a diversity of different creative solutions across cultures to questions of psychological process and development. The African continent which so influenced Jung in relationship to both constructs (images of psychopathology) and process (alchemy), is extremely rich in oracular tradition. The intimate interplay between image, concept, affect, the realities of the moment, and the imagination of the future, combined with an image of truth as constructed and enigmatic, provide for the understanding of symbols and their enactments as symptoms, as both multi-dimensional and contained within the ever-increasing unity of the present moment. Both African oracular tradition and analytic process are quintessentially psychological: encompassing a pluralistic vision of the world and human character, implying a multiplicity of possibilities, choices, doubts, and solutions, with an eye to the unique circumstances of the moment and the individual.

* * *

Cut into stone over the front door of Jung's home is an inscription which translates: 'Called or not called, (the) god will be present', which he took from the Oracle at Delphi. Jung's vision of the psyche interiorized the gods without losing the numinous connection to the constructive and mythopoetic dimensions in psychological process. This was the *genius* of his theory and practice. The *genius* that came to rest in Jung could read the book of time forwards and backwards, backwards into collective and cultural memory, and forward into the prophetic possibilities of psyche's expression. This continuum of psyche's expression is fluid and 'emergent' … speaking through the grammar of mythopoesis, through myth-making and the ongoing creation of images and symbols.

The creative imagination, as it was glimpsed by Jung and the early psychoanalysts, had begun its move into the psyche, into symptoms, complexes and archetypal forms. Now the gods appear materialized outside as well: in our consumer culture and 'goods', cloaked yet fully present in our 'stuff', as well as in our personal and cultural sicknesses. They live in these places now, rather than in their temples and oracles. We can only assume that there is purpose and meaning in this shift of psyche's imagination, and acknowledge that the seemingly egalitarian movement to provide temporary housing for the gods in our diagnostic manuals and shopping malls is just that, no more and no less than temporary housing.

Our own psychoanalytic culture has not been exempt from this movement. We went through a period during which we were so afraid of being labelled a 'cult' or 'occult' that we were in danger of becoming inauthentic in our practice, sometimes hardly recognizable to ourselves. There is still an alarming absence in the clinical literature of what used to be called 'big dreams', even though we are living in a time of collective distress. It is as if what is most important is hidden, that what we do best as analysts is obscured, in plain sight, from our own view. Instead we become embroiled in a search for 'essentials', in both clinical practice and training, or give way to what Toshio Kawai (2006) called 'a casual relationship to truth'. Both these attitudes embody a breakdown of the mythopoetic imagination and are defences against it; compensatory 'correctives' of a sort, characteristic of post-modern cultures. The attempt to take refuge in fundamentalist doctrine, the nostalgic clinging to 'essentials', the privileging of subjectivity and the costume-parade of deconstructed images which it wears, the dissociative 'numbing' as imagination fragments into manic images, into endless 'spin', finally collapsing, exhausted, into what we say in the United States: 'whatever', and 'it's all good'. Sometimes it seems as if the portal into the mythopoetic sensibility and psyche's imagination which opened to Jung and the early psychoanalysts is now just a door … which is closing fast. But 'called or not called', the god is still present.

We found ourselves at a convocation of Jungian analysts in Africa, home of magic, witchcraft, and a rich oracular tradition, all of which resonates with analytic theory and practice. There is a trajectory which runs from Africa to alchemy and into Jung, a shared sensibility, a common ancestry. If we follow it, we re-enter the mythopoetic portal into psychological process, so central to our theory and praxis. Both the oracular tradition and psychoanalysis operate through the mythopoetic psyche, drawing on the field dynamics of affective possession, resonance, and interpretative amplification.

Oracle Figure. Senufo, Ivory Coast, 19thC. Metropolitan Museum of Art, NY, #4

There has always been a diversity of creative solutions across history and cultures to questions of psychological process and meaning, underneath all of them the archetypal play of cosmos and chaos, creation and destruction. As a way of both linking back and moving forward this text was originally accompanied by images of African oracles, many of which were part of an exhibition at the Metropolitan Museum of Art in New York, *Art and Oracle: African Art and Rituals of Divination* (LaGamma 2000). Because of space limitations, only a few could be reproduced here, but most can be accessed directly by linking to www.metmuseum.org/explore/oracle/index.html – the on-line Catalogue numbers are referenced in this text in [brackets].

When I began looking at these images they seemed both familiar and alien. This figure, for example, captures the compelling, yet highly enigmatic quality of African oracles. It's a type of oracle figure, about 3 feet tall, called 'he who speaks the truth', an invisible bush spirit, whose mana has been harnessed. Shrouded and bound, yet emanating energy from its head and feet, the figure expresses the power of archetypal structures to both bind and reveal psychic energy, and the dynamic and uneasy process by which those structures are mediated and translated.

As transitory and liminal experiences, stimulating the imagination to move beyond the limitations of what's fixed, both oracles and analysis also identify and cure disease and difficulty, address social conflict and moral dilemmas, communicate outside the boundaries of conscious awareness, probe destiny, and facilitate wholeness. Both bring unconscious process into play and into focus and endow it with value. Both speak the language of spirits and ancestral memory, signs, symptoms and symbols, dreams, and patterns. Especially patterns. We work towards pattern recognition as we listen to clinical narrative, tuned to the mythical time of origin, the present moment, and the possible futures. At the same time our 'bush souls' become affectively possessed and bound by the dynamisms which inhabit our patients, ourselves, and the world, partially and necessarily identified through *participation mystique*, synchronistically connected, also knowing by being, and being with.

Below is a schematic way of understanding some of the parallel dynamics as they function in both traditions. The predominant modalities in the oracular tradition are possession and interpretation, appealing to the affective and cognitive dimensions respectively. In the analytic, the modalities are better described as resonance and amplification respectively, these being 'other octaves' of the oracular modalities.

Mythopoetic Praxis

Oracular – possession (affective)
  interpretation (cognitive)
Analytic – resonance (affective)
  amplification (cognitive)

The prophetic and oracular dimension of unconscious process was integral to Jung's initial vision of both psyche and analysis. The initial working constructs of our method – teleology, synchronicity, and the Self – all supported the ultimate concern with analysis as a meaning-making endeavour with its functional origins in the imagination. The generation of analysts Jung trained approached 'the Unconscious' almost as an oracle, providing definitive direction to what they saw as the often-benighted conscious personality. This seemed to be an initial wide-stroke compensation to the reductive Freudian model. Historically, the agency of oracular process had been projected onto the action of 'spirits', presenting non-ego images through the oracle in an 'objective' form, provoking and expressing both anxiety and compelling curiosity (Adams 2006). Humanity's initial projections became psychological projects as the gods became conscious, or better said became: 'the Unconscious'. Jung would come to differentiate this 'wisdom of the unconscious' in many specific images: the intuitive knowledge of the 'bush-soul' and the sibylline anima of *Mysterium*, for example. It became highly differentiated dynamically and practically in the method of active imagination, by which the 'other' appears entirely from within.

Our theory gradually moved away from a reified oracular model of Self dynamics, and towards interpersonal and intersubjective process-oriented constructs, methods, and language. Another movement has recently taken place and we now try to understand analysis within a model of unfolding field interactions which collapse all these categories, a beginning attempt at an integrated view of psyche, soul, and nature. We reference the creative imagination and emergent processes, which in turn have been informed by neuroscience and quantum theories. While it is true that a working theory of psychological process which does not account for developments in brain function is obsolete, it is interesting how our theoretical language spirals around again to invisible entities: quarks, prions, and the other particles of spirit. Psychological process, as process, may still be best entered into through the mythopoetic sensibility and the evolving tools of that trade.

These tools go back to our own origins. Psychoanalysis was born in a soup of mediumship, divination, and communication with the 'unseen world'. While working on his dissertation investigating the teleological aspects of mediumship Jung was already under the influence; he was well acquainted with the work of William James, whose *Varieties of Religious Experience* would appear in 1902, and the work of Théodore Flournoy, whose 1899 book about a popular medium served as the model for Jung's dissertation, and of F.W.H. Myers, who coined the terms clairvoyance, pre-cognition, and subliminal imagination. The influential Society for Psychical Research in London, founded in 1882 (of which Myers and James were both presidents, Freud and Jung both members) had a fascination at its inception with the Delphic Oracle, assessing classical scholarship about the Oracle as it pertained to spiritualism and the clairvoyant powers of imagination. This climate was the medium, and the message, which both nurtured Jung's initial formulations and gave rise to the terrific projections which would be brought to bear on women, hysteria, and the anima function by these early psychoanalysts.

In the oracular tradition, the intimate interplay between image, concept, affect, the realities of the moment, and the imagination of the future, combined with an image of 'truth' as constructed and enigmatic, provides for the understanding of symbols and their concrete enactments as symptoms, as both multi-dimensional and contained within the ever-increasing unity of the present moment. The tradition resonates with archetypal aspects of the transference field (Wise Woman, Healer, Shaman) – as well as with the techniques of interpretation and amplification, the relationship of psychological process to culture and context, and our modern understanding of the mythopoetic imagination and fictional narratives. In contrast to other collective traditions which often emphasize definitive solutions to psychological process, many aspects of the oracular tradition are quintessentially psychological: a pluralistic vision of the world and human character, implying a multiplicity of possibilities, choices, doubts, and solutions, with an eye to the unique circumstances of the moment and the individual.

While moving into new theoretical and clinical directions, it may be prudent to remember that going forward often means going backward as well. As analysts we explore both childhood fantasies and psychoanalytic fantasies of childhood, not primarily to recover lost memories or inner children, but rather to commune (back) with the source, with origins and with originators, (and forward) with creators, spirits, the entire archetypal 'ancestry', or as it is all referenced in Africa, with the 'village of truth'.

Baule, Ivory Coast, 19thC. Metropolitan Museum of Art, NY #1

This village is an unfolding field of psychological relationships, a kind of Great Family unconscious (Bynum 1999). It includes the present extended generation, the next generation which has not been born, and up to five past generations of ancestors. The oldest of these ancestors merge into the forces of nature and the gods, which return, in turn, to the village. This couple from 'The Village of Truth' was used by diviners to bring ancestors and spirits from the bush into the village. The ancestors and spirits were flattered and attracted to the idealized figures and came to inhabit them. Thus invested they become oracles.

According to this scheme, we, as the third and fourth generation of analysts out from Jung, are still in the village with him, while 'Jung' is merging into the mythic world. In this context it is interesting to note the curious fact that Jung's life and work continue to function as an oracle for us, which analysts feel the need to consult on a regular basis. I do so in noting that Jung began to consult an oracle himself in the early 1920's, the *I Ching*. He had a significant encounter with it before the trip to Africa in response to the uneasiness and uncertainty which surrounded plans for that trip. He continued to consult the *I Ching* regularly, and apparently about everything, throughout his life. It presaged his interest in mandala symbolism and synchronicity. The whole oracular enterprise is itself symbolic of an attempt to divine the psyche of the cosmos, and from this perspective alone we can imagine how it was very attractive to Jung.

Analysis and the oracular tradition share the methods schematized as possession and interpretation, resonance and amplification. These in turn emerge from common sensibilities referred to below as 'Co-Creation and Uncertainty', the 'One and the Many in the Round', and, borrowing from the alchemists, 'True Imagination'.

Co-Creation and Uncertainty

As he surveyed the Athi Plains of Kenya, Jung became aware of one strand of his own 'myth', an experience he describes in *Memories, Dreams, Reflections* (1961/1989):

> Now I knew what it was, and knew even more: that man is indispensable for the completion of creation; that, in fact, he himself is the second creator of the world, who alone has given to the world its objective existence – without which, unheard, unseen, silently eating, giving birth, dying, heads nodding through hundreds of millions of years, it would have gone on in the profoundest night of non-being down to its unknown end. Human conscious-ness created objective existence and meaning, and man found his indispensable place in the great process of being.
>
> (p. 256)

This mythic event would be followed in a few years by another strand of Jung's myth, alchemy. The alchemical vision echoes the co-creation theme as reflected in the dictum 'what Nature leaves imperfect, Art perfects', although in alchemy there is a struggle with the often intractable base elements, a tortuous process which intimates another sort of relationship, a more dynamic one.

The privileging of consciousness as 'co-creator' of the world has many shadows: inflation and identification with Self dynamics, perverse interiority and narcissism, a stance of non-relatedness and separation from the socio-political psyche, the marginalization of animal species and the inorganic. Jung would later move towards rectifying this imbalance with a synchronistic sensibility, shifting the lens on the subject/object, conscious/unconscious boundary, articulating access through a larger field, into the creation of both meaning and an accountable relationship to what is 'other'. Our informing image now is more like a living web, the interactive and participatory nature of which relativizes the simplistic conscious/unconscious distinction. This has shifted our experience of consciousness, co-creation, the certainty of meaning, and the meaning of uncertainty.

Many oracular procedures trust in chance to reveal the message of the gods. Probability provides the space through which psyche reveals itself. For example, in Azande culture there is a procedure known as 'the poison oracle' in which answers to questions are obtained by giving poison to chickens, the answer being determined by whether or not the chicken survives the procedure. Some die, some survive, and some are entirely unaffected by the same amount of poison. It is the unpredictability and uncertainty of the chicken's reactions to the poison that guarantees the truth, impartiality, and reliability of the procedure. The poison can be deadly or benign, not unlike the way certain comments in analysis have a poison or panacea effect, dependent on intentionality, receptivity, the connection or lack of it with the relevant archetypal ground, and the often obscure meaning of the moment.

In psychological process there is always an embodied surrender to fate and psyche's demands in one form or another; in that sense we are all just chickens. But that response is often also dynamic and calculated, calculated with a co-creative sensibility. In *[Catalogue # 49]* the figure called 'The Shark Who Made the Ocean Waters Tremble' is over 5 feet tall, and depicts the defiant response of a king to the oracular prediction of a difficult reign during a time of foreign occupation. It both refers to the prediction of danger from across the waters and embodies a conscious shape-shift and identification with a predator capable of meeting it. In this case it didn't work.

[Catalogue # 50] is a plaque which commemorates the victory of a 16th century king. The birds which the men are holding, called the 'birds of prophecy', had been traditionally considered harbingers of disaster, and had appeared before a crucial battle. Instead of retreating the king decided to advance and in this case prevailed over both the enemy and the augury. What is interesting is that the meaning of the bird-image flipped after this event to its opposite, coming to indicate the ability to change fate. The men are depicted as striking rods against the beaks of the birds of prophecy. Apparently they can be silenced.

It is the unpredictability and uncertainty of the psyche's archetypal trajectories which provoke counteraction and the co-creativity of conscious awareness. As the play and inclination of unseen factors is alternately revealed and concealed, and we ask ... what and why, the enigmatic factor of archetypal trajectories forces engagement with psyche and events, paradoxically pushing for *dis-identification* from the baleful eye of fate.

One and the Many in the Round

Nothing of much importance took place in traditional Africa without first consulting the gods. It would be virtually impossible to do otherwise, for although there is a boundary between the everyday and the spirit worlds, they are envisioned as a union of autonomous elements in cyclical trajectory – a sensibility in which psyche is experienced as 'One and the Many in the Round', a circulation and interpenetration of archetypal and personal processes; multiplicity within fields of unity. The connection between fields is concurrent, transparent, symbolic, and concrete. The divination kit of gourd and elements [*Catalogue # 22 and 23*] contains natural and man-made objects, bones, seeds, skulls, figurines of people and animals, a microcosm of the universe. When it is shaken, the arrangements of the contents are interpreted as a visual code. The items are multi-referential, inert until ignited by divination. The huge range of organization and patterns possible when the gourd is shaken extends the interpretive and symbolic possibilities exponentially. The meaning of the images comes alive in unfolding juxtaposition to one another, creating an infinite range of narratives. It is similar to the way we work with images and clinical narrative as we presuppose that archetypal forms are finite, but the mythopoetic imagery which expresses them in specific moments and situations almost infinite. The symbolic significance of an image or emotion both remains constant and changes, depending on the context of other images which surround it.

The boundaries of psychological possibility are understood to be both delimited, and enhanced, by this reciprocal connection between individual and archetypal fields. And for everything taken from nature or the spirits, something must be returned.

Accountability, equilibrium, reciprocity, and sacrifice are the dominant dynamisms in play, and these are understood to enhance the power that can be drawn from the gods. As far as I know, there is no image of Promethean torture in African mythology, because creation is not that sort of theft.

In the beautiful image of a Carved Calabash [*Catalogue # 12*] a gourd has been cut to form a cosmos in two halves, the top half the invisible world of spirits and ancestors, the lower half the visible world of the living. They form a unified whole. Existence incarnates in the bottom, departs to the top, then re-incarnates in a cyclical trajectory. The boundary line, the threshold that both bisects and joins the sphere is quite prominent. In Yoruba culture this threshold is presided over by a deity responsible for a venerated system of divination called Ifa. After departing the world, the creator god Ifa passed down palm nuts as a means of communication. The Ifa oracle is a protective agency, like a totem or superior *genius*, a Self imago which reveals and balances the unfolding life and the boundary between fields (Bynum, 1999). The threshold is a dangerous liminal field: an interesting amplification of the analytic field which also serves to open both personal and archetypal ground, to differentiate between them, and to integrate them.

In the system of 'casting Ifa', 16 palm nuts are thrown onto a divining tray or bowl, and the patterns that result form one of 256 derivative octograms. *[Catalogue # 15]* is a Divination Vessel for holding the nuts in tribute and offering to the gods of destiny. Very similar to the *I Ching* oracle, the core of Ifa divination rests in the thousands of memorized verses by which the patterns are interpreted. The verses form a psychological opus of myths, folktales, incantations, songs, proverbs, and riddles. Ifa is the most systematized and largest literary tradition in Africa, an expression of a cultural unconscious which both structures and reflects the mythologems of human experience.

The objective of the divination is to determine what sacrifice is necessary to resolve a client's problem, to receive all due blessings and to mitigate the effects of a bad destiny. The correct sacrifices are contained in the verses, and specified either by describing the sacrifice made by a mythological character under similar circumstances, or by a piece of the verse directed to the client. The former makes recourse to archetypal amplification, and the diviner selects the appropriate verse; in the other method the client finds his own 'answer' by choosing the section in the verse which feels most related to his problems.

Meaning emerges from these song-like stories as it does in analysis. When we amplify with archetypal material we also make a bridge between the 'many-worlds' of personal experience to the 'one world' of the world-soul. This happens on an interpretive dimension and also an affective dimension, as the stories resonate, like voice and music with early, pre-verbal levels of process. Objective and subjective factors intermingle in a familiar way as projection, amplification, association, and dynamisms of the Self move back and forth in interpretation, action, and emotion.

[Catalogue # 13] is a divination tray used for casting Ifa. There is an empty circular area where the nuts will be thrown and the client's individual patterns interpreted. There are images on the border which represent the diversity of interdependent archetypal patterns. This is all 'crowned' by three calabashes and the god of Ifa who faces the client. You can see the open 'channel' between the worlds at the bottom, on the side where the client would be sitting. The interplay

between lived life and archetypal possibility is made visually apparent, and resonates with our experience of multiplicity within a unified field. And there are two familiar warnings about respecting psyche's deep ecology: non-compliance by mythological characters to make the appropriate sacrifice often results in misfortune – one third of the Ifa verses tell these stories. And Ifa as a guardian of time also guards the past; the past has to be guarded because it can be changed. 'Playing with memory', as it is called, is an act which afflicts the world, and 'playing with memory' for self-serving reasons, 'breaking it' by black magic and sorcery, courts fatal retribution.

The last image in this series is a 'Mouse Oracle' *[Catalogue # 17]*. It is part of a legend which tells that in the distant past mice could speak, and lived in the forest. Burrowing under the earth gave them access to earth spirits and ancestors, enabling them to foretell events. So divining specialists came and took them into the villages as oracles. A question is asked, the mice are put into the closed bottom chamber of the vessel, and the upper part is filled with grains or bats' bones. The closed chamber is opened, up they go, and the pattern that is made in the grains as the mice move around and eat is interpreted. They are messengers and agents from 'the field', in which small bits represent the whole, a whole which in turn speaks, in characteristic mythopoetic style, through all the small bits, even mice.

We know from clinical experience that an archetypal field can lodge anywhere in the body or mind of either or both participants in the transference, or even farther afield, in another person, creature, or event. But mice are often interpreted only as a breakthrough of repressed impulses, usually sexual and threatening ego boundaries, a situation we understand in some vague way as potentially 'good'. Amplification of the mouse oracle suggests that there is a specificity to the pattern created by the unfolding of libido, that instinctual libido contains within it and is moving toward the expression of larger, and particular fields of meaning. But you have to follow the trail and let it speak in order to 'get it'. This is the attitude which facilitates emer-gent states of interpenetration between libido, image, and meaning, deepening metabolism in the affective and somatic areas of psyche: the deep 'translation'.

True Imagination

Much of what informs our ideas about psychological practice derives from a trajectory: from Africa to alchemy to Jung. 'Alchemy' derives from '*al-Kemit*', an Arabic term which referred to the science and religion of the early Egyptians, who were called 'Kemits', from the 'Land of the Blacks', or 'The Black Land', the Nile Delta. This Kemitic civilization, which was the classical civilization of Africa, had been fed by indigenous African cultures. The science of alchemy in Egypt was the science of Thoth; Thoth was identified with Hermes in Greece, and then Hermes Trismegistus, the legendary author of magical and alchemical texts.

As one of the allegories for the individuation process in *Mysterium*, Jung described the imaginal journey of a medieval alchemist. The alchemist's journey came to its end at the last of the four directions, 'south', in Africa, which Jung likened to the fourth function, the most heated and unconscious of all, in this case, interestingly, intuition. Satyrs, pans, dog-headed baboons, and 'innumerable species of wild animals' (1963, para. 277) lived in this alchemical 'Africa', as did the mystical phoenix and the Sibyl who foretold the coming of Christ (she is now on the ceiling of the Sistine Chapel). Jung commented on these inhabitants:

> In order to become the ever-living bird of the spirit, the alchemical animal soul needs the transforming fire which is found in 'Africa'. … The mystery alluded to here is not only the encounter with the animal soul but, at the same time and in the same place, the meeting with the anima, a feminine psychopomp who showed him the way to Mercurius and also how to find the phoenix.
>
> (ibid., para. 282)

The Sibyl tells the alchemist to find Mercurius by ascending and then descending the seven planetary spheres, a *circulatio*. There is a transformative triple liaison here: first, the animal or bush-soul completes a quaternity in a first synthesis. When that synthesis meets the anima, the Sibyl, it opens the way to a new personality, the phoenix, image of rebirth. This is the secret of 'resurrection', psychologically understood as transformation of libido, the Stone, the elixir, and most important, the 'medicine'.

The figure of a 'Sibyl and her Medicine Bowl' *[Catalogue # 5]* functioned as a medium providing insights into problems and medicine with which to resolve them. The sibyl and the medicine bowl are one figure. This bowl may have been placed as a guardian in front of a treatment centre for mental disorders, and also contained the whole Society's spirit 'medicine', as a cultural mediator.

The image of 'the medicine' was central to alchemy, the universal panacea which could cure whatever was diseased and afflicted, an image for the transformation process itself, what was needed for the creation of the new personality. The alchemists envisioned the medicine as a physical and quintessential equivalent of the lapis, a Self imago, both concrete and symbolic at the same time it could heal because it was 'like' the illness (Salman 1999). This 'Sibyl and the Medicine Bowl' is a beautiful amplification of aspects of the archetypal transference during which analyst, illness, image, and medicine appear as mirrors of one another.

For example, when the alchemical medicine appears in analysis through projective identification and transference enactments (situations 'like' the illness but not the same as it), what becomes possible from the prospective point of view is both a disidentification from archetypal affects *and* a freeing of the archetypal dimension from complete identity in literality. In the world of *participation mystique* every relationship offers the possibility of a sharing and transformation of essentials through the mythopoetic correspondences between affects, symptoms, and symbols. Real medicine.

A familiar way to amplify the medicine is through the mythology of classical Greece, where the Delphic Oracle stood at the centre of civilization. The east side of the temple was dedicated to Apollo, and the west side to Dionysus. This dual aspect of the oracular sensibility embodied the mythopoetic praxis mentioned before: prophetic interpretation and affective possession. Apollo killed the serpent Python, threw it into a volcanic fissure where it putrefied, came back up as hallucinogenic fumes (the first transformation, a *sublimatio*), the fumes entered the priestess sitting over the fissure, and then emerged again as prophecy (the second transformation). The sequence is a variation on the mythology of the 'serpent power' also found in African Voodoo tradition, where a priestess is also symbolically penetrated by the god in the form of a snake, the synthesis being resonance with archetypal dynamics in the form of oracular power. Jung would further amplify the serpent medicine with images from Eastern tradition in 'The Psychology of Kundalini Yoga'. The transformation of libido takes form in various mythopoetic images: from python to prophecy, from bush soul to phoenix (both somewhat vertical), and here, the sibyl and her medicine as-one. In this last, there is a lovely sense of both the transformation of unconscious identifications, and rooted-ness *in* them, as 'medicinal'.

Personifications of psychodynamic patterns are also made into specific 'medicines', which are like prescriptions. *[Catalogue #7]* figurine personifies an investigative agent which is 'sent out' on missions to divine the cause of afflictions from witchcraft. It is both the divining spirit *and* the victim whose case is being looked into. Women were considered especially vulnerable to being controlled or victimized, and a beautiful woman is often used as an agent since her allure also functions to call out the affliction. *[Catalogue # 43]* is a 'little medicine' symbolically and literally; just a few inches tall, this figurine is for personal use as a power object. Special medicines were inserted into the stomach cavity.

What is significant is that these medicines embody both the person who comes for treatment *and* the spirit which gathers information, and resolves the problem. The fluidity of psychic energy allows unconscious identities and projections to interpenetrate, such that symptom and healing symbol are personified in the same figure, much as we see in dream images and transference dynamics, or in the way in which analysis bridges symptoms and syndromes with larger archetypal patterns underlying, for example, individual victimization. This interpenetration contains, metabolizes and opens-up fixed affective patterns.

Conclusion

When Jung came to Africa, he found a source-point of theory much deeper than the revelation on the Athi Plains of the myth of consciousness. At the same time as consciousness was being privileged, underneath, the dynamics of unconscious process were moving into the foreground: *participation mystique*, field phenomena, the archetypal dimensions of symptom and symbol, synchronicity, the 'medicine'. The parallel nature of these developments, the elevation of consciousness and the coming forward of unconscious process were mirrored in Jung's personal experience.

It is easy to get lost in Africa, as we have all discovered during this Congress, and Jung too lost his bearings here, at the same time as he was finding them. Afraid of 'going black' (Burleson 2006), at the same time re-visioning the significance of the so-called 'primitive mind', he interpreted his own dreams defensively, deciding that 'my European personality must under all circumstances be preserved intact' (1961/1989, p. 273). He collected only one dream from an African – a 'bad sign' from our vantage point – which Jung had explained as due to the ubiquitous 'English problem'. Uncharacteristically, he did not understand it as resonating with a subjective factor in himself. This was all tangled up with the *I Ching* casting before the trip, of the hexagram 'Gradual Progress', in which one of the lines read 'The wild goose gradually draws near the plateau. The man goes forth and does not return. The woman carries a child but does not bring it forth'. Jung took this as a warning and shored up his European personality, but like a good oracle, it also presaged the limits of his understanding at the time.

In the essay 'Archaic man,' written soon after the trip, Jung developed his inter-related ideas about *participation mystique* and projection. What got projected by the imagination was 'mana', what Jung meant by 'libido'. From this point of view, the 'bush soul' is something which has split off completely and taken up its abode in a wild animal. This is the classic, numinous sensibility in which 'In the archaic world everything has soul' (Jung 1933, para. 67) and 'A dream walks in like an animal'. But as it turns out, the pre-logical cast of mind may have more in common with the quantum world which Jung would begin to understand only later through his work with Pauli, as he moved towards an integrated view of psyche, soul, and nature.

But still, Jung had found a 'psychic observation point outside the sphere of the European' (1961/1989, p. 244), and a validation of the mythopoetic nature of psychological process. It also formed a vantage point for his critique of the Western psyche. Whether this qualifies as a 'post-modern' stance is debatable, but it did relativize a particular idealized ego identity. The re-valuing of magical states of mind, the mutual fields of resonance wherein mind, matter, people, animals behave in uncanny and amazing ways, were correctives which Jung insisted on, and moved towards more and more, as he entered first the alchemical field, and later the synchronistic field of psyche and matter.

The trance states of oracular process and the altered states of analytic process encourage affective resonance and the unfolding of archetypal imagination. We open, through our own affective and imaginal capacities, to the reality of another psyche, and to the under-lying archetypal matrix. Although we are no longer fully absorbed or dissolved by the gods, in fields of induction and high affect, archetypal dynamics are felt in the body, heart, and mind. We enter the 'field' with its multiple dimensions of resonance in order to divine and heal psyche's true imagination, to differentiate out and work-through what is in the way of the *circulatio*. The 'truth vs. fiction' question in oracular tradition finds its parallel in the clinical issue of differentiating between the fantasies spun into repetition by complexes and the 'true imagina-tion' of psyche's archetypal trajectories (Salman 2006). We describe this work in many ways: making the unfixed fixed, the fixed unfixed, dissolve and coagulate, find the telos (the medicine) in the symptom, the archetype in the complex.

What is very different now, though, is that oracles, while they ful-filled this function as well, were also the keepers of collective memory and the guardians of collective moral values. Analysis is a more sub-versive activity, i.e. it often serves to *de*construct prevailing collective mythologies. Which must account for our lowered social and financial status compared to our highly-regarded counterparts! For good and ill, our collective situation *as analysts* is not like this 'throne scene' depicted in *[Catalogue # 45]*: an interdependent relationship between transpersonal insight and responsible leadership. Many aspects of the collective and political psyche *are* like this though, with the gods not just on everyone's 'side', but rather, under our rear ends.

Because fields of psyche and matter are made from the same substances there has always been an impressive array of 'correspon-dences' between them which emerge as mirrors, links, and bridges. These correspondences are the grammar of mythopoetic process, and we capitalize on them in all aspects of analysis. It is a kind of 'just so' wherein meaning is already there to be discovered. When we move from the dynamics of *participation mystique* into fields dominated by synchronicity and ego awareness two things emerge: the granting of meaning to the unexpected (a privileging of psyche), and a proliferation of the unexpected which then needs to be granted meaning. In the first field the 'god is called or bidden', in the second 'unbidden'. But it is present in both.

We sometimes romanticize or bias the older traditions and dynamics in our notions of 'primitivity' and borderline psychology, and elevate the newer as 'more psychological'. But a look around the world brings many aspects of this distinction into question. Both appear to prepare the psyche with new attitudes with which to meet the future, reflecting psyche's varied imagination as it constructs new approaches to itself and the world.

References

Adams, M.V. (2006). 'Imaginology: the Jungian Study of the Imagination'. Paper Presented at the International Association for Jungian Studies, London.

Bascom, W. (1969, 1991). *Ifa Divination: Communication between Gods and Men in West Africa.* Indiana University Press.

Burleson, B. (2006). *Jung in Africa.* New York: Continuum.

Bynum, B.(1999). *The African Unconscious: Roots of Ancient Mysticism and Modern Psychology.* New York: Teachers College Press.

Evans-Pritchard, E.E. (1976). *Witchcraft, Oracles, and Magic Among the Azande.* Clarendon Press, Oxford.

Wilhelm, R. (Trans) (1950 / 1967). *I Ching.* NJ: Bollingen Series XIX/ Princeton University Press.

Jung, C.G. (1961 / 1989). Aniela Jaffé: *Memories, Dreams, Reflections by C.G. Jung.* New York: Vintage/ Random House.

– (1933). 'Archaic man'. In *Civilization in Transition.* CW 10.

– (1963). *Mysterium Coniunctionis.* CW 14.

Kawai, T. (2006). 'Postmodern consciousness in psychotherapy'. *Journal of Analytical Psychology,* 51, 3, 437-50.

LaGamma, A. (2000). *Art and Oracle: African Art and Rituals of Divination.* New York: Metropolitan Museum of Art / Harry Abrams.

Salman, S. (1999). 'Dissociation and the Self in the magical pre-Oedipal field'. *Journal of Analytical Psychology,* 44,1, 69-85

– (2006). 'True Imagination'. *Spring: A Journal of Archetype and Culture. Spring Journal,* 74.

Panel: The Idea of the Numinous

Ann Casement
UK (BAP)
Moderator

Introduction

This Panel grew out of a recent book with the same title published by Routledge to which two of the Panel Speakers contributed. Their chapters titles are as follows: 'Rerooting in the Mother: the Numinosity of the Night' by John Dourley, whose paper here is entitled 'Jung, the Numinous, and a Surpassing Myth', and 'On the Importance of Numinous Experience in the Alchemy of Individuation' by Murray Stein, who presents a paper of the same title. The title of Ann Ulanov's paper is 'Before We Were: Creating in Being Created. Encounter and Journey in our Analytic Profession'.

The idea of the numinous is often raised in psychoanalytic and psychodynamic contexts, but it is rarely itself subjected to close scrutiny. The numinous means something like 'awesome' and refers to the emotional quality of religious experience, of being in the presence of the sacred. It has gained currency in the postmodern world, and even materialists and atheists are able to affirm a 'numinous' quality in nature and in experience, whereas before our time, the numinous (from *numen*, Latin for 'will' or 'command') would have been confined to religious discourses. Along with the concept of 'spirituality', which also exists outside formal religion, the numinous has been transformed, and is now included in humanist, secular and scientific views of the world.

In recent times, questions of soul and spirit are being raised in connection with the scientific exploration of the psyche, and especially in the context of psychotherapy. For instance, Jung wrote in a letter of 1945, 'the numinous is the real therapy', which has not been explored in any consistent way though it has led to increasing interest in the ways in which the concerns of therapy and religion overlap. The Panel will explore the numinous in the human psyche and the way in which the overlap between therapeutic and religious interests has led to the creation of a new, third area which is neither exclusively clinical nor exclusively theological. This third area has led to a discourse in which age-old questions are encountered anew. The spirit remains the same, yet its language and expression are changed.

The Panel will attempt to track the 'diffuse' awareness of the numinous in modern and postmodern life where its focus will be not on religion *per se*, but rather the 'religious attitude'.

Jung, the Numinous, and a Surpassing Myth
The Inevitability of the Numinous

John Dourley
Canada (AGAP International)

Jung closely linked numinous experience with his claimed discovery of nothing less than 'the psychic origin of religious phenomena' (*Psychology and Alchemy*, CW 12, para. 9, 16). This claim is a bald, all inclusive affirmation that immediate religious experience and the religions of the world this experience generates derive from the numinous impact of the archetypal unconscious on consciousness. Such powerful impress constitutes the sole source and agency of humanity's individual and collective religious experience and expression. Jung further identified the residual potential for numinous experience in humanity's universally possessed 'authentic religious function'. In his words, 'the careful and scrupulous observation ...' of the numinous expressions of this natural human capacity serves effectively as a private revelation (*Psychology and Religion: West and East*, CW 11, para. 3, 6, 8). Personally, the dream and whatever other media the archetypal may use to make itself manifest become the word of God for the individual thus addressed. Collectively, the religious function also creates, usually through significant individuals, the great cultural revelations whose numinous content compensates society toward its needed balance and stability in the service of the deeper ingression of the archetypal unconscious into historical consciousness. For Jung this process is never ending.

The consequences of the numinous thus understood are far-reaching. Personally it would mean that the numinous power of the individual's dream would derive from the same source as the world's religions, their divinities, and their salvific strategies for humanity. With the sustenance such personal revelation provides, the individual is freed to address whatever archetypal constructions and constrictions create the culture into which one is born. Such response can take the form of endorsement, rejection or modification but will always derive from the power of living into one's unique myth. In a more universal sense Jung's appreciation of the numinous would mean that whether God exists or not humanity cannot rid itself of the sense of God. To the individual the numinous forbids atheism and, to society, a secularity wholly devoid of a religious or ultimate dimension. With Jung the question is never whether individual or society is religious. The question is what the individual or society holds as numinous, or, more in the spirit of Jung, what shape the numinous grip on individual and society assumes at any given historical moment (*Psychology and Religion: West and East*, CW 11, para. 6).

Again, the prevalence of the numinous in human consciousness is what lies behind Jung's repeated references to the '*consensus gentium*', that is, to humanity's collective consent that it is possessed of and by an experiential sense of the divine (*Psychology and Religion: West and East*, CW 11, para. 4). In appealing to their archetypal source, Jung identifies the foundational endurance in variation of unlikely religious and theological statements throughout the history of consciousness (*CW* 12, 17, 20[1]). In the context of humanity's universal sense of ultimacy, Jung's analysis of the ontological argument for God's existence, namely, that humanity has an innate sense of God, joins such moderns as Paul Tillich in the affirmation that the argument is not an argument nor does it prove anything (*Psychological Types*, CW 6, para. 61, 62: ST I, pp. 204-08). Rather it simply points to humanity's universally shared and unmediated experience of the absolute or unconditioned.

More importantly Jung's understanding of the numinous would imply that the Gods create themselves or are created in the interplay between the ego, the archetypal unconscious and whatever conscious imbalance, again individual or societal, the divinities address and seek to remedy in their diverse revelations. Jung's thought here contributes to one of humanity's currently most pressing questions. If the Gods create themselves through the human experience of the numinous has one yet to be created worth a human life? Such a question would be a valuable heuristic resource in furthering the swelling contemporary search for the link between the numinosity of religion and the violence and loss of life it induces in and between the communities it possesses.

Though it is the distinguishing feature of his psychology, theoretically and therapeutically, the numinous thus remained for Jung a profoundly ambiguous force. Here again Jung would agree with Tillich when the latter writes about the intractable numinosity of faith, 'Our ultimate concern can destroy us as it can heal us. But we can never be without it' (Tillich 1957, p. 16). Since humanity can never be free of it, the ambivalence of the numinous demands an examination of its shadow side as well as its potential for the enrichment of human life.

The Numinous as Threat to the Species

Reflection on the shadow side of the numinous engages Jung's political and social psychology and brings it into discussion with contemporary geopolitical thought. Samuel P. Huntington (1996) identifies religion as the operative bonding power of contemporary civilizations. Thus bonded by their religions, contemporary and future

---

[1] *Psychology and Alchemy*, CW 12; *The Development of Personality*, CW 17; *General Index to the Collected Works*, CW 20

wars between civilizations are and will be religious wars. To this point Huntington's analysis of the current geopolitical situation coincides with Jung's in identifying the universal threat communities bonded by the numinous pose to collective survival whenever they come into sustained contact with each other. For the political side of Jung's thought also would affirm with Huntington that archetypal numinosity is the glue of each culture or civilization. More, Jung's social psychology supports a grim psycho-sociological law, namely, the more intense the numinous bonding uniting a community, the tighter its faith and the less conscious and so morally responsible are the individuals thus bonded.

The problem is blatant and acute in the interface of the monotheisms. Three divine transcendental gentlemen currently vie through their communities for an exclusive and all embracing ultimacy. Jung was of the opinion that the epoch of monotheistic consciousness in all its forms had begun its decline with the consciousness evident in the *Book of Job*. He could hardly be more explicit than when he writes,

> An unusual scandal was blowing up in the realm of metaphysics, with supposedly devastating consequences, and nobody was ready with a saving formula which could rescue the monotheistic conception of God from disaster.
> (*Psychology and Religion: West and East*, CW 11, para. 607)

Nevertheless, though the historical evolution of religious consciousness may currently be leaving monotheism in its wake, such evolution has not and cannot outgrow the archetypal unconscious and its drive to become conscious in history through its foundational sponsorship of an ever more inclusive embrace of the totality. If Jung sounds the death knell for the monotheistic mind and epoch, both religiously and politically, his own myth contributes to the overture of a new personal and societal consciousness stemming from a greater profundity and so of greatly extended compass.

New Configurations of the Numinous in a now Emerging Myth

As it is honed in his later work, Jung's myth rests on a sense of radical psychic containment wholly revisioning the human relation to transcendence. Such containment would affirm that the unconscious transcends consciousness infinitely but that nothing transcends the psyche itself. Thus contained, the individual's relation to the divine rests solely on the ego's commerce with archetypally induced numinosity as the basis of all religious experience and its formulation personal and communal (*The Symbolic Life*, CW 18, para. 1664). Psychologically the numinous constitutes the ultimate if not only healing resource available to humanity (Jung 1919/1945, p. 377). To imagine the relationship of the human to the divine as to individual divinities or self-sufficient powers beyond the psyche is hostile to Jung's mature psychology, clearly revealed in the insuperable divide yawning between his psychology and the monotheisms of Buber and White. Effectively Jung's psychology brings down the curtain on all forms of supernaturalism and demands the conscious return of the divine to its psychic origin where a more demanding yet safer dialogue with it continues ushering God into a responsible self-consciousness in its sole possessor, namely, humanity (*Psychology and Religion: West and East*, CW 11, para. 141).

The wholly intra-psychic dialogue between ego and unconscious is at the heart of Jung's fecund but oft neglected understanding of the 'relativity of God' (*Psychological Types*, CW 6, paras. 241-58). Jung's primary understanding of the relativity of God amplified in his work on Job refers to the fact that divinity necessarily creates human consciousness as the sole discriminating agency in existence. Put succinctly, divinity can only become conscious in human self-consciousness (*Psychology and Religion: West and East*, CW 11, para. 595, 642). The principal vocation of each individual and society then becomes the conscious unification in time of the antinomial nature of an unconscious divine power incapable of resolving its self-contradiction in eternity.

The mutual need of divine and human is obvious in this paradigm. Humanity redeems divinity in responding to the divine demand to unite its opposites in humanity itself. Reciprocally divinity redeems humanity in the psychic wealth of such syntheses engendered by the suffering resolution of divinely based conflicts in humanity's historical maturation. Jung dramatically describes this reciprocity in the suffering numinosity of the Christ figure as that of humanity crucified between archetypal opposites. The image is for him both 'psychological' and 'eschatological' (*Psychology and Religion: West and East*, CW 11, para. 408). The process is psychological because it enacts the drive of the archetypal unconscious to unify its opposites in a humanity crucified toward their union. It is eschatological because such progressive unification is the direction in which history moves at the insistence of the archetypal psyche itself.

The relativity of God, thus understood, relates closely to Jung's concise formulation of the evolution of the numinous in Western religion and maybe beyond. In this sequence the many Gods became one. The one God became human and now completes itself in the divinity of 'the common man'. In short the goal of the individuation process is always individual and psychological, yet it also fulfils history as the sole theatre in which God can become conscious (*Psychology and Religion: West and East*, CW 11, para. 141; *The Symbolic Life*, CW 18, para. 1660f).

In this context Jung is explicit in his claim that the unity of divine and human natures, which certain orthodoxies restrict to one exceptional historical life, is a natural truth of every life at least as potential and demand (*Psychology and Religion: West and East, CW* 11, para. 105). The evolution of numinous experience has currently reached a stage in which the sense of the sacred is extending toward the totality in what can only be called a psychic pantheism capable of perceiving the sacred in all that is. Jung makes this explicit when he writes, 'It was only quite late that we realized (or rather, are beginning to realize) that God is reality itself and therefore – last but not least – man. This realization is a millennial process' (*Psychology and Religion: West and East, CW* 11, para. 631).

The process continues in Jung's understanding of the dynamic of incarnation as the matrix of consciousness becoming conscious in it. At times in his late writing he will change terminology and describe incarnation as 'penetration' (*The Symbolic Life, CW* 18, para. 1660). Currently the divine penetration of human consciousness urges a quaternitarian mythology. This supplanting myth recovers the preceding power of the Goddess as the numinous depth of the psyche itself, breaks 'the patriarchal supremacy' (*Psychology and Religion: West and East, CW* 11, para. 627), acknowledges 'the equality of women' (*Psychology and Religion: West and East, CW* 11, para. 753), re-sacralizes the body and embraces the demon. What Jung is talking about is a widening of humanity as an image of God to include the totality of reality as a reflective expression of its source. The Spirit of such a myth would embrace and unite far more as sacred than can the still dominant monotheisms and their limited sense of transparency to the holy from which the totality derives.

A redeeming universal sacramentalism runs through these foundational elements of Jung's psychology, which particular religions, because of their very particularity, cannot convey. The numinosity which attaches to the emerging myth mysteriously combines the individual and the universal, again, at personal and collective levels. The many complexes that make up a personal life would seem to move toward an individual integration with an ever extending compassion for the all. The dynamic of a numinous experience of a unified individuality enlivened by an intensified universal sympathy would seem to describe an immersion or 'baptism' in that transpersonal power Jung describes as the 'pleroma', a primordial fullness (*Psychology and Religion: West and East, CW* 11, para. 677), and elsewhere as the 'eternal Ground of all empirical being' (*Mysterium Coniunctionis, CW* 14, para. 760). Only an experiential dissolution in and consequent residual resonance with what Jung, Goethe and some mystics call that nothing out of which the all 'may grow' can adequately account for the ever deepening personal integration and accompanying compassion toward which processes of individuation and history are now more consciously driven by the nature of the psyche itself (*Civilization in Transition*, CW 10, para. 150).

The path to so intense a universal sentiment is not easy and the alternatives surrounding its birth or failure are stark. Jung identifies them succinctly when he writes, 'We are threatened with universal genocide if we cannot work out the way of salvation by a symbolic death' (*The Symbolic Life*, CW 18, para. 1661). Why is the choice humanity now faces a choice between universal genocide and a symbolic death? It is so because humanity now must grow or die. In context Jung is found to be arguing that species wide genocide is inevitable if communities cannot rid themselves of their current constricted sense of the numinous for a consciousness which would embrace what they cannot, including and particularly other faith communities. But the extension of authentic acceptance to the other as individual or community will entail a symbolic death, that is, a loss of that faith which excludes the other from full natural participation in the ground and origin of all expressions of the numinous.

In a variation of this same theme Jung contends that a consciousness severed from its common source and the life that source provides will lose the will to live. He writes, 'Nevertheless, when a living organism is cut off from its roots, it loses the connections with the foundations of its existence and must necessarily perish. When that happens anamnesis of the origins is a matter of life and death' (*Aion*, CW 9ii, para. 279). In these words Jung suggests that unless humanity can recover that numinosity which only the memory of its native and universal divinity can provide as the power informing a now emerging myth of more total embrace, then its forgetfulness will prompt the loss of the will to live.

In Jung's view the recovery of this numinous memory remained problematic. In his late work on Job he writes, 'Everything now depends on man ...' (*Psychology and Religion: West and East*, CW 11, para. 745). With this statement he puts the ball squarely in humanity's court. In the end the most one can responsibly say is that Jung has given humanity the chance to see what is at stake in the fearsome option, forced now by the psyche itself, either to cling to current constrictive faiths or to lose them toward a more universal sympathy. In the end we can do little more than hope that the gentle suasion of Jung's mythology with its vastly deepened and extended sense of the numinous will be a significant contributor to humanity's option to choose life.

References

Huntington, S.P. (1996). *The Clash of Civilization and the Remaking of World Order.*   New York: Simon & Schuster.

Jung, C.G. (1919/1945). *Letters. Vol 1, 1906-1950.* Eds. G. Adler & A. Jaffé. Princeton: Princeton University Press, 1973.

Tillich, P. (1957). *Dynamics of Faith.* New York: Harper & Row.

On the Importance of Numinous Experience in the Alchemy of Individuation

Murray Stein
USA (AGAP, SGAP)

In a letter to P.W. Martin (20 August 1945), the founder of the International Study Centre of Applied Psychology in Oxted, England, C.G. Jung confirmed the centrality of numinous experience in his life and work:

> It always seemed to me as if the real milestones were certain symbolic events characterized by a strong emotional tone. You are quite right; the main interest of my work is not concerned with the treatment of neuroses but rather with the approach to the numinous. But the fact is that the approach to the numinous is the real therapy and inasmuch as you attain to the numinous experiences you are released from the curse of pathology. Even the very disease takes on a numinous character.
>
> (Jung 1973, 1, p. 377)

The question is: How are such momentous experiences related to and used within the context of analysis?

On Healing and Numinous Experience

We can begin by investigating how attaining to numinous experiences releases a person from the curse of pathology, as Jung claims in his letter to P.W. Martin. Generally speaking, an 'approach to the numinous' is considered a religious undertaking, a pilgrimage. The 'attainment to the numinous experiences' that Jung speaks of refers to religious experiences of a quasi-mystical nature. By itself, this attainment might well persuade a person that life is meaningful. Numinous experience creates a convincing link to the transcendent, and this may well lead to the feeling that character flaws like addictions or behavioural disorders are trivial by comparison with the grand visions imparted in the mystical state. The pathological symptom can be interpreted as an incitement to go on the spiritual quest, or even as a paradoxical doorway into transcendence, and this can donate meaning to the malady itself. Perhaps some degree of pathology is needed, in fact, in order for a person to feel strongly enough motivated to set out on a spiritual quest to begin with. In this case, attainment to numinous experiences would bring about a change in the feeling that pathology is a *curse*, even if it did not result in curing the pathology itself, although it might lead to this as well.

For modern and psychologically astute people, however, such a spiritual development might not signify more than a temporary Band Aid and is by no means a definitive solution to the problems created by neurosis. For such people, who tend to be the ones who seek out analysis rather than spiritual guidance or religious pilgrimages, spiritual awareness by itself is not enough. So how would an approach to the numinous and the attainment of numinous experiences contribute to the more far-reaching project of bringing about significant change in analysis?

Generally speaking, a numinous experience is a 'hint', as Jung defines it in several passages. It is a hint that larger, non-egoic powers exist in the psyche, which need to be considered and ultimately brought into contact with consciousness.

The movement of analysis includes dissolving attachments not only to parents and other personalities but also to religious objects, traditional practices, and childish theologies. It is one of the primary achievements of analysis to arrive at a type of fluidity in consciousness that is free from identities that were created early in childhood and adolescence and then became cemented in place through ongoing attachments, loves, loyalties, and the need to belong and to be a member of the collective. Consciousness must be freed from this contamination if a person is to gain individuality and true uniqueness.

The reality of psychological life requires that in analysis we confront voices and images that communicate feeling and emotion; we do not confront inner structures as such. It is in considering the voices and images as they are experienced concretely within the psyche, which influence and at times even take possession of consciousness, that we come upon the mythic dimension, which is only a small step away from the experience of a *numen*.

This profound realization of the psyche's archetypal foundations leads directly to the view that pathological symptoms also contain (and often conceal) an archetypal element. Human psychopathologies are not only individual and personal acquisitions. They are typical outcomes of human interaction with environments of many types, and they disguise or represent basic human needs, including spiritual ones.

Numinosity enters this discussion in relation to the role that archetypal influences play in pathological states of mind. As Jung writes in a letter, dated 30 January 1961, to William Wilson, co-founder of *Alcoholics Anonymous*: 'His [i.e., Roland's, Jung's patient] craving for alcohol was the equivalent on a low level of the spiritual thirst of our being for wholeness, expressed in medieval language: the union with God' (Jung 1973, 2, p. 624). In Bill W's case, as Wilson is referred to in the literature of AA, the approach to the numinous and the attainment to numinous experiences changed him when he was able to free himself from the notion that opening himself to the numinous would oblige him to go back to the familiar religion of his childhood and to its prescribed teaching and dogmatic structures. Since he could not do this, his path to the integration of the numinous was blocked. For Bill W., his religious tradition had become, as it has for modern people generally, Procrustean. The key came in the spontaneous advice from an alcoholic friend who had found a way to spirituality: 'Why don't you choose your own conception of God?' (*Alcoholics Anonymous*: 12). Giving the ego choice and responsibility, rather than insisting on submission to dogma, was the answer to his religious conflict. Once the true underlying craving for spirit was effectively addressed and integrated into daily life, the desire for alcoholic ecstasy could be held in check.

Are not all addictions, one wonders after having seen such a wide variety of them in clinical practice, a search for something so elusive as to be considered somehow 'of the spirit'? A search for ultimate satisfaction and fulfilment?

Numinous Experiences and Individuation: Hints and Signals for Integration

The psychological explanation for numinous experiences like those Rudolf Otto describes in his writings lies with projection, whereby deeply unconscious, especially archetypal, contents are 'found' in the physical objects, rituals, or sounds that elicit them. In religious experience, the psychologist claims, the ego is experiencing a content of the unconscious in projection. The stronger the experience, the more archetypal is the content. Such experiences link conscious-ness to the unconscious and offer 'hints' that may be deciphered as communications. These hints can lead to a deeper perspective on life from the viewpoint of the collective unconscious and are essential for the psychological process of individuation if they can be brought forward and made conscious. This transformation from one state (the spiritual) to another (the psychological) falls under a process called sublimation. To cite von Franz:

> [Sublimation] comes from alchemy. Freud took it out of alchemy, out of chemistry. For example, when you boil water, it becomes steam. Steam is sublimated water. It is another aggregate state. Chemically, steam is not different from water. But qualitatively it manifests itself in another way. It has a higher potential. In steam, the water molecules are more alive; they whirl more about and therefore give the impression of steam instead of water.
>
> (von Franz 2004, p. 167).

Sublimated, the archetypal images become woven into the fabric of a person's conscious identity. They become integrated. As sublimated spirit and transcendence, these images and ideas offer healing. They release a person from the limitations of the purely personal and time-bound framework of the ego and thereby contribute essentially to the formation of the transcendent function, a psychological structure of identity made up of personal and archetypal elements.

'It is altogether amazing how little most people reflect on numinous objects and attempt to come to terms with them', Jung exclaims in his famous theological outburst, *Answer to Job*, 'and how laborious such an undertaking is once we have embarked upon it. The numinosity of the object makes it difficult to handle intellectually, since our affectivity is always involved' (Jung 1954, para. 735). Sublimation and integration of this type is a difficult task but absolutely essential to the *opus* of deep analysis.

In this approach, the psychological embraces (i.e., takes up, integrates) the religious in such a way that its spiritual value is not damaged or reduced. It is sublimated. In fact, the spiritual becomes confirmed and amplified through the psychological. Psyche is not seen as limited to brain chemistry, early childhood, or learning potentials. It is rather an ultimate term, an *ousia* as Jung says in a letter to Victor White, with an infinite horizon, which does not in principle exclude the metaphysical grounding of unconscious contents.

The 'hints' Jung speaks of repeatedly in reference to numinous experiences may be taken as similar to what the sociologist and student of modernity, Peter Berger, has in mind with his phrase, 'signal of transcendence':

> To speak of a signal of transcendence is neither to deny nor to idealize the often harsh empirical facts that make up our lives in the world. It is rather to try for a glimpse of the grace that is to be found 'in, with, and under' the empirical reality of our lives.
>
> (Berger 1977, p. 212)

In contemporary art, too, this has begun to come to the fore again in the boldly symbolic paintings of Anselm Kiefer and in the later films of Wim Wenders, where hints and signals of transcendence shine through the fabric of everyday life.

In conclusion, the attainments to the numinous experiences, if sublimated and integrated by consciousness, are major milestones and often constitute sharp turning points in the analytic process. Most importantly, they go into the creation of the transcendent function. The arduous task is to make them conscious and to bring them into relation with other aspects of the self, and thereby to attain approximate wholeness.

References

Jung, C.G. (1954). 'Answer to Job'. *CW* 11.
– (1973). *Letters*. Vols. 1 & 11. Bollingen Series.
Berger, P. (1977). 'New York City 1976: A signal of transcendence'. In *Facing up to Modernity: Excursion in Society, Politics and Religion*. New York: Basic Books.
Von Franz, M.-L. (2004). 'Conversations on "*Aion*"' (with Claudia Drey). In *Lectures on Jung's Aion*. B. Hannah & M.-L. von Franz. Wilmette, Ill: Chiron Publications.

Before We Were: Creating in Being Created Encounter and Journey in Our Analytic Profession

Ann Belford Ulanov
USA (JPA)

My focus is on the numinous and the analyst, in the making of us, the breaking of us, in what got us going in this profession before we were. Jung describes the numinous as something beyond the human will that alters consciousness; it is a quality belonging to a visible object – what we call mana, or genius, and is 'extraordinarily potent'; it is the influence of an invisible presence which impacts us, arrests us, addresses us (Jung 1954/1960, para. 383, 441; 1937/1958, para. 6). We may not understand such an encounter, but we never forget it. How does it alter our consciousness? We alert to something there, an unknown X that sheds its own peculiar light, what Jung calls 'luminosity' (1954/1960, para. 388), sparks in the soul, scintillae in the unconscious.

The Dark Side of the Numinous through Wounds

I begin with the dark side of this light, with the negative of its positive awe inspiring nature, the wound it inflicts that brings us, analysts, into analysis in the first place, before we were professionals of long standing, or newly accredited analysts, or analysts still in training. For the mana power, the unknown X, may strike into us in ways we find confounding, humiliating, and lead us to seek analysis. Many of us did not know we would come into this profession; we only knew we were caught and held fast, pierced; it was before we were, and we did not know something was also creating us by undoing us. We came into this profession through wounding by the numinous, through its darkest side – the fascination of a fetish or a sexual hook, the compelling need for middle of the night food, the repeated linking up with the wrong partner, or the undertow of dead places inside us that we could not bring alive. We sought analysis as patients. Those of us who began analysis to train as analysts just took longer to arrive at the abysmal entry point of being a patient first, no longer rising above nor dodging out of the way of being addressed at the nadir point of ourselves.

As Augustine says, you cannot give what you do not have, and so we could not be creating as analysts for others until we were first being created as patients. As Jung says, 'the life of the spirit on the highest levels is a return to the beginnings' (Jung 1946/1954, 439) and 'inasmuch as you attain to the numinous experiences you are released from the curse of pathology. Even the very disease takes on a numinous character' (Jung 1973, 1, 20 August 1945, p. 377). Before we were, the numinous came in the back door, through our wound, and only wrestling with it, and being wrestled by it, did we discover something beyond our ego living there, creating us.

The Numinous as Transcending the Ego

Reflecting upon this wound that resists our will and intellect turns our suffering into an encounter with something that transcends our ego. All of us here share the unfolding into becoming analysts. Who would have thought this possible?! Who would have known there was balm in Gilead, a jewel in the wound, a resurrection after the crucifixion? The numinous is present in our becoming analysts.

Precisely here is the extra something Jung's approach offers analysands. The numinous is that which transcends our egos and compels our attention, often positive in a moment of stunning light or peace or bliss, but also even through the back door of our problems. This is a first meaning of numinous: it is beyond our ego and confronts us, positively or negatively; we cannot grasp it in ego terms; it evokes awe. With this sense of encounter a journey begins. The problems that beset us, serious as they may be, contain within them a something else, a bidding, a summons, an engineering by something transcending our egos that point us toward a door through which we come to create what is already being created on both an individual and collective level. For many of us, it is precisely encounter with the numinous that unfolded into our becoming analysts.

Individually, the wound that is an entry point is peculiar to ourselves. The work of analysis pays close attention to a person's particular details. The importance of the small thing, the tiny features which really make the process alive for the patient, leads analysand and analyst to come upon what needs to happen for something to be created (see Balint 1993, p. 223, 227). When a woman, for example, says she lives in the posture of a 'karate crouch', she conveys at once her defensive fear and her resilient aggression, a combination distinct to herself, not to women in general. Imaginative perception, that is, a sense of creating what we experience, yields increasing awareness that it witnesses that we are being created.

Collectively, wounds we sustain as a people, a tribe, a nation, are also encounters with the numinous in its darkest forms. A stark example of our opening decade in this new century are terrorist attacks in subways, office buildings, commuter trains, restaurants, that shock us as being outside patterns of war we have known. Here the victim *is* the innocent bystander, not seen now as regrettable collateral damage, but instead as the intended target for the attack.

The perpetrator here is not the soldier in arms following a hierarchy of order from commander down to infantryman, but instead one's neighbour, a gentle person, now incomprehensibly transmogrified into a mass murderer. Here the terrorist is not criminal or crazy in the accustomed meanings of those terms, but one caught up into archetypal energies that include a religious zeal exciting the ultimate sacrifice of his or her life. Here religion is not about compassion and service of others, but instead self-murder and murder of countless others, making them dead in the name of a living God.

Of all the groups responding to terrorism, as analysts we are called to look into such events to discern what addresses us through this collective wounding. What wounds give rise to this horrific enactment of wounding on a mass scale? Is this a poor man's way of waging war, as effective as a rich man's planes and bombs? What identifications operate here that lead young people, sometimes with children and mates, to give over their egos into the power of the Self in its crushing forms? What do we encounter here, that when reflected upon may indicate an unfolding path, a journey we find ourselves already on, but when identified with unconsciously, vault people into enacting the furies' vengeance? Asking these sorts of questions comprises one of our tasks and contributions to society.

Looking into the numinous wounds, that is, wounds so profound to us as persons and in society that they hold us in their grip, means seeing something in the background stepping forward. The wound becomes an encounter with something in the background. To try to discern it, to come into more direct relationship with this background, can only be for the good. Our greatest danger is to avoid this hard paying attention. Then we live in fear, in reactive retaliations, in conscious over insistence, and we are vulnerable to becoming assimilated to the Self. The change that comes when trying to perceive that the background is the impersonal becomes more of a personal encounter that may yield a direction, a path to our journeying.

Trying to perceive the formless background makes us see our foreground newly, as if standing on another point on the circle that contains everything. This containing circle, that Jung calls the *unus mundus*, 'a potential archetypal world plan in the mind of God' before God began creation where all the opposites are still unified, manifests sporadically in moments of synchronicity (von Franz 1992, p. 217). Then we glimpse the underlying unity of psyche and matter, of inner and outer, of meaningful coherence of reality as an interconnected whole. In those moments we see what Jung calls the *creatio continua*, the acts of creating going on right now, displaying 'a pattern that exists from all eternity', yet which is not determined by any antecedents (Jung 1952/1960, para. 967 and n. 17).

To perceive these glimpses is to participate in creating as we are created. Such synchronistic experiences that touch the heart as well as the mind, that bring great clarity as well as beholding something ineffable, link our personal experiences of the numinous with the numinous as the background of our collective life, our shared existence with others, and give us a momentary perception of our part in the scheme of the whole, what religions call the will of God (see von Franz 1992, p. 257; Jung 1952/1960, para. 924, 931, 948). Our participation, by our encountering what rests in our wounds, whether personal or national, initiates a second experience of the numinous.

The Numinous Entering the Ego

The numinous does not always stay in the background, but steps over into concrete ego life within the bounds of space and time, historical and cultural location, with all the accompanying personal details. Mana comes into the ego and gradually decathects as we make something of the experience and assimilate some of the object's power to ourselves. We absorb our projections onto the numinous. Looked at from the side of the numinous, so to speak, this process of absorbing and giving form to the influx of potent formlessness of the ineffable contributes to the transformation of the God-image over the ages.

Here I want to focus on the ego side of the experience. As Jung says, in consciousness our complexes slough off their mythic envelope and enter into adaptive processes; they are personalized and rationalized, so dialectical discussion becomes possible (1954/1960, para. 384). The unknown X begins to be known; we create relation to it as we find it creating us; we name it as it reveals its hidden form, its 'pure inconceivable *esse*', God's *hecceitas* which manifests in our existence in 'continuous activation of the Divine Names' the *ipseities* (von Franz 1992, p. 301). We are the ones who call on these names, make narratives of our congress with them, and create meaning out of our encounters with what creates us. For Jung, encounter with 'the personified God-image in [our] psyche is *the* essential meaning of [our] existence. (von Franz 1992, p. 283).

Failure to connect with the background numinous leaves the ego high and dry in a desert of meaninglessness. This is illustrated by the plight of a man in his early twenties, in the grip of depression from which suicide appears as the only way out to peace. He says of his life, there is nothing happening; he is in a nothing job, with no chance to get a good job; he feels nothing, there is nothing in his future. He has suffered a catastrophic disillusionment that life could hold possibility and gave up around the age of twelve that he could make any difference. The hostility hidden in his passivity turns up in gruesome dreams of killing and nearly being killed, of having to pass a test and despairing that he can do so. In the transference he watches me like a hawk to perceive if I have any hope for him, and is ready to resist it quietly and completely if he spies hope in any of my responses. It is as if there is no numinous for him, except in the form of No-thing: nothingness blanketing his life, threatening to suffocate its beginning. He cannot, yet, make a narrative, a conversation, a form of the formless, a conversation between ego and Self.

At the other end of the spectrum is a woman in her nineties, remarkable in her achievement as a clinician and a social activist through her work in the community, and in drawing on her African American religious heritage to move her generation and that of her children out from the slavery of her grandmother. She comes for a specific symptom of hearing tunes, often the hymns or spirituals of her religion, and experiences them as communications. Can they be from the Spirit? At the same time, being medically trained herself, she seeks consultations on possible neurological causes of these auditory events. She is in dialogue with this numinous happening. Sometimes she sings back; sometimes she argues with what the tunes say; sometimes she responds with thoughts they inspire. In our sessions, I feel the background very much surrounding the foreground, as if she is approaching the border between life and death, and it is quite possible for her to entertain simultaneously that this symptom is nothing but an organic disorder and also a means God is using to speak to her. She is nimble enough to make something meaningful out of this hearing of tunes and enter the joy of it, while at the same time investigate it scientifically. She is in conversation, continuing her narrative of life right up to the moment of death.

When the numinous comes into the ego, the ego changes and so does our perception of the numinous. We build up forms for the formless and enter into dialogue with it, finding the ineffable in daily ordinary events of our lives. This enriches living. We feel we come to witness some presence witnessing us. Creating is going on in relation to what creates us. A double discourse may develop, from both sides, so to speak, one in words and symbols, the other in scintillae, synchronicities, emerging moments of absolute knowledge. This conversation confers unity on scattered parts of the psyche and of the world, so that we meet, for example as we are now, in conferences to exchange perceptions of the intersection, the conjunction of the Vast and the All with the here and now.

The precious ingredient in such *coniunctio* moments is our ego. We come again into touch with what was and is before we were, but now with consciousness, ready to make something of what we experience. This is the key on which everything turns, for without this willing consciousness, but instead a blind identification, we risk destruction.

If our identification is unconscious, then our distinctly human ego is at the mercy of the archetypal.

Jung's warning is frighteningly apt right now: if we are unwilling to undergo symbolic death, universal genocide will ensue (Jung 1956-57/1976, 1661). But to suffer symbolic death, there must be consciousness, an ego capable of making a narrative, a symbolic discourse advancing from encounter with the numinous. We make a hut, an ark, a tabernacle, an earthly house for the divine. The Self finds in the ego a receiver and a transmitter. For symbolic death to occur that could spare the world genocides, which we have already seen in massacres, holocausts, forced marches, systematic starvations, and oppressions of whole peoples based on race or religion or politics, we need egos full of readiness to respond to the numinous that already has engaged them.

As analysts, we have something to say here that can make a difference to the survival of the world. The first meaning of the numinous is that it is something powerful that transcends our ego consciousness to which we must pay close attention. The second meaning of the numinous is its entering into our ego consciousness and changing it to enlarge it and /or to defeat it (Jung 1963, para. 778). The third meaning of the numinous is *its* enlarged manifestation as a result of our egos engaging with it. The discourse doubles.

The Objective Numinous

In the secular option at this third meaning of the numinous, which we see in postmodernism (Anderson 1990, chapter 1), we focus on the ego's narratives, representations that depict our various registerings of the numinous and let its objective presence go. The question is not who is there, or even, is there a there there, but rather, what do I, we, make of it? Focusing on our language creations for experience of the numinous, we let it, in itself, go. We involve ourselves with ways we are creating what we are describing. Representation captures our focus, over what is being represented. We emphasize our creating and leave off our being created, our dependence on an antecedent creator. This option does not lead to symbolic death, but is the underside of postmodernism retreating into the ego world.

Symbolic death is to build relation to what is there as well as to our forms of representation for it, to include both the ego and the numinous as dialogue partners, and then to suffer their unravelling in the gap between our symbols and what they point to. We build up symbols, names, pictures for the numinous and converse with it in particular, personal and social rituals. The ego builds up readiness by which I mean consciously gathering the bits and pieces of what we know, assembling them to present ourselves attentive to the numinous.

The New Testament parable of the wedding feast comes to mind (Matthew 22:1-13). Jesus invites guests to the wedding feast who do not come. Their business or farm calls; they make light of the invitation and go their ways. Then Jesus instructs his servants to go out to the highways and invite strangers along the road. They do come in – the homeless, the unemployed, a free meal, an occasion! But one of them does not wear a wedding garment and he is seized and thrown out into outer darkness. The point is thus forcefully made. Once we know that the numinous is, that the numinous bids us through our wounds, that the numinous impresses us as transcending our ego, that the numinous in momentous experience enters our ego consciousness, then we must dress up to meet it. It is not how grand our dress is; we may own little; but it is dressing up, readying ourselves in our finest to meet the finest, the most, the momentous; it is willingness to honour what presents itself in the numinous encounter. The ninety-year-old patient brought such flair to our sessions where she spoke of the numinous speaking to her: she sported a delicate violet feather on her head to match her purple dress.

The dressing up is creating our forms to represent the numinous, to value it, to corral our lives in their disparate activities to organize around this central conversation with what transcends us and yet speaks to us. Engaging in this conversation is what Jung calls the symbolic life. Religions go further into the precincts of the sacramental life (Ulanov & Ulanov 1975, chapter 4). Jung describes the religious attitude as 'careful consideration and observation of certain dynamic factors that are conceived as 'powers': spirits, daemons, gods, laws, ideas, ideals, or whatever name man has given to such factors in his world as he has found powerful, or dangerous, or helpful enough to be taken into careful consideration, or grand, beautiful, and meaningful enough to be devoutly worshipped and loved' (Jung 1937/1958, para. 8).

Symbolic death means we create as much as we can to house and express what is the most important, that around which our life and life itself revolves, and then we suffer its dismemberment, dissolution, destruction, because our forms, however grand, are finite constructions, mortal (see Ulanov 2007, chapter 9). We create as much as we can of what we name as ultimate, as God, as Self-experience, as Truth, Beauty, and we know that none of it, all of it, is not it. What we create is dust.

The Numinous in Itself

Such a symbolic death that introduces a gap of nothingness, of mortality, between us and everything we have given our lives to build, if endured, launches us into a new consciousness. In our profession, an example would be learning all we can, training hard, working on theory, putting in the hours of analysis, supervision, case consultations, self analysis, and putting it aside. As Jung says, 'forget everything when you face your patient' (Jung 1960/1964, para. 882). We sacrifice the ultimacy of what we are creating, and we go on creating it as if it is ultimate.

Paradox supervenes over intellect: we lose our rational constructions. We do opposite things simultaneously: 'Paradox ... does more justice to the *unknowable* than clarity can do, for uniformity of meaning robs the mystery of its darkness and sets it up as something that is *known*. That is usurpation ... by pretending that ... the intellect has got hold of the transcendent mystery by a cognitive act and has 'grasped' it. The paradox ... reflects a higher level of intellect ... by not forcibly representing the unknowable as known ...' (Jung 1954/1958, para. 417). We identify what really matters and commit ourselves to its vital importance, while at the same time we know it is not the first thing, not the utmost, the supreme endpoint. While committed wholeheartedly, we disidentify from our values. A space exists between us and them, dependent on the living numinous creating us as we are creating. We explore the underlying real, the primary real, the *hecceitas* through its various and numerous names, its *ipseities*, its forms of communication. We commit to purposes at the same time we sense a background purposiveness that may unravel them. We withdraw our projections at the same time we entertain them as visions that make the whole visible, that bring within range the 'Farnearness' – what Marguerite of Porete of the 13th century calls God (Babinsky 1993, p. 155).

Our images of the heavenly city, of the peaceful lying down of the lion with the lamb, of the Kaaba at the centre of the universe bring the mystery in view, at the same time we know the mystery is none of these things. We 'become as little children' again for whom 'the opposites lie close together', but now with consciousness, 'not the unconscious child we would like to remain' (Jung 1952/1958, para. 742). This is the paradoxical consciousness of the child 'born from the maturity of the adult' (ibid.). We are at once 'never more than [our] own limited ego before the One who dwells within [us], whose form has no knowable boundaries, who encompasses [us] on all sides, fathomless as the abysms of the earth and vast as the sky' (ibid., para. 758). This One, grand and magnificent, also brings through the backdoor, the wild thing, always alive and untameable, the All far beyond our comprehension yet whom we know best in the tiny particulars of our personal journey and the cultural forms of our particular time. It dethrones our ego, wounding it, defeating it: 'Whoever has suffered once from an intrusion of the unconscious has at least a scar if not an open wound ... the wholeness of his ego personality, has been badly damaged ... a fatal blow to his own monarchy' (Jung 1988, 1233). Through that wound enters the '*influxis divinus*' and Jung says we 'do better to disidentify ... from the small voice within ... through which the divine spirit manifests itself' and listen to it attentively to find a middle way between its opposites (Jung 1956-57/1976, para. 1661).

This something reveals itself more as other than the forms we make for it which it graciously consents to while also remaining a wild thing. We analysts touch it in the joy we feel in the work we do. Beyond the necessity of our virtuous effort to be a good analyst, is the joy of it, that makes the virtuous life, for all its value, seem sterile in comparison.

Marguerite of Porete writes of the country of peace. This lies beneath or beyond the unconscious of tumultuous affects and conflicting instincts that Jung and Freud describe. We reach this joy through a momentary spark that is also a brief aperture that shows the 'glory of the soul' and the peace that remains 'is so delicious that Truth calls it glorious food' (Babinsky 1993, pp. 135-36). As a result one is 'very free and unencumbered from all things', dwelling in freeness from feebleness and fear (ibid., p. 153). This is a passionate living with 'The Ravishing Most High who overtakes me and joins me to the center of the marrow of divine Love in whom I am melted' (ibid., p. 155).

The alchemist Dorn describes the peace of eternity that breathes into the temporal world through the *spiraculum aeternitatis*, a sort of air hole where 'the personal realm of the psyche', our particular wounds and potentiality', touches the collective unconscious, Self meeting ego (von Franz 1980, pp. 109-10; Jung 1963, para. 670). From this pivot point, 'from this nowhere comes everything which is newly created' (ibid., p. 110).

Here we find our moments of joy, of our perceiving before we were: being created as we are creating.

References

Anderson, W. T. (1990). *Reality Isn't What It Used to Be*. San Francisco: Harper.

Babinsky, E. L. (1993). *Marguerite of Porete The Mirror of Simple Souls*. Mahwah, NJ: Paulist.

Balint, E. (1993). *Before I Was I: Psychoanalysis and the Imagination*. Eds. Juliet Mitchell & Michael Parsons. London: Free Association Press.

Jung, C.G. (1937/1958). 'Psychology and religion'. In *Psychology and Religion: West and East*, CW 11.

– (1946/1954). 'Psychology of the transference'. In *The Practice of Psychotherapy. CW* 16.

– (1952/1958). 'Answer to Job'. *CW* 11.

– (1952/1960). 'Synchronicity: an acausal connecting principle'. In *The Structure and Dynamics of the Psyche. CW* 8.

– (1954/1958). 'Transformation symbolism in the mass'. *CW* 11.

– (1954/1960). 'On the nature of the psyche'. *CW* 8.

– (1956-57/1976). 'Jung and religious belief'. In *The Symbolic Life. CW* 18.

– (1960/1964). 'Good and evil in analytical psychology'. In *Civilization in Transition. CW* 10.

– (1963). *Mysterium Coniunctionis. CW* 14.

– (1973). *Letters*. Vol. 1 of 2. Eds. Gerhard Adler and Aniela Jaffé.

– (1988). *Nietzsche's Zarathustra*. Princeton NJ: Princeton University Press.

Ulanov, A. B. (2007). *Aliveness/Deadness: The Unshuttered Heart: Opening to Aliveness and Deadness in the Self*. Nashville, Tn: Abingdon Press.

Ulanov, A. & Ulanov, B. (1975). *Religion and the Unconscious*. Louisville, Ky: John Knox/Westminster Press.

von Franz, M-L. (1980). *On Divination and Synchronicity*. Toronto: Inner City Books.

– (1992). *Psyche and Matter*. Boston: Shambhala.

Closing Remarks

Astrid Berg
Vice-President (2004-2007)
Chair of the Organizing Committee

At the beginning of this Congress I said to you that it was my most fervent wish that we learn from each other. I do hope that we have been able to bring our different worlds together, not in order to make them the same, not to imitate them, but to celebrate the richness of human cultures and to know that in the end we are all equal and that the same deep structures underpin our inner landscapes.

I wish you a safe journey back home.

The IAAP Looks Far Ahead
President's Farewell Address

Christian Gaillard
France (SFPA)
President (2004-2007)

When my Fellow Officers not so gently reminded me that I must absolutely give a final address on the last day of the Congress, I must admit I was very reluctant.

How, and more importantly why, should I force a speech on you after five days of intense work, and the evening before a well-earned time of rest, which you will no doubt spend getting to know better the country that hosts our Congress, South Africa, and which impresses and attracts us all?

My reluctance soon provoked a strong inclination towards introversion. And the introversion rapidly turned into a profound regression – a rather dark regression.

So what was I to do? At this point I hesitated between two methods: consulting the Yi King, or turning to an exercise quite often practised in the Jungian milieu, the exercise of active imagination.

I chose the second method. To be honest, I do not really know why. I will have to try and understand this choice – perhaps with the help of a good analyst! I know many of those, still in the Jungian milieu of course.

So what is my internal, intimate, representation of the IAAP? This was the question I started with in this exercise.

And this is what appeared.

The IAAP is a funny sort of bird. It can fly and even, theoretically, fly away. But it keeps its feet on the ground. Sometimes, even rather solidly.

This funny sort of bird has, so it is said, a

tendency to isolate itself. But it has a keen eye. And more importantly, as you can see here, this funny creature first and foremost takes care of its offspring, the members of its own family.

Some of them are still in the egg – we often call them 'candidates'. Some are in groups – we call them 'group members', and others are more isolated – we call them 'individual members'.

They are waiting, sometimes impatiently, to hatch out of their eggs, and stand on their own legs. I have even been told that some of them, to liberate themselves, attack the shell that protects them.

Certain others have already hatched. I ask myself whether those are not our young Russian colleagues that we can see here, already grown.

It must be known that this funny bird is careful not to put all its eggs in the same basket. It is of course implanted solidly in the countries and regions of the world where it has been thriving for a long time – in Western Europe, the United States of America, in some Latin American countries, and even in Australia, South Africa, and Japan.

But we can also find it now, as the species disseminates, in many other parts of the world, in Eastern Europe, China, other Latin American countries, North Africa. The IAAP, in its most recent evolutions, has given much more attention to its distant offspring, for whom it has great expectations, including some for its own future.

The IAAP is looking far ahead.

The paths of active imagination are unpredictable. Here is another image, another scene that came to me:

Perhaps because it is a family photograph. A photograph that you know well, and that comes to us from way back.

We are in 1911. Here is the psychoanalytic family of the beginnings. With, of course, Sigmund Freud in the middle. Because he was rather small, he was standing on a stool. But what authority he radiates! He is truly the centre, the axis, of the whole group.

Except to his left, who can we see but our own Carl Gustav Jung. You can see that he is going to move out of the frame.

I mean to say out of the Vienna circle. And he is right to do so. I am not of the same mind as those who think that the psychoanalytic movement should have been, or should be, an indivisible whole.

On the contrary, I believe that it was beneficial that Jung left the Freudian school, where he none the less had a good position. His leaving and others leaving after him contributed to the diversity of the psychoanalytic movement. Among other happy consequences, it freed us from the orthodox mentality of obedience that is definitively incompatible with the practice of analysis and encouraged the deployment of theoretical thought that this practice demands.

It was beneficial that Jung should break away from Freud and his version of psychoanalysis, not simply because their age difference – 19 years – was insufficient for the two researchers and colleagues to benefit from the distance of a generation, which would have allowed one to be the father and the other the son, as both men had dreamt. Nor simply because Jung's psychiatric experience and his cultural and personal references were obviously different from Freud's, so that he had to find, or rather create, his own way of working as a clinician, and his own way of thinking, his Analytical Psychology.

But most of all because if the past, and history, were less important to Jung than it was to Freud, he had none the less a different point of view. He had a different perspective concerning the processes involved in clinical work, and in everyday life.

Jung looks at the processes we are involved in and the direction they are taking. And he looks far ahead. If the IAAP is looking far ahead, as we have just seen, it is because Jung himself was looking far ahead.

His relationship to the unconscious is prospective. He shows as much here in this family scene, as early as 1911, even if he would need another forty years to write his *Answer to Job* and *Aion*.

Here a debate has opened, in which I would be glad to see you participate. This debate was developed one evening between members of the Executive Committee.

For you must not imagine that we talk exclusively about you, about the current affairs of the IAAP. We also sometimes debate, heatedly at times, on clinical or theoretical questions – and these are for me some of the most pleasurable moments of our work together.

In this particular case the debate concerned this term, this adjective that I have just used to characterize Jung's approach, and our own, 'prospective'. I propose, indeed, that in future we use this term rather than 'teleological', which is more traditional, but has the disadvantage of giving the impression that we know more than we really do about the object of this process of the relationship to the unconscious. Whereas describing it as a prospective approach indicates as clearly, but more simply, and I believe in more concrete terms, that our attention is decidedly oriented towards the future, or rather that which is becoming.

Indeed, I think that Jung himself, as you can see him here, would say I was right – but I hope you will give me your own opinions on this question of vocabulary, which I believe is rather important.

In any case, this orientation of Jungian analysis towards that which is becoming is for me one of the major characteristics of our way of practising analysis. It is also a starting point for developing our own theoretical thinking, in comparison with that of most of our Freudian colleagues.

The experience I have acquired of the work of our Freudian colleagues has convinced me that it is by taking our differences as the starting point that we can apprehend and develop those elements that are specific to us, and the points we truly have in common with them. This is true for clinical questions or about historical questions, as I regularly see in Paris, and as was the case last month in Berlin during the IPA congress. Or in yet other areas of research, as was the case here on Monday, concerning prehistoric art.

Despite all this, even if our Jungian approach is prospective, it did not really enable us to foresee the whirlwind development of the Jungian community across the world.

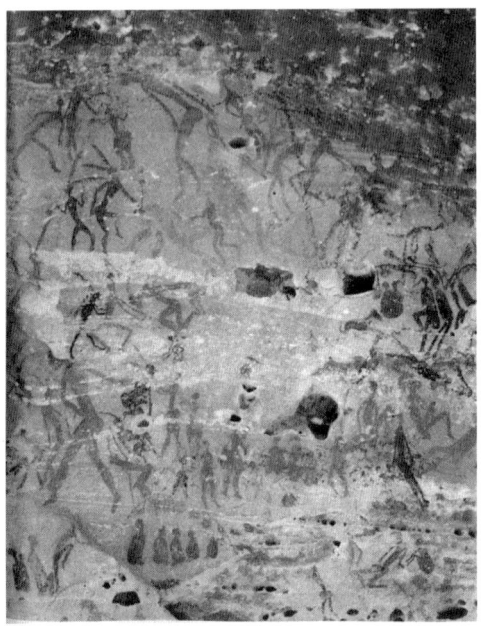

Here is a picture of the whirlwind movement of the contemporary Jungian community seen from Barnes in South Africa.

The whirlwind is movement, it is life. But at certain times, some structure is necessary.

Here another debate is opened. What is the role of our main bodies – the member Societies – in this task of creating structure, and what is the role of our central governing body?

I must say that I am all the more attentive to this question in that I myself am Swiss. I am French too, of course – and have been for over forty years. But more fundamentally I am Swiss, and have been for over six centuries. That is to say that I am particularly attached to the federal character of our institutions. Many of my colleagues, particularly the Americans, of course, share this attachment – it is one of our many points in common, along with the care to always distinguish between the executive powers of our Executive Committee, the legislative powers of our Delegates Assembly, and the judicial powers of our Ethics Committee.

In practice, this will be, I think, one of the most important and delicate questions to be worked on and debated in the years to come: how can we go about making sure that the actions undertaken by the Executive Committee really emanate from our member Societies, from the work with them, rather than being parachuted in from above, even as Guidelines?

It can be noted in passing that it is fascinating to observe that the same questions are currently being asked in the construction of the institutional body of the European Union.

In this federal mindset, one of our particularities is that our distaste for orthodoxy – which, as I have said, is a good thing – leads us to prefer a diversity of internal orientations: the development of the IAAP is not made up of one unique whirlwind movement, but many, with each being a pole of attraction and growth, each with its own theoretical base, often its own revues and colloquiums, and even its own clinical practice. The IAAP is polycentric.

I wonder whether this evolution of the Jungian world has not left Jung a little pensive.

I like this photograph of Jung very much. I only discovered it a little while ago. One of my daughters brought it back from Switzerland for me. And I am all the more attached to this portrait because, in this photograph, Jung resembles rather uncannily my own grandfather. Yet another family story.

But a family story well situated in time, and in history. We belong to the third, if not the fourth generation after Jung. And in this sense, we are all post-Jungian.

With the particularity that today we have moved from geographical poles – starting, historically, with Zurich and London – to an internal multi-polarity. Each of us, each Jungian analyst, each of our Institutes, is engaged in continuous internal debate that now places the discussion about our different orientations inside each one of us.

Here yet another debate emerges that will certainly hold us in its grip in the future. How, under these conditions, are we to train future Jungian analysts? What are our criteria, our points of reference? What have they been so far? And are they still applicable in the areas of the world where we are present today – in Tunisia, Saint Petersburg, Moscow, Kiev or Tbilisi, or in China, Hong Kong, Guangzhou, Shanghai, or in Colombia?

My position on this question is one of method. I propose that before promoting any rule as far as training is concerned, even as Guidelines, we should begin by setting up a system of observation, as practical and complete as possible, to assess the training systems currently in use, the experience acquired by our members in their own Societies, and of course the experience acquired by our new members and candidates in the regions of the world where our Developing Groups are now working.

I see that Carl Gustav Jung still looks a little pensive. As if to lighten his mood and worries, another family photograph then came to mind.

Here, gathered around my predecessor as President, is the team that helped me most in preparing to preside over the IAAP.

I owe much to Murray – Murray Stein – here, especially concerning the sharing out of tasks and responsibilities.

Since Luigi Zoja was president, indeed, the government of the IAAP has been organized into sub-committees, each having its own field of thinking and action, and its own responsibilities.

I myself have further accentuated this movement, by proposing to our Executive Committee that a few of these sub-committees be largely autonomous, including their financial responsibilities.

And to thank Murray for showing himself to be so competent in running our affairs, we have nominated him to be a member of the new working body, the Advisory Board for Institutional Issues and Congresses, where he has actively participated, with our indispensable and incredibly polyvalent Honorary Secretary, Tom Kelly. This has been extremely valuable to all of us, and to me in particular.

I believe I am able to say that our IAAP is remarkably wise in its choice of officials, which is a clear sign of the lucidity and good health of an institution.

We have even encouraged the most active participation of your elected representatives in the different sub-committees of our Executive Committee. This is a working method that is, I think, now solidly written into the contemporary history of the IAAP.

And as you can see in this family photograph, we all look happy. The then president first and foremost. When I saw this, I said to myself, and also to my Honorary Secretary at the time of my election, that I had a simple and clear principle of governance: *the president presides, and does not work.*

This principle is excellent. I recommend it to my successors. But it is difficult to apply as my predecessors will agree with me.

In fact, the daily tasks of the president are weighty, multiple and everyday – especially just before one of our meetings, and even more so in the run up to a congress. So I address my warmest wishes of good health to Hester Solomon, who is now going to take up the task.

You will no doubt also notice in this photograph the clear connection between my predecessor and myself as I speak to you today. In fact, at every stage of my work as president, and for each of the often delicate questions that I have had to raise with my Fellow Officers, I have often been able to consult Murray, and also Luigi Zoja, Verena Kast, and Tom Kirsch, whom I would like to thank warmly here for their help and friendship.

Talking of encounters and connections, another image, another scene now comes to be associated with the previous ones.

We are now in China. In Shanghai. This was last May. You will recognize our colleague Heyong Shen, who is here among us in Cape Town, and with whom I have had the pleasure to work on several occasions over the last three years.

I know that some of us are surprised by the efforts we have been making, for a few years now, to set up personal and professional training programmes in places where we do not have, or at least not yet, a Society of analysts. I even hear criticism of our work with and for our Developing Groups across the world. To all of you, I would like to say: Come and join us in this work. Agree to travel, regularly if possible, to these regions of the world that are calling us. Come and prepare a public conference where you can demonstrate your ideas and your experience as an analyst.

Agree to give individual sessions of clinical work which cannot, of course, aspire to being analysis sessions like those you can give in your Institutes, but they are a chance for our correspondents to express themselves, and for us to hear them more closely.

Or, better still, arrange to be able to travel far away from where you live to give analysis sessions as regularly as possible, or group or individual supervision sessions, as our British colleagues do so admirably in Russia, and as many of us do elsewhere in the world.

It is a privilege for us to be able to encounter a country, a culture, not as tourists, but from the inside, sharing closely with clinicians who live and work in conditions quite unlike our own, all that we have truly in common with them, over and above our differences.

You will see that this work, to which I have given a significant amount of time and energy over many years, enables us to rethink profoundly the differences that manifest themselves in the different orientations of Analytical Psychology and Jungian analysis, and also to rethink our own institutions.

What is more, if I ended up travelling to Shanghai, it was, of course, to meet our Groups in China, but it was also because I had been invited to participate in a large congress of academics and psychotherapists, mainly Chinese, and to give a lecture at the University of Fudan. At this university in Shanghai, one of the best in China, I also met teachers and students who are already studying with our colleague Heyong Shen, and who are waiting for us.

Our active presence – alas still too slight – in academia and research and our exchanges with other psychotherapists are another two current dimensions of the IAAP, and yet more questions to work at in the future.

This is where, I think, this next image comes from, this other rather pleasant reality that then came to me. The very elegant and very thorough membership directory:

The multi-polar whirlwind that I spoke of earlier has now taken a more organized turn. Here we can find the current composition of our member Societies, but also, of course, the list of our Developing Groups and the details of those of us who are most actively involved with them, the list of our Individual Members, the colleagues who have trained with us and are often waiting to be numerous enough to make up a new Society of the IAAP, as is now the case in Russia, for example.

Every entry, and everyone, is exactly in its right place, thanks especially to the special care of our Communications Officer, Joe Cambray.

Everything is in its right place, but for these strong winds that, as you can see here, are blowing across our Jungian world. So what are these currents? Where do they come from, these storms from outside that might just perturb us somewhat in the future, and even seriously threaten us? They come, in my opinion, from two places, from two different sources.

On the one hand, they come from the shadowy dimension of the multi-centrism that I spoke of earlier, that is to say from a misunderstood and superficial cultural relativism, which can easily lead, if we are not careful, to a sort of communitarian attitude towards the very fact of the diversity of the Jungian movement throughout the world.

Is the relationship to the unconscious, and the unconscious itself, radically different in China, Latin America, the United States of America, or Europe, as we sometimes hear, even in our own Jungian circles? In this case our ways of thinking and exercising analysis would be so different that only our institutions could bring together our different ways of being Jungian – and no doubt only for a limited amount of time.

My experience of the Jungian world in all its diversity thus far leads me to think that only deeper and regular exchanges between analysts of different origins, and especially between those who train future analysts, allow us to respect our differences while developing the aspect of our concept and practice of the unconscious that is radically universal.

I hope, then, for my part, that regular and cross-disciplinary gatherings can be organized between older and younger generations of analysts, especially if they are involved in training future analysts. These working gatherings should be first and foremost centred on clinical questions and questions of training. Our congresses, of course, contribute to these matters. But we no doubt need to think about creating a specific framework within which to address these questions, in Russia, in China, and everywhere where new members of the IAAP are now working.

As for the other currents that are ominously threatening us, if they seem to come from outside, they have nevertheless managed to sweep inside our Jungian world. Here I am thinking of the increasingly pressing demand for short courses to meet the demands for help that are themselves impatient and short-term.

Individuation, as we well know, is a long-term process. How then are we to reconcile the time, inevitably limited, allowed for the training of analysts with the necessarily long and slow rhythms of personal transformation?

This is a truly difficult question, and a challenge to be taken up, not only as far as our Individual Members across the world are concerned, but also within most of our 'old' Societies.

How can we imagine and exercise efficient and modern professional training of Jungian analysts, and at the same time constantly work on these long-term processes that we call individuation? Here, I reckon, is subject matter to stimulate us earnestly in the years to come.

I can see that in referring to these crosswinds my discourse has become darker. But do not think for a moment that at the end of my mandate as president, I have myself become gloomy. Quite the contrary. I find these questions that I have just spoken of truly stimulating.

It is in any case an attitude quite different from hiding one's head in the sand, as some say ostriches are apt to do.

In fact, I think that if we keep our eyes wide open to the present and the future that is taking shape, and if we are ordinarily exacting as to ourselves and our representatives, we can be truly optimistic as to the future of the Jungian movement.

In any case, as far as I am concerned, I am clearly optimistic; especially after what this congress has offered us, thanks to the

competence and devotion of Joe Cambray, in his role as chair of the Programme Committee, and thanks to the qualities of Astrid Berg, who with the Organization Committee that seconds her, has shown such warmth in her welcome, and has organized our encounters and working sessions so well.

I can see that the IAAP will soon have to round new capes. But I also know that here in South Africa, we have never been so close to the Cape of Good Hope.

And I can see that the Jungian movement is well constructed and solid enough. It is true to its course. Our institutions are sufficiently strong, and they are also increasingly open. We can look without fear to the different directions of our future, while staying firmly together.

So I wish the IAAP 'Bon Voyage' with its new captain, Hester Solomon, and its new crew – who, I can assure you, already know the manoeuvres!

Bon voyage to all of you, to all of us!

Author Index

BARCELONA 2004
Edges of Experience: Memory and Emergence
Proceedings of the 16th International Congress for Analytical Psychology
edited by Lyn Cowan
illustrated, 240 printed pages, 1380 pages on CD, ISBN 978-3-85630-700-4

CAMBRIDGE 2001
Relevant themes of politics in today's world, racism, the reading of collective events were being discussed and "2001" was in the air: it was just days before "911". This volume carries the record of what concerns Jungians at the onset of the Millennium. 768 pages, paperback, ISBN 978-3-85630-609-0

FLORENCE 1998: DESTRUCTION AND CREATION
Proceedings of the 14th International Congress for Analytical Psychology in Florence,
edited by Mary Ann Mattoon, 620 pages, illustrated
hardbound: ISBN 978-3-85630-584-0 / paperback: ISBN 978-3-85630-583-3

ZURICH 1995: OPEN QUESTIONS IN ANALYTICAL PSYCHOLOGY
Proceedings of the 13th International Congress for Analytical Psychology
edited by Mary Ann Mattoon
All of the papers from the Zurich Congress of August, 1995.
752 pages, illustrated, hardbound: ISBN 978-3-85630-555-0
paperback: ISBN 978-3-85630-556-7

CHICAGO 1992
The Transcendent Function: Individual and Collective Aspects
edited by Mary Ann Mattoon
Sixty presentations were made by Jungian analysts from around the world, and they appear in their entirety. 560 pages, illustrated
hardbound: ISBN 978-3-85630-537-6 / paperback: ISBN 978-3-85630-538-3

PARIS 1989
Personal and Archetypal Dynamics in the Analytical Relationship.
edited by Mary Ann Mattoon
This gathering was controversial, provocative and stimulating. All the papers are presented, many richly illustrated. 510 pages, illustrated
hardbound: ISBN 978-3-85630-529-1 / paperback: ISBN 978-3-85630-524-6

BERLIN 1986
The Archetype of Shadow in a Split World
edited by Mary Ann Mattoon
The 10th International Congress of Analytical Psychology was held in Berlin, September 2 – 9, 1986. 456 pages, numerous illustrations and diagrams
hardbound: ISBN 978-3-85630-514-7 / paperback: ISBN 978-3-85630-506-2

JERUSALEM 1983
Symbolic and Clinical Approaches in Theory and Practice
edited by Luigi Zoja and Robert Hinshaw
This handsome volume, drawn from the 9th International Congress of Analytical Psychology in Jerusalem, contains contributions reflecting on the meaning and significance of contemporary analytical work from 25 prominent Jungian analysts from around the world.
375 pages, hardbound, illustrated, ISBN 978-3-85630-504-8

Eva Wertenschlag-Birkhäuser

Windows on Eternity

The Paintings of Peter Birkhäuser

Peter Birkhäuser's paintings frequently give form to overwhelming contents from the collective unconscious whose sense only becomes apparent when seen in the context of the spiritual predicament of our times. Birkhäuser was uniquely sensitive to the subliminal issues of the age. His whole career demonstrated that his special calling as an artist was to dedicate his abilities to a greater creative spirit and use his art to reveal, not only the crisis and infirmity of our times, but more importantly the reactions and healing impulses of the autonomous psyche. His pictures act as mirrors of the soul, where things hidden within us and our age become visible. In the major themes of the paintings we can observe something resembling a collective process of individuation. This is religious art, a manifestation of an image of God originating in the unconscious, striving to become real as part of a new consciousness. The artist's own personal individuation process becomes a gestation in paintings that circumscribe the birth of a new myth.

(200 pages, with 53 color plates, ISBN 978-3-85630-715-8)

Fred Gustafson

The Black Madonna of Einsiedeln

An Ancient Image for our Present Time

What is the Black Madonna? One answer leads to more questions which in turn demand more explanations. A possible reason for this turmoil lies in the difficulty our culture has always had in consciously integrating the feminine side of life, and especially its dark side. Another reason is the nature of the dark feminine itself, which defies attempts to give eternally fixed limits to what she represents. The Black Madonna of Einsiedeln stands among the many Black Virgins that seem to imagistically express this dark side of the feminine in a creative transformational manner for both the individual and the collective.

Beginning with a history of the Einsiedeln Madonna, Dr. Gustafson broadens his analysis into a psychological and historical examination of the Black Madonna, from her roots in pagan rites and the Great Mother archetype, to her resurgence as the Virgin in the Middle Ages, to her life today as the unheeded unconscious archetype of the feminine.

(176 pages, ISBN 978-3-85630-720-2)

English Titles from Daimon

Jane Reid - *Jung, My Mother and I: The Analytic Diaries*
of Catharine Rush Cabot
R.M. Rilke - *Duino Elegies*
Miguel Serrano - *C.G. Jung and Hermann Hesse*
Helene Shulman - *Living at the Edge of Chaos*
D. Slattery / L. Corbet (Eds.) - *Depth Psychology: Meditations on the Field*
D. Slattery / G. Slater (Eds.) - *Varieties of Mythic Experience*
David Tacey - *Edge of the Sacred: Jung, Psyche, Earth*
Susan Tiberghien - *Looking for Gold*
Ann Ulanov - *Spirit in Jung*
- *Spiritual Aspects of Clinical Work*
- *Picturing God*
- *Receiving Woman*
- *The Female Ancestors of Christ*
- *The Wisdom of the Psyche*
- *The Wizards' Gate, Picturing Consciousness*
Ann & Barry Ulanov - *Cinderella and her Sisters*
- *Healing Imagination: Psyche and Soul*
Erlo van Waveren - *Pilgrimage to the Rebirth*
Eva Wertenschlag-Birkhäuser - *Windows on Eternity:*
The Paintings of Peter Birkhäuser
Harry Wilmer - *How Dreams Help*
- *Quest for Silence*
Luigi Zoja - *Drugs, Addiction and Initiation*
Luigi Zoja & Donald Williams - *Jungian Reflections on September 11*
Jungian Congress Papers - *Jerusalem 1983: Symbolic & Clinical Approaches*
- *Berlin 1986: Archetype of Shadow in a Split World*
- *Paris 1989: Dynamics in Relationship*
- *Chicago 1992: The Transcendent Function*
- *Zürich 1995: Open Questions*
- *Florence 1998: Destruction and Creation*
- *Cambridge 2001*
- *Barcelona 2004: Edges of Experience*
- *Cape Town 2007: Journeys, Encounters*

Available from your bookstore or from our distributors:

AtlasBooks
30 Amberwood Parkway
Ashland OH 44805, USA
Phone: 419-281-5100
Fax: 419-281-0200
E-mail: order@atlasbooks.com
www.AtlasBooksDistribution.com

Gazelle Book Services Ltd.
White Cross Mills, High Town
Lancaster LA1 4XS, UK
Tel: +44(0)152468765
Fax: +44(0)152463232
Email: Sales@gazellebooks.co.uk
www.gazellebooks.co.uk

Daimon Verlag - Hauptstrasse 85 - CH-8840 Einsiedeln - Switzerland
Phone: (41)(55) 412 2266   Fax: (41)(55) 412 2231
email: info@daimon.ch
Visit our website: **www.daimon.ch** *or write for our complete catalog*